ONE NATION
UNDER STRESS
The Trouble with Stress as an Idea

Dana Becker

OXFORD
UNIVERSITY PRESS

OXFORD
UNIVERSITY PRESS

Oxford University Press is a department of the University of Oxford.
It furthers the University's objective of excellence in research, scholarship,
and education by publishing worldwide.

Oxford   New York
Auckland   Cape Town   Dar es Salaam   Hong Kong   Karachi
Kuala Lumpur   Madrid   Melbourne   Mexico City   Nairobi
New Delhi   Shanghai   Taipei   Toronto

With offices in
Argentina   Austria   Brazil   Chile   Czech Republic   France   Greece
Guatemala   Hungary   Italy   Japan   Poland   Portugal   Singapore
South Korea   Switzerland   Thailand   Turkey   Ukraine   Vietnam

Oxford is a registered trademark of Oxford University Press in the UK and certain other countries.

Published in the United States of America by
Oxford University Press
198 Madison Avenue, New York, NY 10016

Library of Congress Cataloging-in-Publication Data
Becker, Dana.
    One nation under stress : social uses of the stress concept / Dana Becker.
    p. cm.
    Includes bibliographical references and index.
    ISBN 978-0-19-974291-2 (hardback : alk. paper)—ISBN 978-0-19-997177-0 (updf)
    ISBN 978-0-19-997178-7 (epub)   1. Stress (Psychology)   2. Stress management—21st century.
    3. Post-traumatic stress disorder.   I. Title.
BF575.S75B343 2013
155.9'0420973—dc23
2012029879

9 8 7 6 5 4 3
Printed in the United States of America
on acid-free paper

For my mother,
Betty Becker

CONTENTS

ACKNOWLEDGMENTS

Many people have supported this project. Special thanks go to Jeanne Marecek, Eva Magnusson, and Sharon Lamb. There are others to thank whose encouragement for my work over the years has been truly heartening: Frank Richardson, Nicola Gavey, Rachel Hare-Mustin, Paula Caplan, Leonore Tiefer. Even though she was not there at the finish, Maura Roessner, my first editor at Oxford, was enthusiastic about this project from its incipient stages and helped shepherd it—and me—through the process from proposal to the first draft chapters. Many thanks to Dana Bliss and Nicholas Liu, who took over and made the book's trajectory from draft manuscript to publication a seamless one. Thanks also to Jillian Graves for her research assistance on Chapter 6. I could not have completed the book without generous leaves funded by Bryn Mawr College and supported by Dean Darlyne Bailey and Provost Kim Cassidy. And, as always, my love and thanks to Stan.

One Nation Under Stress

CHAPTER 1

Stress: The New Black Death?

Katy, who is going off to college as a freshman this fall, is "stressed out" because everything will be new and she doesn't want to be separated from her boyfriend Brad, who is going to another college; her parents are stressed out because their adjustable rate mortgage just shot up and now they're not sure they can pay it, take care of Katy's tuition, and handle the expenses of raising their other three, especially when there could be layoffs at Katy's dad's company. Emily down the street is stressed waiting for the doctor's office to call with the results of her breast biopsy. Sarah, who lives in the large home at the end of the cul de sac, doesn't know why she agreed to host 15 kids and their parents for Josh's fourth birthday, so she's stressed out about whether the clown she hired is going to turn up on time. Across town, Maria, who has a new job with a 90-minute commute, is worried that her mother won't be able to take care of her baby and her two-year-old because her mother has high blood pressure and the kids just stress her out too much. Maria's niece, Tiffany, is stressed out because she was caught texting in math class yesterday. Two blocks away, John, home from Afghanistan for nearly a year, is still living with his parents because he hasn't been up to looking for a job. He's been drinking a lot—even more now that he's begun having the flashbacks again. They're saying he has posttraumatic stress disorder. Janet is telling her friend Charlene how stressed she is because her son Jerome is in trouble at school again, and she doesn't know how she's going to keep him away from the kids dealing drugs down the block when he starts high school next year. She's short on money to pay the bills this month, and the big electric bill that'll be coming any day now has her feeling stressed.

It doesn't take long to figure out that the common denominator among such different life stories is the concept of stress. People say they experience stress for all kinds of reasons. Thousands of academic articles are published every year examining the effects of stress on body and mind, and this number has been growing exponentially. From 1970 to 1980, there were 2,326 academic publications in the social sciences with the word *stress* in the title. In the decade between 2000 and 2010, there were 21,750.[1] The mass media have dined out on the wild popularity of the stress concept ever since 1976, when the *New York Times* published its first article about stress.

We are bombarded with frightening stories about the harm stress can do to our health and our emotional states and how we can manage stress or fight its effects. Over the past 60 years or so, and particularly over the last several decades, the concept of stress has been applied to nearly every condition or situation that people encounter. Stress is a protean concept that can represent a situation or event, a psychological or physiological state, or an emotion. This diffuseness gives the stress concept great versatility when it comes to explaining human dilemmas. Contemporary ideas about stress hearken back to the nineteenth century when George Beard made an alarming connection between nervous illness and the stress of middle-class life, insisting that the amount and character of the stress that Americans experienced was exceptional. From a cultural standpoint, the middle-class American take on stress mingles a certain pride in the fast pace of life with worry about its effects. But some of these anxieties about stress take up more space in the public forum than others. For example, there is more public hand-wringing over the stresses of middle-class life than over the stresses of a life in poverty; there is more worry about the stressful nature of mothers' attempts to balance work and family life than there is about fathers.[3]

England's *Daily Mail* recently called stress the "Black Death of the 21st century."[2] Comparing stress to a plague that hit Europe in 1348 and eventually killed roughly 25 million people may sound extreme, but we don't seem able to go far enough in expressing our fears about what life can do to us. The "Black Death" article, accompanied by a picture of a man sitting in front of his laptop with his head in his hands, cites stress, particularly in the form of financial pressures and fears about layoffs, as the most common reason employees give for long absences from work. Elevating stress to the status of an actual disease, the author of the article reports that stress has "eclipsed stroke, heart attack, cancer and back problems" as a reason for worker absenteeism, and Professor Cary Cooper, author of *The Science of Occupational Health*, says that symptoms of stress include behavior changes such as poor concentration, "losing your sense of humor or losing your temper more quickly than usual."

As I was reading this piece, it occurred to me that perhaps if the occupations themselves were "healthy" from an economic standpoint, Professor Cooper wouldn't have to be talking about stress, but job growth obviously isn't what he meant by "occupational health." I spent more time than seemed reasonable mulling this over, thinking about what the stress concept conceals—a practice I've engaged in for some time as I've worked on this book. Whereas Professor Cooper is thinking about occupational health in terms of job stress, I'm thinking about "occupational health" in terms of an unhealthy economy. In the first case, getting people to do things on their own to relieve stress seems to make sense; in the second, tackling political, social, and economic problems that bring uncertainty and financial pressure seems logical. These days, "stress" often seems to stand in for people's uncertainty and fear. The stress concept draws the outside in—and in such a way that we end up believing that we need to change ourselves so that we can adjust to societal conditions, rather than changing the conditions themselves. And the chameleon-like nature of the stress concept makes it possible to obscure or conceal social problems by individualizing them in ways that most disadvantage those who have the least to gain from the status quo—among them, women and the poor.

STRESS AS METAPHOR

Stress has had many different meanings over the centuries, and because of this, the way we talk about "stress" now bears only a shadow of a resemblance to the way people talked about stress long ago. At one time, stress was a name for "what was hard and had to be endured," as Robert Kugelmann has noted.[3] Stress demanded strength and fortitude. The image that was often invoked was that of a ship tossed about by the stress of bad weather, and in that image Kugelmann sees the difference between the stress of then and the stress of now. The storm-tossed ship represented something that neither challenged the forces outside it nor was wholly separate from those forces. Stress was what "proved the strength, power, and virtue of ship and crew."[4] It was occasional, like the wintery blasts that assailed that metaphorical ship; stress signified hardship, and endurance was needed to deal with it. Now, particularly in the middle class, we "work" to overcome stress; we don't suffer it. And stress is not considered a sometime thing in contemporary Western societies; it is believed to be constant.

Early engineering gave us the ideas of stress and strain, and from these followed the metaphor of the body as a machine with a finite store of energy and with parts that life could grind down.[5] The 1949 edition of the *Merriam Webster Collegiate Dictionary* defined stress completely without reference to human beings, as the "action of external forces; especially to overstrain." Today, the definition reads like this: "a physical, chemical, or emotional factor that causes bodily or mental tensions and may be a factor in disease causation" and "a state resulting from a stress; especially one of bodily or mental tension resulting from factors that tend to alter an existent equilibrium." Stress now derives from physics, where it refers to the force that can transform material in ways that cause it to change its form or to break. In our vernacular, stress can be both a cause ("It was stress that caused his heart attack") and an effect ("When the plane was late I was so stressed out"). But although we refer to stress as both a force outside the person and an inner state, recently it is the inner state that has been getting the primary emphasis.

In Middle English, stress denoted "hardship or force exerted on a person for the purpose of compulsion,"[6] suggesting that stress was someone else's will forced on the individual rather than, as today, something we conceive of as integral to the "self." Today's stress concept owes a great deal to the dominant ideology of liberal individualism in which human beings are seen as free to act in accordance with their own judgment. It is an ideology that prizes not only individual freedom, but also individual success and self-actualization.[7] The "self" has become something we can think and talk about—something we can even remake, if necessary.[8] But individualism or no, the self is not separate from social expectations and norms; it can't be considered apart from the way it is talked about and judged, as British psychologist Nikolas Rose has pointed out.[9] Many of the events in our lives (marriage, unemployment, combat) are open to judgments about how we have coped with or adjusted to them,[10] and these judgments are steeped in a psychological language that has slipped its middle-class moorings to become the currency of our time. People say, "I'm a commitment-phobe" or "I didn't used to have any self-esteem," or "I'm pretty obsessive about it," or, more to the purposes of this book, "I'm stressed out." These statements and the language they're couched in didn't come out of thin air, a function merely of our unique personalities and family histories; these are the available terms through which many of us come to understand ourselves. As philosopher Ian Hacking has noted, certain ideas play a part in how we are "made up" as people.[11] They become part of who we are and what we do. And we are made up at a particular time in history and in a culture that subscribes to certain ideas and practices that themselves have a history.[12]

We can say that the concept of stress "makes up" or produces people who can act and think about themselves in certain ways and not in others. People who are "stressed" can feel in certain ways: they can be anxious, irritable, depressed. They can behave in certain ways: overeat or drink too much or not take care of themselves. They can develop illnesses because their immune systems are out of whack. They can see themselves as overwhelmed and/or out of control. Of course, this does not describe the entire universe of how "stressed" people can feel, behave, or perceive themselves, but you get the idea. I'm not saying here that experiences aren't stressful or that people don't experience something called stress. What I am saying is that at other times in our history, when the stress concept didn't exist, we couldn't experience ourselves in the way that stress both describes and delimits.

When people believe that feeling "stressed" ruins their relationships, their work lives, and/or their health, they feel impelled to do something about it. The idea that people should constantly monitor themselves for signs of stress speaks to what Michel Foucault termed "technologies of the self," practices that, as he put it, enable people to "operate on their own bodies and souls, thoughts, conduct, and way of being, so as to transform themselves in order to attain a certain state of happiness, purity, wisdom, perfection, or immortality."[13] Of course, Foucault wasn't referring to actual technology in the form of iPhone apps—though there are apps out there that purport to monitor stress. That's right; one app asks you questions to determine how stressed out you are, and you can repeat this ritual daily until you have a "progress report on your stress-reduction efforts." Another requires you to put your finger on the smartphone's camera lens so the camera can detect your pulse, turning the phone into a heart rate and blood-oxygen level monitor (of course, heart rate and blood-oxygen levels can vary for many reasons and are not reliable indicators of stress, but this did not deter the app developer). Depending on the reading, the application dispenses advice, generally of the not-so-profound variety: "Take a deep breath, a walk or a few deep breaths and slow down."[14] The media and their expert consultants—psychiatrists, psychologists, and other helping professionals—encourage people to maintain vigilance over their mental and physical states so they can transform those states when they judge they're stressed out. They can avoid certain risks; take certain measures to monitor their health; use relaxation techniques, yoga, medication, meditation, psychotherapy, journaling, or organizing. These technologies, as I argue throughout the book, are middle-class answers to primarily middle-class problems. But, as generally happens, dominant cultural ideas eventually become more widely influential. And as people take in the prevailing ideas about stress and its effects, they become adept at monitoring themselves for signs of stress and selecting stress management strategies from the available cultural menu of options.

We understand stress primarily through the science that explains it to us, particularly neurobiology, neuropsychology, cognitive psychology, and psychoneuroimmunology. But I think there's a case to be made, and I try to make it in this book, that although explanations about how stress affects the mind and body are located in the psychological and biological domains, we can also explain the stress concept with reference to the often-neglected moral domain. When we say, for example, that poverty is stressful (in fact, in the academic literature, poverty is often called a *stressor*), we're saying that people subjectively experience poverty as stressful; one person's stress is another's challenge. But poverty is not merely—or mainly—a subjective experience. Unfortunately, the psychological, or "psy,"[15] professions don't give much weight to the kind of experience that makes subjectivity a *social* phenomenon, that is, the experience that derives from people's positions in a specific culture and in both the smaller and larger political and economic worlds.[16] The stress concept often obscures injustices and inequalities by seducing us into viewing those injustices and inequalities as individual problems.

As I discuss throughout the book, more and more social phenomena are currently being transformed into disease entities through a process sociologists have termed *medicalization*. An unwavering faith in the power of scientific explanation from the nineteenth century[17] onward has created a fertile ground in the United States for biomedical solutions to societal problems as dissimilar as working motherhood, poverty, and road rage. As the fields of neurobiology and psychoneuroimmunology have grown, increasingly emphasizing the deleterious effects of stress on the immune system, our attention is diverted from changing the social conditions that create stress toward the management of our own health. In what Rose calls the "age of susceptibility," we are all theoretically at risk, no matter how healthy we are.[18] As I'll discuss in Chapter 3, the obligation to guard our health has become a significant ethical value, and we are encouraged to practice behaviors, adopt attitudes, and purchase products that will decrease our stress. What today's stress concept obscures, however, are the social underpinnings of the "stresses" we bemoan. For example, in the National Geographic documentary *Stress: Portrait of a Killer*, we see the chief of cardiology at Kaiser Richmond Medical Center as he drives through a poverty-stricken urban neighborhood, looking through his windshield at poor people as he talks about how residents of this area "are living a more stressful life" in a "community that produces high stress hormones in people."[19] The context of poverty—the economic, political, and social forces that create it—is almost entirely blotted out when the focus is on communities as producers of stress hormones.

Many people continue to hang on to the now-discredited belief that stress actually causes cancer. Increasingly, the way stress operates on the body is explained as a chain of events propelled by emotional distress, leading to a physiological response. For example, a recent radio report about a local nonprofit agency offering psychological services to cancer patients explained that cancer can result in "overwhelming emotions"; that these emotions can lead to stress; that stress can result in sleep problems; and that sleep problems can interfere with recovery from cancer. In her 1977 essay, *Illness as Metaphor*, Susan Sontag asserted that "Disease imagery is used to express concern for social order, and health is something everyone is presumed to know about."[20] Unlike cancer, of course, stress isn't a disease, but I believe that the stress concept has become a new metaphor for social and moral tensions and ills at this time in our history.

STRESS AND THE PRESS

Fear of Stress or Fear of Life? Stress in the News

In 1963, at a symposium on stress, Stanley J. Sarnoff of the National Institutes of Health (NIH) was quoted as saying, "Stress is the process of living." At the same symposium, Hans Selye, the principal architect of the stress concept as we know it, remarked: "One cannot be cured of stress, but can only learn to enjoy it."[21] Further, a neurophysiologist at the symposium was reported to have said that "mental stress" was "good for the mind." I can hardly imagine experts saying these things today. Although a Harvard psychiatrist who was present *did* make the point that "intolerable stress leading to suicide will kill more than 19,000 in the U.S. this year," it was clear to everyone attending the symposium that the level of stress had to be astronomical in order to be considered "intolerable."

Fast-forward 46 years, to 2009, when Mary Carmichael, a journalist for *Newsweek*, began asking researchers about "good stress." She reported that "many of them said it essentially didn't exist." According to Carmichael, one researcher said, "We never tell people stress is good for them..." Another allowed that it might be, but only in small ways, in the short term.[22] When Carmichael asked whether this was also true for ER doctors, air traffic controllers, and others who seem to feel they do well in high-stress environments, this is what she got by way of response: "No, those people are unhealthy. This business of people saying they 'thrive on stress? It's nuts.'" This comment was made by Bruce Rabin, a psychoneuroimmunologist whom Carmichael then asked whether he thought these people actually had a disease: "You can absolutely say that. Yes, you can say that,'" Rabin replied, after taking a minute to think about it. Carmichael said she could see Selye, the man who viewed stress as "the salt of life" that makes us fully human, tossing in his grave.

A piece on MSNBC's website entitled "Can Stress Actually Be Good for You?" also tells us something about the gulf between Selye's ideas about stress and our own:

> Stress can be positive, but get too much of it—when the flood of hormones bombards your body longer than 24 hours, doctors say—and all kinds of bad things start to happen [high blood pressure; heart disease; exhaustion; depression]. 'Over time, if you're constantly in fight-or-flight, if your heart muscles and valves are awash in epinephrine, it causes changes in the arteries…,' says Dr. [Lynne] Tan. The problem is, it's difficult to shut off the onslaught of stress hormones when they become harmful. People can't control how high their hormones go when they experience a difficult situation. 'What we can do is change the way our brains respond to [stress] with coping techniques such as deep breathing, meditation and exercise,' says Dr. Bruce Rabin. The goal isn't an absence of stress. It's an unavoidable reality. Besides, without it, life would be a pretty dull existence. The key is channeling stress energy into productive action instead of feeling overwhelmed, experts say."[23]

We've come to recognize this language and these themes in many media reports on stress. Here's the reference to the bowdlerized version of Walter Cannon's original ideas about how the body responds to fear (I'll say more about Cannon and his "fight or flight" theory in Chapter 2). Here's the concern that too much stress (here it's stress that lasts even for one day; elsewhere it's "too much" or "chronic," often without an reference to how much this is) can destroy the body, and there's the war rhetoric that goes with it ("bombards"; "onslaught"). Add to this the theme of vulnerability and lack of control, and humans seem to be at the mercy of physiological and psychological forces ("flood of hormones"; "overwhelmed"). And there's the insistence on how we have to take charge of stress and conquer it ("people can't control how high their hormones go," but they can take the "stress energy" and use it in "productive" ways). Naturally, a list of stress-reducing technologies to help in these endeavors follows ("deep breathing, meditation and exercise"). And here come the experts, including the ubiquitous Dr. Rabin. As we read a posting about how stress can be *good* for us, we get the message that we're in physiological and psychological jeopardy if we don't act to combat the potentially corrosive effects of stress. When we hear someone like neurobiologist Robert Sapolsky, who has been studying the stress responses of baboons for decades, say that we are "marinating in stress hormones," or when we hear talk of how stress can be "lethal," how it can "shrink our brains," "kill brain cells," and "unravel chromosomes,"[24] we know we're in the land of fear.

Although many people probably aren't familiar with the growing field of psychoneuroimmunology, psychology has been fused with brain science and immunology in ways that many of us readily recognize from scores of media reports. We've become familiar with the talk of "stress hormones" and, as I discuss in Chapter 3, middle-class Americans are practically on speaking terms with their immune systems. The drumbeat of personal responsibility strikes an oddly discordant note in the suggestion that people can control their own neurobiological processes, as when seniors are first warned that "excess cortisol, [experts] suspect, may suppress neurogenesis, the brain's ability to create and support new brain cells," and are then asked: "So how can you turn off the cortisol [a.k.a. the stress hormone]?"[25] Steven Brown has theorized that the more people think of their lives in terms of stress, the more they see themselves as needing to "cope" effectively with it; and the more they make changes in their everyday lives to reduce or eliminate stress, the more they need explanations about what causes stress in order to justify the changes they've made.[26] And the media are happy to oblige.

Stress Inflation

There are certainly viable connections to be made between physical disease and what we now call stress, but the media often create a closer association between stress and its purported effects on body and mind than research evidence supports, creating unnecessary panic. The narrowest academic studies can be springboards for making the most general conclusions about and prescriptions for human behavior. That many research studies on stress have used primates and rodents rather than human beings as their subjects has not deterred either researchers or members of the press from this practice. Although primate research has been incredibly useful in its medical applications, the business of making inferences about psychological states, whether from studying human brains or monkey brains, is pretty dicey. To give an example of the monkey-to-human inferential process, we have only to look at a piece in the women's magazine *Elle* that asks, "Is the best way to raise resilient kids protecting them from stress or allowing them to deal with limited amounts of it?" It cites a Stanford University study in which monkeys removed from their family group were compared with monkeys who had not been removed. The journalist, explaining the Stanford study, writes, "By and large, the young monkeys exposed to intermittent stress [by being taken from their family group] explored more gamely. (Their stress hormone levels were also lower)." Karen Parker, Ph.D., the Stanford researcher who had performed the study, was invited by the reporter to make inferences about parenting that were well beyond the scope of her research. "I do think it's important to allow kids to learn to cope with challenges and changes," she said, while at the same time warning that "all animal research should be interpreted with caution."[27] But all the caveats in the world are pretty worthless when "KIDS AND STRESS" is the screaming headline and there's an expert on board.[28] It's a fair bet that in magazine and newspaper articles of this kind, interviewers will continue to ask the expert to apply her or his results to humans, and nothing will prevent the expert from gamely taking on that mission.

Stress inflation takes some strange forms. For example, the headline "Stress Ages Women Faster" seems to imply that stress ages women faster than men—yes? But if you went to read the research study on which it was based, "Accelerated Telomere Shortening in Response to Life Stress" (a journal article that you probably wouldn't want to find on your nightstand unless you were suffering from insomnia), you'd learn that all 58 participants in the study were women.[29] So, women are aging faster than *whom*?[30] There are dire warnings about the "toll" stress can take on teeth,[32] how it can turn our hair gray,[31] how it can prevent skin from healing,[33] and more. Of course, the connections between stress and aging, stress and dental problems, stress and _____ (fill in the blank) are only *associations*, not actual cause-and-effect relationships. But don't let *that* stress you out.

Stress Throughout the Life Span: A Cultural Phenomenon

Press coverage about stress is pre-womb to tomb, from stories about how women's stress can adversely affect their fertility[34] and how mothers' stress influences their babies' hormone levels in the womb[35] to the adverse effects of stress on brain growth in children,[36] to the stresses of a digital age that produces "Blackberry-toting toddlers"[37] and the "counterproductive stress" that pressures for academic achievement can place on children.[38] I think you get my drift. Here's an article in the *New York Times* about Lisa D'Annolfo Levey, who's on the phone with a parent coach, having told her two dueling sons only moments before, "This is stressing me out, guys. You can sword [fight], but I'm feeling compromised here."[39] And here's a *New York Times* report about a high school principal in Massachusetts who meets regularly with the school Stress Reduction Committee and has made yoga classes a requirement for all seniors.[40] Did you know that "more than 92 percent of students say they occasionally feel overwhelmed by all the tasks they have to perform,"[41] or that there's a "quarterlife crisis" afflicting stressed-out twenty-somethings? As one journalist put it, "Forget waiting till midlife to panic. There's pressure enough halfway there."[42]

Stress and the "Psy" Professions

More and more experts seem to be needed to help Americans deal with stress. The graver the stressful situation or event, the more vigorously psychological remedies are urged upon the public. As I discuss in Chapter 6, when terrorists attacked the World Trade Center in September 2001, the first offer of help for ordinary citizens came from mental health professionals who warned that an epidemic of posttraumatic stress disorder (PTSD) was on its way. Human dramas provide an opportunity for the most well-intentioned of "psy" professionals to enlarge their sway. For example, in 2008 the house publication of the American Psychological Association (APA), *Monitor on Psychology*, titled a short article on APA's survey on stress in America "A Growth Area for Psychology." A 2011 issue of the *Monitor* reported that "America's workers are stressed by the continued economic turmoil," but that "psychologists are poised to help."[43] Territorial imperatives in psychiatry, psychology, social work, and counseling have not only created and sustained a booming therapeutic industry in the United States but have helped shape a therapeutic culture that has gathered momentum in other Western countries. In Britain, whose embrace of popular psychology and psychotherapy has been slow relative to that of the United States, newspaper citations of the word "stress" rose from under 1,000 in 1993 to 24,000 in 2000.[44]

Lifestyle and Stress: A Pairing Made for the Middle Class

The relationship between stress and "lifestyle" is an intimate one, since decreasing stress is often cited as the rationale for making lifestyle changes. Boom or bust—it doesn't matter, when it comes to the ongoing discussion of how people must change their lifestyles in order to reduce stress. In 2004, when economic times were good, it was clear that "All This Progress Is Killing Us" (e.g., that high productivity leads to the loss of more jobs; increased car ownership causes people to walk less; and that these kinds of things can create severe health problems). Turn around, and in 2007, when the recession and middle-class job insecurity were just on the horizon, the theme was the same: that year we read, "America: A Toxic Lifestyle?"[45] You might not have known that "TLC" doesn't stand for "tender loving care;" it's now psychologese for *therapeutic lifestyle change.* Moving beyond public health exhortations to change people's lifestyles, the "psy" professions are now offering "lifestyle treatments."[46]

Public health campaigns targeted at reducing what is almost universally referred to as the "epidemic" of obesity in the U.S. offer examples of the lifestyle/stress connection: stress leads to overeating and overeating leads to obesity, which leads to diabetes and coronary heart disease. The public health goal is for Americans to achieve "healthy lifestyles." But not all Americans have time to exercise or access to decent healthcare, fresh fruits and vegetables, and safe neighborhoods. The achievement of a "healthy lifestyle" requires more than individual "healthy choices." When the "stressor" is poverty, we need to reckon with inequities that make the universal attainment of a healthy lifestyle so elusive.

In 2011, the American Psychological Association's annual survey, "Stressed in America," reported that the number one stressor in America was money. Of course, money in itself is not stressful, although expressions like "financial stress"[47] appear to make it so. It is the lack of money that creates problems for people, and financial worries are big news in the dog days of a recession that affects the middle class. But money—the getting of it—has always been a problem for people on the bottom of the economic ladder. Managing "financial stress" by taking a hot bath or going for a brisk walk in the neighborhood is no solution to the problem of poverty. The idea of lifestyle is a middle-class development,[48] and the push to eliminate stress through lifestyle changes is only one of the middle-class adjustment strategies that have been promoted since the early twentieth century, as I discuss in Chapter 2. As Steven Brown notes, lifestyle advice on how to reduce stress creates a "product" in the form of a person's newly "serviced" and "re-engineered" self.[49]

The Dialogue about Difference: Gender and Stress

In 2009, quite a bit of dust was kicked up in the wake of a paper written by economists Betsey Stevenson and Justin Wolfers. In "The Paradox of Declining Female Happiness," documenting trends in men's and women's well-being over the past 35 years, Stevenson and Wolfers concluded that whereas women of the 1970s were more content than men, men were eclipsing women in subjective well-being.[50] The study gave fuel to those who blamed the women's movement for sowing the seeds of discontent: women have too many choices; they're overwhelmed; they're stressed; they're "liberated and unhappy."[51] On the other side of the debate, critics like Barbara Ehrenreich pooh-poohed Stevenson's and Wolfers's study, pointing out what an elusive phenomenon happiness is to measure.[52] The banner headline on the website jezebel.com read, "'Declining Female Happiness' May Be Just Another Way to Sell S—t" to women.[53] When interviewed, Stevenson herself said that she didn't hold the women's liberation movement responsible for the happiness decline: "It's not the women's movement that's made us so unhappy, but the failures of the women's movement" like the persisting wage gap between men and women.[54]

Early on in the life of the stress concept, men's stress was of much greater public concern than women's; after all, men were straining their grey flannel suits against the bulwarks of capitalism every day. In 1957 one could read about "Colonel M.B., who worked for an unreasonable, hostile boss. His cholesterol level was high, but diet and exercise didn't help. [But] when [his] boss was taken to the hospital..., Colonel M.B.'s cholesterol level showed a remarkable drop."[55] Ever since the 1970s, when middle-class women began entering the paid workforce in larger numbers, however, the subject of women's stress has moved front and center. Here's Amber McCracken, director of communications for the National Women's Health Resource Center, talking about women's stress: "Women must manage not only their own health, but they are considered the health-care managers of their families.... [E]ach aspect of care brings stress. Unfortunately, too often women do not take the necessary steps to alleviate their stress, and their own physical health suffers."[56] As I discuss in Chapter 5, these same themes are salient in much of what is said and written about women and stress: women must manage their stress so that they can continue to be the primary caregivers in our society; women are to blame for not taking good enough care of themselves. The fault lies in self-care, not in the burden of care that women assume on behalf of a society reluctant to look at gender inequality at the societal level.

As the largest consumers of self-help books and lifestyle magazines, women have become primary targets both for advice on how to manage stress and for advertisements for products holding out the promise of stress relief. Women are encouraged to "diagnose" their "stress type" ("Hyperdrive?" "Dash and Crash?" "Fried and Frazzled?")[57] so they can formulate an individualized plan for managing stress. We hear that, unlike men, women overeat when "stressed," bringing on a host of potential health problems:[58] "Packing a bit of a spare tire? It could be from cortisol, a stress-related hormone that makes you store belly fat. To help your body cope more efficiently, increase your intake of stress-easing B vitamins."[59] And "High cortisol levels may also put a damper on feel-good neurotransmitters, such as dopamine and serotonin, moving you into a vicious bad mood/stressed-out cycle. Take a few minutes to ease the stress with deep breathing, a bit of music, and these relaxing stretches."[60] Of course, there's also a lot of talk about how mothers' stress not only affects *them*; it affects their children as well (that old "vicious bad mood/stressed-out cycle"), particularly when women "juggle" paid work and motherhood. In Chapter 5 we'll look at how it's women's job to maintain the "balance" between paid work and home. In fact, warnings to middle-class mothers, particularly white middle-class mothers, about combining outside work and motherhood are so pervasive that mothers may find themselves having to work hard to resist feeling guilty about failing in one domain or the other. And it's difficult not to feel like a failure when white middle-class expectations for what constitutes good parenting have reached an all-time high.

In *Time* magazine's special issue, "The State of the American Woman," a poll showed that the majority of men and women believe the ideal family arrangement is to have a father at work and a mother at home.[61] Self-help gurus like John Gray, the original *Men Are from Mars, Women Are from Venus* guy, argue in effect that innate differences between men and women ideally suit them for traditional roles, disregarding egregious flaws in the science of "brain differences" between men and women that render many of those differences questionable.[62] I'll tackle some of the "difference" assumptions in Chapter 4, where I argue that the stress concept fuels a quasi-obsessional concern with difference that encourages women to keep their place in the domestic order. Perhaps a poll on traditional roles might have a different outcome if the work of caring were an overarching societal value that drove policies such as universal childcare and paid family leave for both men and women.

Stressism: A Definition for Our Time

Over 20 years ago, Steven Brown argued that most types of suffering and "dis-ease" have been transformed into the experience of stress. While I agree, I'd add that now there is a tremendous emphasis not only on the *emotional* "dis-ease" of stress, but on the potential of stress to induce *actual* disease. The connection between external events and disease is now so well forged that sometimes an adverse event and its physiological effects are strangely comingled, as in this article on the tensions of the holiday season:

> The holidays are hard on your amygdala, a primitive little part of your brain that gets activated whenever you experience a feeling. Emotions— both good and bad—give the amygdala such a workout this time of year

that your frontal lobe, a more recently evolved part of the brain that acts as a rational brake on your primal impulses, has to work extra hard to keep you on an even keel, says Ruben Gur, a University of Pennsylvania neuropsychology professor.[63]

As emotions themselves are medicalized, and stress, emotion, and disease are fused in the public imagination, the stress concept has become an important means of thinking about life's difficulties and our personal vulnerability to risk, disaster, and death. In the documentary I mentioned earlier, one expert insisted that "[stress] is not an abstract concept." I beg to disagree. It is the thoroughly abstract and diffuse nature of the stress concept that makes it such a useful container for societal tensions and individual fears. Some ideas perform what Mary Poovey calls "ideological work," managing or containing contradictions in ways that make for the widespread acceptance of certain overarching ideas as common sense.[64] I believe that, among other things, the stress concept performs ideological work for us by managing much of our uneasiness about social change, whether in the pace of life in the wake of technological advancements, in gender arrangements as a result of the rise in dual-career marriages, or in the number and nature of uncontrollable external events such as the terrorist attacks of 9/11.

Stress is "real" in the sense that people experience it and may suffer as a result of it, but it also can be said that the concept of stress has been created (and re-created) at certain places and times in our history[65] and that it performs certain functions for our society. Although I'm critical of the stress concept and of the degree to which the "psy" professions (of which I am a member) have fallen under its spell, I am mindful that there are many who experience stress and who suffer its effects, and also that there are many professionals who are there to help people in distress. I'm also mindful that it's very hard to talk about stress and trauma without invoking the words *stress* and *trauma* themselves, creating a sort of tautological thicket that can be difficult to avoid.

This book doesn't claim to be a comprehensive history of stress or stress research. Such histories are out there to be read.[66] Unfortunately, those histories don't have much to say about the meaning of our contemporary reliance on the stress concept. I've written this book, at least in part, to try to fill that gap.[67] I believe that in order to understand stress as a bellwether cultural concept, we need to understand what accounts for its widespread appeal; what social purposes it serves; what social problems it solves; why stress sometimes appears to be owned by the white middle class. The anchoring frameworks from which I draw in grappling with these questions are social constructionism, critical psychology, and feminism. The disciplines from which I derive support for many of the ideas presented in this book include sociology, the history of medicine, and medical anthropology.

In the chapters that follow, I've chosen to highlight diverse aspects of the stress concept's cultural influence. Chapter 2 explores a particularly American attachment to ideas about how people can cope with the fast pace of life that progress brings with it. Chapter 3 explains how the stress concept offers protection from fear of disease and death through a mandate to reduce risks and manage our health, obscuring the problem of health inequalities arising from differences in social class. Chapters 4 and 5 aim to show how the stress concept helps keep traditional ideas about men's and women's natures and responsibilities from unraveling in ways that might create actual changes in social policy and in the division of care work. Chapter 6 lays out how, in a society allergic to existential doubt, the concept of traumatic stress helps stifle disturbing moral ambiguities, whether in relation to war, child abuse, terrorism, or male-to-female violence.

I've coined the word *stressism* to describe the current belief that the tensions of contemporary life are primarily individual lifestyle problems to be solved through managing stress, as opposed to the belief that these tensions are linked to social forces and need to be resolved primarily through social and political means. Analysis of stressism brings into sharp focus significant polarities in Western thought, principally the sharp divisions between mind and body, health and illness, public and private, social responsibility and individual self-actualization. Examining stress brings to light many of our cherished cultural preoccupations and predispositions, exposing existing tensions and inequities related to class and gender; and our increasing dependence on stress to explain our lives has consequences for the way we see ourselves and the world, the way we act, and the world we create as a consequence of that vision and those actions.

CHAPTER 2

Getting and Spending

The Wear and Tear of Modern Life

> O born in days when wits were fresh and clear,
> And life ran gaily as the sparkling Thames;
> Before this strange disease of modern life,
> With its sick hurry, its divided aims,
> Its heads o'ertax'd, its palsied hearts, was rife—
> —Matthew Arnold, *The Scholar Gipsy* (1853)

We Americans never tire of telling the story of how we've built what we've built—and what it's cost us. Ever since the Gilded Age, we've ruminated about how the pace of change is leading to our loss of virtue or our crumbling piety or our tendency toward overwork, or, Heaven forbid, to the decline of the family dinner hour, all in the name of progress—a progress, mind you, that we also celebrate (and endlessly); a progress that is supposed to define us as uniquely American. In the United States, this allegory about the human costs of progress has taken many forms over 150 years or so, but it generally serves the same cultural purpose: to help us get past our worries about what is happening to moral values and social practices during times of social and/or economic upheaval. Change—and the inevitable advancement that comes with it—is worth the price we have to pay for it. And there's always some action we can take—some individual, some personal action each of us can take to grease the rails of our forward trajectory. If we're stressed, we can relax; if we're overworking, we can pull back—just not enough to stall the engines of progress. And so it goes.

The story of the price of progress is an old and unalterably optimistic tale about how humans have conquered the material world and created civilized societies. It is a story about how, with the same persistence and ingenuity they used to build those societies in the first place, human beings can undo any harm they may have inflicted on themselves in the process of construction. Its ambiguity has allowed the allegory to be appropriated across two centuries by critics and champions of the social order alike.[1] Whether we call the price of progress *nervousness* or *stress* is not particularly important. But it *has* seemed important to Americans to have a focus for our anxieties that keeps the social structures of our society intact. We apply the term *crumbling infrastructure* to bridges, roads, and sewers. But when it comes to the near meltdown of our economy or the poverty of our inner cities, we talk about stress and illness.

Two themes have dominated the American progress-and-pathology story.[2] The first of these is that excessive anxiety is damaging, and that the damaging effects of worry increase as the pace of life increases. The *damage* theme once took the form of medical and popular hand-wringing over "nerves" and nervous disease. Now it is given endless expression in discussions—public and private—about how stress affects our health. The second theme is that all of us are individually responsible for managing ourselves so that we can make a reasonable adjustment to the conditions of modern life, however stressful. This *adjustment* theme had its origins in the Mental Hygiene Movement that peaked in the 1930s, and it is easy to spot today in talk about how we need to achieve "balance" in our hectic lives.

The *damage* scenario emphasizes the possibility that society can destroy our health and well-being; the *adjustment* scenario emphasizes the possibility that if we fail to adapt to the conditions imposed by our culture we will ruin ourselves. These themes give the stress concept its dual nature,[3] but in practice they do not have equal weight. Generally, it is the *adjustment* scenario that carries the day.[4] In our culture it is no accident that people believe they are to blame if they cannot adjust "successfully" to stressful circumstances. We are schooled to look to ourselves for both the causes of our problems and the solutions to them when things go wrong. How could it be otherwise? The worth of the individual and the value of individual achievement are fundamental to a national identity shaped in the tradition of liberal individualism. It is not by chance that we continue to place a high value on autonomy, self-fulfillment, and choice.[5]

The question of whether society or the individual is responsible for managing the fallout from industrial, technological, or social "progress" is one of the questions that the idea of stress resolves in favor of the individual.[6] The "stressed out" person comes to stand for all our relationships with the social structures that make up modern life as we know it.[7] That "stressed" person becomes the cultural embodiment of—and, in a sense, the scapegoat for—all our ideas about how people relate to society. In talking about the "stressed out" person, or about stress itself, we're talking about that person/society relationship. But we focus on the *person*, because when we talk about the person/society relationship we're *not* generally talking about inequalities in the economic system, or men's and women's family responsibilities, or what's wrong with the ethos of success, achievement, and competition. Throughout our history, especially during times of social and economic transformation, worrying about nervous illness or Type A behavior or keeping our immune systems in top condition has helped us avoid tackling larger social problems. Finding solutions to those problems might force us to make substantive structural changes in our society, and it is easier to try to change ourselves and each other than to change the social or political environment; far easier to talk about the "stressed" African American single mother, say, than to think about the effects of de facto school segregation in our cities, or the effects of discrimination on employment opportunities, or the shortage of affordable childcare.

If today the "stressed out" person embodies our relationships with the institutions in our society, in mid- to late nineteenth-century America the neurasthenic man or woman represented his or her society's relationship to rapid social and economic change. With the shift from an agricultural to a commercial economy came changes in the roles of men and women and in the meaning of work and success, among other things. Broad public discussion of nervousness in its myriad forms effectively paved over the structural fault lines that threatened to appear as a result of the social transformations and dislocations that accompanied the growth of industry and consumerism.

NINETEENTH-CENTURY NERVOUSNESS

Americans have long believed that circumstances and events can make people sick. In the eighteenth century, good Jeffersonians made the connection between social well-being and health.[8] Dr. Benjamin Rush, noting that many Loyalists had become dangerously ill, presumably from the strain of being on the wrong side in the Revolutionary War, named that illness "Revolutiana."[9] During the Jacksonian, era "moral management"[10] of the insane was predicated on the idea that certain emotions and stressful conditions, particularly the pressures of urban commerce and industry, could induce mental illness.[11]

But in the late nineteenth century, obsessive concern about nerves and nervous illness swept through the country with gale force. Silas Weir Mitchell, a neurologist and specialist in the treatment of nervous disorders, wrote about the conditions of life that he and many of his peers believed were responsible for the outbreak of nervous disease. In 1871 he fretted:

> Have we lived too fast? The settlers here, as elsewhere, had ample room, and lived sturdily by their own hands, little troubled for the most part with those intense competitions which make it hard to live nowadays and embitter the daily bread of life. Neither had they the thousand intricate problems to solve which perplex those who struggle to-day [sic] in our teeming city hives.[12]

To read the medical and popular literature of the day is to be struck with the sense that never before in history had a people experienced anything like the problems faced by Americans at the turn of the century. What made concerns about nervousness and the stresses of civilized existence seem to spring full-blown from nineteenth-century culture? More than anything else, it was the ever enlarging gaze of science, seizing on everything from the harmful impact of urban life to the question of women's proper place in society.[13]

Americans' veneration of science and scientific opinion had reached a new zenith.[14] Not surprisingly, it was an American neurologist, George M. Beard, who became the popularizer-in-chief—on both sides of the Atlantic—of the nervous disease called neurasthenia.[15] Social Darwinist to the core, Beard believed that the rate of cultural evolution was outstripping the ability of people to keep up with it. From the late nineteenth-century until the 1920s, neurasthenia ("nerve weakness," translated from the Greek) was the label chosen for a host of wildly divergent symptoms, from insomnia to fear of lightning to tooth decay.[16] More frequent symptoms of neurasthenia were fatigue, poor concentration, pain, digestive problems, and anxiety. To Beard and his contemporaries, every bodily function was in competition for a limited store of energy, such that using too much in one area temporarily weakened others.[17] According to Beard, this vital energy had to be carefully conserved:[18] "The force in this nervous system... is limited; and when new functions are interposed in the circuit, as modern civilization is constantly requiring us to do, there comes a period, sooner or later... when the amount of force is insufficient to keep all lamps actively burning."[19] It was clear that the human battery needed constant recharging.[20]

Although neurasthenia was by no means a disease restricted solely to Americans,[21] Beard viewed it as a particularly American disease. Its causes, according Beard, were the stressors of the day: "steampower, the periodical press, the telegraphy [sic], the sciences, and the mental activity of women," the cruelly competitive marketplace, the pressures of urban life, and the climate of the American Northeast.[22] The commotion over neurasthenia expressed a characteristically American ambivalence—both optimism about where progress could lead and a persistent cultural insecurity.[23] Beard sided with the optimists: the "evil of American nervousness," he insisted, "tends, within certain limits, to correct itself.... Social customs with the needs of the times shall be modified, and as a consequence... strength and vigor shall be developed at the same time with... debility and nervousness."[24] The majority of Americans saw it Beard's way. They believed that although they were enduring the most stressful conditions ever known, their sacrifices were worth it; their efforts now would benefit future generations.[25]

For all the talk about how the fast pace of life was leading to nervous disease, no one was suggesting that the engines of American progress and prosperity should be shut down. Indeed, Beard himself, with some pride it seems, viewed the nervous problems of some members of the educated elite as natural developments in a free and advanced society. Americans were free to rise above the social station into which they had been born and to achieve fame and fortune on their own merits, and this did not come without cost.[26] The neurasthenic embodied both the upward trajectory of American life *and* the high price Americans were paying for rapid industrial growth and increasing materialism.[27] As historian Tom Lutz has pointed out, neurasthenia was more than a medical condition: it offered writers, academics, and journalists a way to talk about social, psychological, and economic change—change in the relationships people had with institutions and in the institutions themselves. In justifying the status quo, neurasthenia gave Americans a way to regain their balance,[28] while at the same time endorsing, for the first time in our history, the idea that Americans could manage their symptoms by making what we would now call "lifestyle changes," engaging in activities outside the compass of their daily duties.[29]

At least a portion of neurasthenia's popularity can be attributed to the way it comforted the comfortable—reassuring men, in particular, about their powerful place in society. Early on, neurasthenia was seen as a disease of the well-off, even a credit to those afflicted with it.[30],[31] Neurasthenic metaphors underscored the connection between nervous disease and the stuff of American capitalism: masculine earning and owning.[32] The "capital of vitality" could be drained by the daily wear and tear of life in the cities as the nervous system became "sorely overtaxed."[33] And all of this could lead to "nervous bankruptcy."[34]

Then, as now, the stresses of American middle- and upper-class life merited more attention than the pressing problems of the working class and the poor. In the nineteenth century, the general assumption that women were "naturally" meant only to devote themselves to domestic responsibilities and child rearing took no account of the lives of the hundreds of thousands of working-class women who ventured out into the world every day to earn their bread.[35] It was not until the 1980s, when middle-class women began to enter the workforce in significant numbers, that the "stresses" of balancing home and work became the stuff of public concern, even though for centuries poor and low-income women had been working both in and outside the home at the sametime.

Neurasthenia confirmed the essential rightness of applying Darwin's ideas to humans. Evolutionary biology, newly in vogue in the latter portion of the nineteenth century, seemed to "prove" that the better class of men was more highly evolved—that middle-class nervous systems were more sensitive than those of the poor. Servants and day laborers were responsible for their disadvantage through their own lack of fitness—of body, mind, or morals. In the evolutionary scheme of things, women's nervous systems were underdeveloped because through the ages they had needed all their available energies to reproduce the race and serve mankind.[36] Their brains were smaller than men's, and since they were ruled by their reproductive systems, they were by nature more emotional.[37]

As a result of rapid industrial growth, the nature of work was changing and, with it, the roles of men and women. The middle-class family that had once pulled together to produce goods for itself and its neighbors in an agricultural economy had to adjust to father's leaving home for work every morning in the "teeming city hive." His home, complete with servants, a wifely "angel of the hearth," and scrubbed and smiling children, was expected to be a place of refuge from the tensions of the workday.[38] A changing economy supported what historians have called the ideology of the separate spheres—the notion that men were constitutionally suited for engagement in the public realm and women for home and hearth. And that division between public and private, man and woman, was helped along by the evolutionary confirmation of women's inferior brain development.

The apparent contradiction between the depiction of the middle- and upper-class mother as the strong, heroic, moral center of the family and as a physiologically fragile vessel requiring male protection did not seem particularly troubling at the time, perhaps because women's heroism was self-abnegating and her role subordinate.[39] These days, as I'll discuss further in Chapters 4 and 5, we overlook similar contradictions. These days, middle-class women are depicted as heroically coping with the pressures that accompany their multiple roles and responsibilities, while at the same time they're bombarded with "expert" advice on how to cope better with the stress caused by those same roles and responsibilities.

Anxious Men and Nervous Women

In the early days of its popularity, neurasthenia gave some breathing room to middle-class men who had to make a transition[40] from a life grounded in a severe Protestant work ethic to a life centered around an ethos of competition and "compulsive industry."[41] The world of business, thought by their ancestors to be "common," was not a comfortable fit for some men, and these men sank into a depressive lassitude. At a time when the standard of masculine strength denied them any permissible signs of weakness, men could be given the "scientific," respectable diagnosis of neurasthenia.[42] But even though the mission of doctors was to get men on their feet and back to work—in Beard's words, "to put these patients into working order"[43]—doctors had real ambivalence about a competitive atmosphere that emphasized getting ahead no matter the cost. On the one hand, physicians were all for hard work: they repudiated idleness and felt compassion for men felled by overwork. On the other hand, they knew enough about the ways of their countrymen to fear where wild ambition, cut-throat competition, and the mania for money-making might lead the nation in the long run.[44]

The period when men were granted permission to show their sensitivities in the form of nervous disease was to be short-lived. Male fatigue and "nerves" made men seem passive and irresolute; these symptoms were too womanish to be socially sanctioned. Social Darwinism confirmed that only the hardy survived life's ordeals, so doctors found a way to explain men's nervous illness that restored the distinction between real men and weaklings. Instead of insisting that men's nervous exhaustion *created* weakness of the will, they determined that weakness was the *cause* of men's nervous problems. The weak now could be blamed as well as pitied.[45] In a society continually worried about stripping men of their masculinity, the story of the price of progress has had to be told very carefully. And differences between men and women—in their skills, their strengths, their weaknesses—have had to be continually emphasized in the interest of maintaining the status quo.

Although case literature of the period between 1870 and 1910 shows that the number of male and female neurasthenic patients was almost identical,[46] Beard and his fellow physicians observed that more women suffered from neurasthenia than men.[47] And even though the symptoms of hysteria and neurasthenia were confusingly similar, women were thought to be especially prone to hysteria (considered the less refined of the two diseases).[48] Doctors shied away from applying the label of hysteria to men because of its association with women. Beard wrote of hysteria: "Symptoms acute, intense, violent, positive. Usually associated with great emotional activity and unbalanced mental organization.

Very rare in males."[49] The female hysteric was noisier and more difficult than the neurasthenic, who was, in Silas Weir Mitchell's words, "just the kind of woman one likes to meet with—sensible, not over sensitive or emotional, exhibiting a proper amount of illness . . . and a willingness to perform their share of work quietly."[50]

Even the same nervous disease had different symptoms and treatments for men and women. Men often had acute and obvious "breakdowns," easily spotted in the disruption of their daily routines and regular work responsibilities. But because middle-class women had no work outside the home, their decline was not so readily noticed, and the onset of their illness was generally more gradual—more like a chronic depressive or anxious state that could persist for years before it was noted or treated.[51] On the treatment side, since men could not usually be spared from work for long periods of time, they were often advised to take up rugged outdoor activities, whereas women were usually prescribed indoor "rest cures" that isolated and infantilized them. Silas Weir Mitchell was well known for confining his women patients to bed for six weeks or more and having them fattened up with rich foods, sometimes through force feeding.[52]

As middle-class men girded themselves for the new world of business, their wives were making the transition to lives of greater leisure than ever before. But within their more or less gilded cages, these women were suffering from nervous ailments in alarming numbers.[53] When Mitchell, the most prominent chronicler of the treatment of neurasthenia, ordered women's rights advocate and author Charlotte Perkins Gilman, who was suffering acutely from a nervous disorder, to put down her pen and never write again (she egregiously disobeyed), the battle over women's "nerves" that continues to this day was joined.

It was assumed that women were less well "nervously prepared" to handle stress than men and thus more prone to nervous illnesses and more easily traumatized.[54] As noted earlier, nervousness in the "weaker sex" was tied to women's reproductive physiology. Puberty and childbirth made women vulnerable. Because physicians believed that women had even less nerve force than men, they were constantly cau-tioning women against expending too much energy. At the same time as they were saying that higher education could prove deadly for women, doctors pooh-poohed the idea that domestic duties could cause nervous disease. They believed that only *crushing* responsibilities at home could affect women's nerves. Crushing domestic responsibilities, of course, were more often the lot of women who couldn't afford servants—poor women who were often servants themselves.[55] Margaret Cleaves, a physician and herself a former neurasthenic, took the lonely position that neurasthenia was induced when women of high intelligence and education tried to carry on a life of the mind while simultaneously managing their obligations as wives, mothers, housekeepers, and hostesses. "Women, more than men," Cleaves insisted, "are handicapped at the outset, not necessarily because they are women, but because, suddenly and without the previous preparation that men for generations have had, they attempt to fulfill certain conditions and are expected to qualify themselves for certain work and distinctions."[56]

Nervous women caused problems for everyone. They were failures as women, and some were refractory patients who gave their doctors headaches. Mitchell said his clientele was "well known to every physician, —nervous women, who, as a rule, are thin and lack blood. Most of them have…passed through many hands…, but…remained at the end…invalids, unable to attend to the duties of life,… sources alike of discomfort to themselves and anxiety to others."[57] Doctors did their valiant best to help women resume their ordained jobs as wives and mothers, believing that by returning women to their domestic labors they had found the solution to, rather than the cause of, the problem.[58] Since physicians persisted, even into the twentieth century, in seeing whatever was connected with reproduction as a physical or mental handicap, hysteria and neurasthenia opened the way for the women's brains—their psychology—rather than their reproductive organs to become the arena for scientific expertise. Things changed in the twentieth century, but not as much as might have been expected. Now the battle is joined not over what women are *capable* of doing, but what they *should* do.[59] Today, much of the medical and non-medical advice given to women about how to deal with stress—to devise a "to do" list, make time for a soak in an aromatic bath, take antidepressants to combat premenstrual moodiness that might interfere with service to the family—also contains implicit messages about what she *shouldn't* do—nag, yell, demand too much, or in any way inconvenience those in her care. Like the advice of nineteenth-century physicians, these suggestions have served a similarly stabilizing social function.

Physicians' continuing inability to find cures for the nonspecific symptoms of nervous illnesses finally brought the age of neurasthenia to a close. But the progress-and-pathology saga was not over. Other ways of explaining the relationship between the person and society became even more instrumental in helping form our contemporary ideas about stress. In fact, just when the excitement over neurasthenia was at its peak, a new movement was in its infancy that would soon dictate what "normal" adjustment to society should look like.

The Mental Hygiene Movement embraced the broad goal of curing the ills of society through promoting wholesome habits of mind.[60] It had sprung to life in 1912, propelled by the reformist energies of the day, backed by the U.S. Public Health Service, and supported by such luminaries as the psychologist and philosopher William James and prominent psychiatrist Adolf Meyer.[61] For Meyer, mental health constituted adjustment, characterized as the ability to look objectively at life, act with decisiveness, and live up to middle-class societal standards.[62] Meyer believed that prevention of severe mental illness must take place in the community, where people at risk for mental illness could be found. Meyer also recommended that outpatient clinics be established for people with mental disorders, so that they could more easily return to society. There was no need to wait until people became acutely mentally ill and then shunt them off to asylums; now, in the interest of society at large, people could be helped to adjust to society before they reached this state. Anyone who didn't fit the social standard of adjustment was presumably a candidate for treatment. Unsurprisingly, defining mental health and mental illness in terms of social adjustment broadened the reach of the psychiatric profession considerably.

A minority of very early mental hygienists thought there were problems to be solved beyond those of individual adjustment. As the first medical director of the National Committee of Mental Hygiene, Thomas Salmon, put it, society, too, "has its diseases."[63] This theme was resurrected when, during a period of increasing labor unrest, there was a moment when an unusual convergence among workers' needs and professionals' sense of moral purpose fueled the mental hygienists' reformist spirit.[64] Rejecting the Gilded Age view that poverty resulted from individual defects, many mental hygiene reformers of that era joined

Progressives in understanding that conditions outside the individual—unemployment, bad neighborhoods, and the like—were responsible for human misery and had to be transformed.

But the historical moment for social reform was fleeting. By 1930, Dr. Frederick A. Allen, a child psychiatrist, baldly stated that the Mental Hygiene Movement's philosophy "presupposes the existence of an ideal about the social order and the individuals who constitute it."[65] That ideal was nothing less than perfect adjustment to what was often referred to as "Reality," and reality appeared synonymous with the status quo.[66] Over time, movement leaders tried to influence major American institutions—schools, hospitals, and the like—to adopt a mental health agenda.[67] Little by little, adjustment came to mean individual intrapsychic adjustment. This was hardly Jane Addams's progressivism; Meyer, who had so energetically put his shoulder to the wheel of the movement, felt his spirits sink. Altruism was to be a casualty of the materialism sweeping the country following World War I.[68]

In the United States, the impulse for social improvement is invariably coupled with the urge for social control, and mental hygiene proved the rule.[69] At the urging of movement leaders, mental hygiene researchers plunged into scientific studies of "the sources of human happiness and efficiency"[70] to show how personalities are formed by the environment. But the environment they referred to was not environment writ large; the researchers were not referring to the structure of society.[71] They didn't find the critical elements that shaped personality in the workplace or in the larger economy or in the educational system: they found them in the emotional environment of the home. Scientific child-rearing methods would ensure that children were well adapted to the needs of the economy and society at large.[72]

Charlotte Perkins Gilman harbored the hope (a vain one, as it turned out) that science would eventually lead to greater freedom for women. In her view, the innovative technologies that had brought other forms of social progress had not done enough for women:

> The domestic hearth, with its undying flame, has given way to the gilded pipes of the steam heater and the flickering evanescence of the gas range. But the sentiment about the domestic hearth is still in play. The original necessity for the ceaseless presence of the woman to maintain that

altar fire…has passed…but the *feeling* that women should stay at home is with us yet.[73]

Elevating women's work to a science, she believed, could free society from the mother-worship—the "matriolatry," as she called it—that had long ensnared women in the sticky web of domesticity. At first blush it looked as though mental hygiene's ideas about scientific child-rearing practices could offer women a new, improved status. But in the end, science did not offer women the autonomy that Gilman and others had hoped for. The idea of motherhood as scientific enterprise seemed only to confirm that women should be trained for motherhood and nothing else,[74] reaffirming middle-class women's place in the home. The New Woman of early twentieth-century America may have set her sights on self-actualization, employment opportunities, and sexual freedom; after all, Edna St. Vincent Millay *did* arrive in Greenwich village to write poetry and slept with whomever she chose. But to most women and men, women were only daughters, wives, and mothers.[75]

Mental Hygiene's Legacy

Joel Kovel has suggested that, sadly, the most important contribution made by the Mental Hygiene Movement may have been the very idea embodied in the term *mental hygiene* itself, the idea that what was "mental"—human psychology—could be surgically separated from the history and context of that same psychology.[76] Beyond this, I believe that the psychology of adjustment touted by the mental hygienists lives on in the notion, enshrined in the stress concept, that social problems can be resolved by improving the mental functioning of individuals. Echoing down through the decades, mental hygiene's message of adaptation and adjustment has helped shape the fields of psychiatry, psychology, and social work.

The idea of adaptation was used to explain how, even in the absence of outside pathogens, the wrong kind of adaptation—adaptation to adverse external conditions—could cause disease.[77] And these ideas about adaptation fueled the work of the physiologists, endocrinologists, and cardiologists who brought the idea of stress closer and closer to its present meaning. As individual adjustment to the demands of life became a pressing social concern, these professionals began to ask questions about how we achieve balance between what is inside the body and what is outside it. And the stress concept as we understand it today gradually came to be.

STRESS COMES INTO ITS OWN

For all its ideological precursors in the nervous diseases of the nineteenth century, the concept of stress did not enter popular culture until the mid-twentieth century. But, as early as 1914, Walter Cannon, a Harvard physiologist, had used the term *stress*. Cannon was greatly influenced by a French physician, Claude Bernard, who had argued in 1878 that in order to manage conditions in the *external* environment, the body's *internal* environment had to be constant.[78] Cannon studied the physiology of cats when they were in the presence of dogs, their natural rivals. Applying what he had learned about cats to humans, he concluded that in response to rage and fear (what he called "disturbing" conditions), the body released adrenalin,[79] the heartbeat sped up, and blood sugar rose. He noted that, despite these potentially disruptive effects, the body was able to keep "on an even course," returning, like a thermostat, to a steady state.[80] Cannon called this state *homeostasis*. He marveled at the "wisdom of the body," how "the natural mechanisms of the body operate to shield it against harm and to repair and restore it in case of actual injury."[81]

Tremendously influenced by Darwinian thought, Cannon believed that rage and fear were gradual evolutionary adjustments that had prepared the body of the Stone Age man or woman for fight or flight in the face of danger. But, despite the (small "c") canonization of the "fight or flight" response to stress (and "fight or flight" seems to be mentioned at some point in nearly every popular discussion of the stress response), Cannon's use of the term *stress* was different from today's. His focus was not on the relationship between disease and the fast pace of life. Cannon described stress in terms of heat, hunger, oxygen deprivation, and other phenomena that can cause predictable physiological responses. Because he defined stress in physiological terms, questions have been raised as to whether Cannon can justifiably be called the "founding father" of stress.[82] Whether or not Cannon would agree with later interpretations—and appropriations—of his work, it is generally agreed that, after Cannon, all stress theories were based at least in part on his ideas about homeostasis.[83] Cannon's work lives on in the popular idea that there is an ongoing battle between our out-of-date physiology and the demands of modern life. We make biological "adjustments" that are no longer functional: we react to an angry boss the way our Stone Age counterparts reacted to a saber-tooth tiger, but we can't run away. So, in the modern age, the argument goes, constant fight-or-flight reactions will produce excessive bodily wear and tear.[84]

Hans Selye: Reaping the Whirlwind of Stress

Cannon may have been first to use the term *stress*, but Hans Selye, an endocrinologist born in Czechoslovakia, believed that in creating his theory of stress, he had made a discovery on a par with that of Columbus and Louis Pasteur. This initial "discovery" came about as a result of his attempts in the early 1930s to find new female hormones by injecting rats with a variety of tissue extracts. When, to his dismay, he found that all the different extracts caused the same response in the rats,[85] he started to think that the body might have a general response to noxious agents introduced to it, and he began to call these agents "stress."[86] By the late 1930s, Selye was convinced that a set of reactions he had observed, which he called the General Adaptation Syndrome (G.A.S.), was universal. In his formulation, the stress response was a general (nonspecific) response to any demand. The G.A.S. consisted of three stages: an initial *alarm stage*, in which the body prepared either for fight or flight by, among other things, increasing blood sugar, perspiration, and heart rate and releasing hormones that would increase heart rate; a *resistance stage* in which these changes were essentially repaired; and, if stressful external conditions persisted, a stage of *exhaustion* when adaptive processes began to break down and disease or even death might ensue.

As late as 1940, Selye used the term *stress*, much as Cannon had done, to describe the external forces that influenced the body's homeostasis. But, by 1950, he was describing stress as a "response to a condition evoked by 'stressors.'"[87] In his book *The Stress of Life*, written for a popular audience, he calls stress "the rate of wear and tear caused by life."[88] He used the new term *stressor* to refer to the "agent that produces the G.A.S."[89] This revised theory was no longer a theory of general adaptation; it was a theory of stress.[90] For Selye, health represented successful adaptation to the environment; disease, unsuccessful adaptation. He wrote that "disease is not just suffering, but a fight to maintain the homeostatic balance of our tissues, despite damage."

According to Selye, he purposely had not used *stress* in his early papers because the term had been greeted with "violently adverse public opinion."[91] But, as Selye related, little by little "the term slipped into common usage...through habit rather than logic."[92] What Selye did not discuss was his role in creating that "habit." A tireless promoter of the stress concept, Selye sold and resold it over the years in popular and professional venues—in his best-selling books *The Story of the Adaptation Syndrome* and *The Stress of Life*, in talks to doctors' groups in Canada and United States, and at meetings of the American Psychological Association. In the 1950s and 1960s, Selye's connection with the military helped move the stress concept outside the laboratory.[93] Speaking at the U.S. Army's 1953 "Symposium on Stress," Selye urged the military to study stress in order to prevent "neuropsychiatric casualties."[94] In this case, his salesmanship hit its mark. By the 1970s, approximately a third of all stress researchers were military men.[95]

Selye's popularization of the stress concept resurrected both old and new themes. Warning that "our reserve of adaptation energy is an inherited finite amount, which cannot be regenerated,"[96] Selye echoed both the nerve doctors' idea of nervous energy as capital[97] and the mental hygienists' emphasis on adaptation. Selye's focus on individual achievement and self-fulfillment was in step with the times. For Selye, stress was part of "the evolution of individuality, of the need for self- expression, and the urge to work for rewards."[98] "Man's ultimate aim is to *express himself as fully as possible, according to his own lights*" (Selye's italics).[99] In order to do this, he told his readers, "you must first find your optimum stress-level [*sic*], and then use your adaptation energy at a rate and in a direction adjusted to the innate structure of your mind and body."[100] Selye wanted to elevate stress to the position of the most important problem facing sociology and psychology in his time, and by constantly asserting that stress could cause health problems and disease, he tried to make it so.[101]

In one respect, Selye's sales pitch worked: the stress concept was broadly embraced in the popular culture. Very different groups used it to buttress their very different points of view. Conservative industrial and commercial interests found in stress the validation of dearly held capitalist credos, while cultural critics found in it an indictment of those same interests and the society they bred.[102] But it was as a champion of capitalism that Selye, hardly an anti-establishment figure, gathered to himself his most powerful supporters.

On the heels of the Great Depression in the United States and the expansion of fascism in Europe, prominent social scientists worried about the potential for social instability. Selye, too, had his concerns.[103] On the one hand, the "fight" was one that the individual waged against what Selye called "diseases of civilization," such as heart disease.[104] But Selye also had a vision of how his ideas about stress could be employed in the larger fight against social instability: people needed to adjust successfully "to the ever-changing conditions on this globe; the penalties for failure in this great process of adaptation are disease and unhappiness."[105] Men must work. Work, Selye insisted, was biologically necessary:[106] "Without the incentive to take on his role as *homo faber* [working man], a person is likely to seek destructive, revolutionary outlets to satisfy the basic human need for self-assertive activity."[107] Selye must have had no trouble finding a willing audience for these ideas: worker efficiency and worker docility weren't a hard sell in postwar America.

Earlier on, Cannon had also applied his ideas about physiology to society. But Cannon's examination of the relationship between human aggression and social instability was no argument in favor of the status quo. *His* working man needed to have security and steady wages. Writing before the advent of the New Deal, Cannon spoke up in support of unemployment compensation, regulation of working hours, and the eradication of child labor.[108] In contrast, for all his talk of "society," Selye barely betrayed a social conscience. In *Stress Without Distress*, he argued that natural selection was a product of egotism from the cell upward. But, he maintained men—or cells—are not islands. Selye had the idea that safety and prosperity in numbers could be achieved through what he called "altruistic egotism."[109] Just as "the best interests" of the body are served when cells work together harmoniously, so the best interests of humankind are served when we each look out for "ourselves first, without feeling guilt," he told a reporter from the *Montreal Gazette*.[110] Taking care of their health was the best thing people could do for their fellow humans. A 1956 *Time* magazine interview with Selye underscored his focus on the individual:

> A man can be drunk with his own hormones, according to Endocri-nologist [*sic*] Selye, who adds: "This sort of drunkenness has caused much more harm to society than the other kind.... In all our actions throughout the day we must consciously look for signs of being keyed up too much—and we must learn to stop in time."[111]

Selye was by no means the only champion of the stress concept in the 1960s and 1970s. In 1967 two psychiatrists, Thomas H. Holmes and Richard H. Rahe, published the *Social Readjustment Rating Scale* (*SRRS*), a questionnaire that ranked stressful life events on a scale from 0 to 100.[112] Each event was valued as having a specific number of "life change units" (LCUs). Christmas earned 12 points; marital separation 65. Whether the event was pleasant or extremely distressing was of no consequence; in accord with Selye's framework, what mattered was the degree of adaptation the stressor entailed. The total number of points determined a person's risk for illness and disease.[113] The *SSRS* was wildly popular, both with the public and with academic psychologists. Until the late 1970s, when Holmes's and Rahe's ideas were cast into doubt, their work spurred on many researchers to make connections between stress and disease.

The Fall of Selye and the Rise of the Stress Concept

A major stumbling block for Selye was his failure to get colleagues in his own field to accept his ideas. Early on, some critics found stress too elusive, too difficult to measure; others found the idea of nonspecific adaptation too amorphous. Cannon himself did not accept Selye's findings. Fellow scientists critical of his theories and research methods were equally put off by Selye's outsized ego.[114] Undaunted by the failure to have his ideas accepted unequivocally, Selye went on the road to popularize the stress concept. His tireless work in bringing stress to the public's attention not only satisfied his messianic ambitions; it had the paradoxical effect of bringing stress back into the scientific fold via psychology. When Selye stopped describing stress in strictly physiological terms and sold it as a part of human life that needed to be studied scientifically, he began to win converts among professional psychologists. In Russell Viner's words, "stress had been translated from a story told to the masses by a scientist, into an experience told to scientists by the common person."[115] The *idea* of stress had not been rejected by physiologists in the 1970s—only Selye's model of it. Selye continued to fight the repudiation of his model tooth and nail, revising his popular books and writing new ones.[116] In *Stress Without Distress,* he called for "philosophers, psychologists, economists, and statesmen" to "readjust" the "motivation" of the public, and for the "communications media" to "drive the lesson home." From there, politicians could craft "a national or even international policy" to guide society toward a "better, healthier philosophy."[117] In fact, this actually happened, to some extent: the people and institutions named by Selye made stress an indispensable part of the way people talked and thought about life and health. The stress concept had something for everyone: for the person on the street, for industry, for the military; for physicians, psychologists, and research scientists. But in an irony that didn't escape Selye's notice, his popularization of stress was so successful that his theories about stress became irrelevant. After having written some 40 books and 1500 articles and after having created an institute for the study of stress, Selye did not see his specific formulations of stress accepted.

Just as in the case of neurasthenia, the "truth" of the stress concept and the American embrace of it did not come about through scientific agreement or through medical cures for "stress-related" diseases. It was stress's popularity that *made* it "true."[118] And because of the "truth" of the stress concept, it is studied and talked about and sold again and again as the source of the many problems Americans face in the twenty-first century. Stress may have outlived his theoretical formulation of it, but Selye's success in selling the public on the association between stress and disease made the concept robust enough to survive all the uses to which it has been put since. And the association between stress and heart disease has been one of the sturdiest of those associations.

Bar and Bishop had both been by-standers…, and as Mr. Merdle was swept away by the crowd, they made their remarks…to the Physician. Bar said, there was a certain point of mental strain beyond which no man could go.…

Charles Dickens, *Little Dorrit*

Success, Stress, and the Driven Man: The Medicalization of Masculinity

To Benjamin Franklin, as to the Puritans before him, prosperity and success did not signify wealth alone: they meant social usefulness, wisdom, good reputation, and health, among other things. But in the nineteenth century, success required more of men than wisdom and virtue: the new bureaucratic culture made a "glad hand" necessary.[119] Personal charm, a sense of confidence, and plenty of interpersonal knowhow were the order of the day. By the time Dale Carnegie published his bestselling *How to Win Friends and Influence People* in 1936, success had been completely decoupled from the Protestant virtues. It had become its own reward.

Following the Second World War, many men were able to achieve the house in the suburbs with attached wife and garage. This lifestyle was purchased to some degree at the cost of a return to conservatism in gender roles. Rosie the Riveter, urged to go to work during the war, was pressured to quit her job to make room for G. I. Joe when he came home.[120] If the middle-class wife, standing in her suburban kitchen, became tense or upset, her psychiatrist might prescribe tranquilizers (called "mother's little helpers"). But this type of treatment would hardly do for her husband. The strong, military-sounding word *stress* sounded better than the weak and womanish *depression* or *anxiety*.[121] Many men immersed in the white-collar "rat race" seemed to be pushing themselves beyond endurance in the 1950s and 1960s, and they earned their own label: "Type A personality." As at the turn of the century, it was the striving, the competition, the tensions—in a word, the *stress* of men's lives—that was held responsible for their health problems. But I'm getting ahead of myself.

The Life of the Type A Man

Sir William Osler's[122] 1910 description of the type of person most prone to heart disease eerily foreshadows later portraits of the middle-aged managerial man whose "Type A" behavior seemed to make him a prime candidate for heart disease in the postwar period and beyond: "the robust, the vigorous in mind and body, and the keen ambitious man, the indicator of whose engines is always at 'full speed ahead'... —the well 'set' man of from 45 to 55 years of age, with military bearing, iron-grey hair, and florid complexion."[123] In 1944, *Time* magazine ran a story about two 56-year-old identical twins. One of the twins, G. G., weighed 250 pounds and had high blood pressure and a 12-year history of angina. His brother, R. G., weighed 175 pounds, had low blood pressure and no major health problems. G. G.'s friends called him "Speed Up George" and R. G.'s friends called him "Lead in the Pants." Meyer Friedman and a cardiologist colleague of his were confounded. After thoroughly examining the twins, they were unable to find "biological differences" between them. As reported in *Time*, they came to believe that George had "hardened his arteries solely by his 'tension and drive'" and that "bad psychological habits" alone could be responsible for bringing on heart disease.[124] In the mid-1950s, Friedman and Ray Rosenman began to explore what forces might be contributing to the development of coronary heart disease (CHD) among legions of middle-class managerial types. They paid particular attention to extreme competitiveness and what they called "emotional stress."[125]

In his book *Type A Behavior and Your Heart*, Friedman recounted the following story about the origins of the cardiologists' "Type A hypothesis." Searching for potential causes of the epidemic of coronary heart disease, he and Rosenman set about examining the dietary habits of San Francisco Junior League women and their husbands. They believed that if they could show that the women ate lower cholesterol foods than their husbands, this would explain sex differences in CHD. Their thesis did not prove out, but in the middle of what Friedman later called a profound "mental stew" over the results of their study, a conversation with the president of the Junior League gave them a brand new perspective, as Friedman later recounted:

> [Junior League president]: "If you really want to know what is giving our husbands heart attacks, I'll tell you."

"And what is that?" we asked, possibly a bit patronizingly (as doctors can't help behaving at times when confronted with laymen who are certain that they know the immediate answers to age-old medical puzzles).

"It's stress, the stress they receive in their work, that's what's doing it," she quickly responded.

And that's when our concept of Type A Behavior Pattern and its probable relationship to coronary heart disease was born.[126]

In 1960, on the crest of their revelation, Friedman and Rosenman began an 8½-year study of 3,500 healthy men ages 39 to 59. They divided the men into "A" and "B" groups using a structured interview that they believed scientifically and objectively captured the essence of a behavior pattern they called "type A."[127] "Group A" men had "an intense, sustained drive..., [a] profound inclination...to compete, persistent desire for recognition and advancement,...constantly subject to time restrictions,...and extraordinary mental and physical alertness."[128] The results of the 1960 study, showing significantly more coronary heart disease in group A men than in the men of group B, seemed robust.

By 1971, Friedman and Rosenman were referring to the "Type A man" and describing him as "invariably punctual and greatly annoyed if kept waiting." He had little time for hobbies and found "routine jobs" a waste of his time. He walked fast, ate rapidly, and didn't stay long at the dinner table.[129] This wasn't a husband who lingered over coffee to hold his wife's hand, a partner who took his own plate to the sink, or a father who patiently played with his children. In fact, he hated losing "any sort of contest, even with his own children."[130] According to Friedman and Rosenman, Type A man's desire to achieve was bottomless, and he had so much aggression that "it frequently evolve[d] into free-floating hostility." Yet he often "[kept] such feelings and impulses under deep cover."[131]

Was all this the result of the "tear" part of the "wear and tear" that Silas Weir Mitchell and Hans Selye had talked about? Were these the effects of that chronic strain? At the beginning of the siege of neurasthenia, rapid change from rural to urban ways had been blamed for men's nervous disease. Men had been jolted, as Mitchell had put it, by "those intense competitions which make it hard to live nowadays and embitter the daily bread of life."[132] But by the 1950s and 1960s, middle-class men had been out in business world for decades, so the culture of business transacted in the "teeming city hives" could hardly be blamed for their plight.

It may have struck the reader that Friedman's and Rosenman's Type A man was a pretty typical middle-class working man of the period. In the postwar era, excessive conformity to American masculine values and attributes seemed to account for men's vulnerability to coronary heart disease.[133] As *Time* magazine put it, perhaps this was just "the cost of getting ahead": "Many a young man rising fast in his profession is sinking fast physically."[134] But some men were "sinking" and others were not. How could this be explained? Perhaps some men had adapted—conformed—better than others to the demands of the rat race. Rosenman and Friedman, echoing the nineteenth-century theme that people were "forced to live and work continuously faster," advised men to find ways to accommodate to the *constant change* to which they were exposed.[135] This was something of a new idea. The almost oxymoronic notion of "constant change" gave even more life to the story of the cost of progress.

Women's Place in the Heart

When Friedman and Rosenman told men that they needed to accommodate to the hurried pace of life with its constant change, they didn't mean that men should work more, harder, or faster. What they had in mind was for men to adapt by making changes in their behavior so they wouldn't have to pay the price of progress. Work hard but relax, they advised; your wife can be a boon to you in this endeavor. The little woman herself, it was thought, was an unlikely candidate for coronary heart disease because women were not being run ragged on the treadmill of a capitalist society, "the contemporary economic and professional milieu that nourishes the development of the Type A Behavior Pattern," as Friedman and Rosenman described it.[136]

In the 1950s and 1960s, women were urged to make sure their hubbies didn't become Type A casualties. The angel of the hearth might have acquired central heating, but not much else had changed. A 1958

New York Times article put it this way: "The woman who, despite the pressures of her own day, can insure a relaxed mealtime atmosphere is doing more than providing an appropriate prelude to a quiet evening. She is helping to build a line of defense not only against jangled nerves in family members, but against actual disease as well."[137] In 1961, Fred Kerner pointed out in *Stress and Your Heart* that "in spite of the many responsibilities involved, a woman's work at home apparently does not entail the same type of strain which most men undergo from day to day while working.... Just the realization of the responsibility is enough to make many men feel tense and anxious at all times." And since, unlike men, women were already at home, they could "take time to rest during the day."[138] Breadwinning had it all over cake baking and childcare in the stress department.

One thing that *had* changed for women was their mortality. What had been lethal in 1860 wasn't lethal in 1960—not childbearing, not tuberculosis, not pneumonia. Now the big killers were coronary heart disease, stroke, and cancer. The tables had turned; from the standpoint of mortality, men rather than women were the "weaker sex."[139] By the 1970s, women were living longer than men.[140] But as women's workforce participation increased from 28 percent to 42 percent between 1950 to 1978, concern spread that CHD would also increase among women and that they would lose their longevity advantage.[141] It didn't happen. From 1970 to 1980, mortality rates from CHD fell for both men and women. In fact, they fell even more for women than men. In light of these conclusions—conclusions that emerged from the enormous, long-running Framingham Heart Study—researchers decided to compare housewives with women who worked outside the home in order to examine the relationship between employment and women's vulnerability to CHD.[142] The researchers examined the women for moodiness, ambitiousness, and "situational stress" such as work overload, marital conflict, and worries.

In 1980 the results of the researchers' analyses were published. What they had found was that working outside the home in itself did not lead to increased risk for CHD.[143] But there was more: the married clerical workers with children had rates of CHD twice as high as those of the housewives and non-clerical workers. The researchers remarked on the fact that the clerical workers had very little autonomy in their jobs and negligible control over their working conditions. In thrall to unsupportive bosses, their abilities were underutilized and their accomplishments went unrecognized. They seemed to be swallowing quite a bit of hostility. The researchers speculated that these conditions, in tandem with family caregiving, might have contributed to the clerical workers' high incidence of CHD.[144]

A few years later another large study, the Minnesota Heart Survey, looked at gender differences among employed men and women with Type A behavioral patterns (TAPBs). This time, researchers concluded that gender differences came about principally because jobs held by women (this was in the mid-1980s) didn't give women opportunities for advancement, or because many women were only working part time or intermittently in an effort to manage their family responsibilities.[145] Although the variety of jobs available to women has certainly expanded greatly since the 1980s, many women continue to work part-time or intermittently. In Chapter 5, I'll talk more about the marginalization of mothers in the world of paid work. The phenomenon of middle-class working motherhood has turned working mothers into the latest targets of discussions about stress and CHD.

From Behavior to Personality

The 1970s and 1980s saw an explosion of interest in the Type A hypothesis. A typical *New York Times* article of the period cited Friedman and Rosenman's research and issued warnings about the dangers of Type A behavior: "Dr. James Gill [a Harvard University Health Services psychiatrist] . . . cited the case of one accountant [a previous heart attack survivor] who failed to heed the group's advice that he set a limit on clients accepted before the Federal income-tax deadline. . . . We buried him several days before April 15."[146] Journalists of the period rarely mentioned anything outside the individual that might have contributed to the Type A-ness. Far from it. In the same *New York Times* article, a psychologist described how she had succeeded in helping Type As to reduce stress by "selling" them on the idea that their style of approaching things was "inefficient" and "rob[bed] them of productivity."[147] In this instance, Type A salesmanship was used to combat Type A behavior. Any examination of the relationship between our economic system and ideas of success and achievement that might have contributed to Type A drivenness? America's infatuation with the individual and individual achievement? Not in evidence. Class bias? Hardly.[148] References to rigid gender distinctions that had for decade upon decade discouraged middle-class women from entering the workplace? You guessed it—none.

Although these questions weren't being raised in the popular press, they *were* being considered by sociologists. But the sociologists did not prevail; in fact, it wasn't long before a narrow psychological outlook on stress achieved dominance.[149] Barbara Ehrenreich has said that what was beautiful about stress as an explanation for why businessmen were dropping like flies was its ability to make "a bridge between vague emotional states and observable physiological change."[150] This is true. But that bridge was not completely traversed until the psychologists came onto the scene.

Enter the Type A Personality

The entrance of psychologists into the debates about the Type A man marked a critical juncture in American thinking about stress and what should be done about it.[151] It paved a road barely sketched out in Friedman and Rosenman's earliest research: the idea that the most important change in the lives of Type A men had to come from within. Type A was now not just a set of behaviors, but a "personality." Explaining the connection among men's stress, overwork, and coronary heart disease in internal, individual terms, psychologists worked around the question of what external conditions might be responsible for the Type A man's predicament and how these might be altered. The mid-1960s invention of Type A as a personality style had huge implications for how we study and talk about stress, and we can trace the current framing of "lifestyle" and "psychosocial factors" as risk factors to this period. As Robert Aronowitz has pointed out, Type A was the first of many attempts to quantify the social and psychological nature of our society in terms of the individual.[152]

Stress and Heart Disease: The Association That Didn't Die

By the 1980s, the Type A man had company. The connections forged between stress and coronary heart disease remained sturdy; now anyone might have a Type A personality. The nation was even fretting over Type A children.[153] Although studies began to appear by the late 1970s that did not support the Type A hypothesis,[154] it wasn't until the late 1980s that the popular press began to bring the research debates into the open,[155] and even then reports of the demise of the Type A personality were premature. *InStyle*, a women's fashion magazine, featured this advice in 2008: "Stop Stressing! Attention, Type A personalities: Put down that Blackberry and strike a downward dog pose. If you don't learn how to relax, stress hormones will shrink your brain's memory center."[156]

Now that CHD hasn't been found to be associated with some of Rosenman and Friedman's original Type A behaviors (e.g., excessive competitiveness, fast speech, and impatience), researchers have turned their attention to how other individual factors, particularly anger and hostility, might influence coronary heart disease.[157] In 2009, a *Time* magazine reporter insisted: "We all know that anger can stress your heart." He went on to make a distinction that seems familiarly protective of the American way of competition: "Aggression and just being aggressive" are very different things. "Your type A co-workers who are annoyingly ambitious and dutiful are not more likely to have a heart attack than you are. Rather, it's the seething, angry types with underlying hostility who are the ticking time bombs. Anger, it turns out, is physiologically toxic."[158] And another recent *Time* article limns a relationship between anxiety and heart attacks: "It's no secret that men with angry, explosive personalities are at a higher risk of a heart attack. But they're not alone: Nervous, withdrawn and chronically worried people are courting coronary problems, too."[159] Big Pharma has a stake (if the bad pun can be forgiven) in the heart/stress connection. Reading a long piece on stress and heart disease on *Time*'s website, I almost didn't notice the faint emblem of the "sponsor" of the piece—AstraZeneca, maker of Crestor, a cholesterol-lowering drug.[160]

The story of the Type A personality does not conclude this history of how the effects of social transformations, problems, and conditions became the private psychological properties of individuals. There's yet one more story to tell: the story of how stress came to be increasingly linked with emotion and subjectivity.

STRESS GETS EMOTIONALLY INVOLVED

Master of All the Stress He Surveys: Lazarus Rises

When Friedman and Rosenman compared Type Bs with Type As in their early studies, they said that Type As were the exact opposites of Type Bs.[161] But later on Rosenman made it clear that Type Bs were not just more relaxed or less hostile than Type As; they had a different *style of coping* that didn't generally lead to hostile, impatient, or competitive behaviors.[162] This relationship between coping and stress has been the life work of Richard Lazarus, arguably the most eminent psychologist of the past 40 or more years to tackle the problem of stress.[163] In their influential 1984 book, *Stress, Appraisal and Coping*, Lazarus and Susan Folkman defined psychological stress as "a particular relationship between the person and the environment that is appraised by the person as taxing or exceeding his or her resources and endangering his or her well-being," and said that "[o]ur immediate concern must be with what causes psychological stress in different persons."[164] In his writings, Lazarus continually refers to this person/environment relationship. But to Lazarus, the stressful event or circumstance itself is not what determines a person's response; what matters is how the person *appraises* the stressor and how he or she copes with it. What is important is the meaning the event or circumstance has for the individual. The significance of class or culture, for example, lies in the way these are evaluated psychologically.

For researchers following Lazarus's line of thought, the demarcation between exposure to stress and individual vulnerability can become quite indistinct, as Gore and Colten suggest:

> For example, when a loss of a loved one means loss of a sole supportive tie, versus when it means the end of a [sic] stressful caretaking, these differences will be accounted for in the cognitive appraisal process. Although this formulation solves the problem of meaning by blurring

the lines around the "stress exposure" construct, this conception of stress takes what is really a finetuning of the exposure construct and places it within the individual difference domain, making it, in effect, a personal vulnerability factor.[165]

Lazarus was moved to focus on individual differences in the ways people appraise and cope with stressful situations, in response to what he saw as the sociologists' failure to account for those differences. He insisted that the sociologists had gone too far in emphasizing the influence of the environment on the person; that their view of the person/society relationship was "structural and static,"[166] whereas his view of that relationship was variable and dynamic. There is no question that individual differences needed to be brought into the person/environment equation, and Lazarus genuinely seemed to want to correct the balance. But over the years, as he talked more and more about the person, some researchers accused Lazarus of going too far. Patently false assertions such as "all measures of somatic health are dependent on self-reports," inflamed debate.[167] Other researchers questioned Lazarus's assumption that there is no such thing as an objective environmental event—his idea that the subjective evaluation of the event alone produces stress. Surely there are *some* situations, conditions, and/or events that most people would find stressful, critics insisted. And certainly some characteristics of the events and environmental conditions themselves—controllability, predictability, or pervasiveness—influence how we appraise them.[168] At the same time, instruments that merely measured stressful life events were being criticized on the grounds that life events are structured by social circumstances.[169]

These debates didn't become any less heated when, in the early 1990s, Lazarus began studying emotional and cognitive processes almost exclusively and embraced the position that stress was "a subset of emotion."[170] In Lazarus's words, the aim of his revised theory was, among other things, "to convert...person-environment relationships into personal meanings."[171] These days, he views stress as an entirely internal, psychological experience: "If we know only that a person is experiencing psychological stress, we have useful information, but it is far more useful to know that a person feels angry, anxious, guilty, sad.... Each of these emotional states *says something different about the conditions being faced*" (italics added).[172] In this formulation, we come to know the conditions out there (in the environment) via the emotions in here (personal experience; subjectivity; psychology). Lazarus is not denying that there *is* an environment and that it affects us, but the fact that he is *only* interested in the emotion generated in people's encounters with the environment has trained the gaze of many young stress researchers principally on aspects of the human psyche.

We don't need to look very far to see where Lazarus's current formulations can take us. A 2009 health note in the *Philadelphia Inquirer* cited research showing that men who didn't stand up for themselves at work were more likely than assertive men to have heart attacks or to die from coronary heart disease. The study's investigators suggested that more research was needed "to determine if efforts to reduce the amount of *covert coping* would also lower the risk of heart attacks and deaths."[173] What is "covert coping," after all, but behavior gone underground? No longer identified as behavior, coping itself is identified as emotion.

Over a period of 150 years or so, American thinking about stress has been shaped by traditional American values of individualism and capitalism. We have seen how both the *damage* and the *adjustment* scenarios helped maintain the status quo through a seemingly inexorable tilt toward the individual as the cause of and the solution to the pressures brought by change, whether sudden or "constant." The Type A hypothesis is proof positive of a historical bias in favor of intrapsychic over psychosocial risk factors.[174] It isn't hard to see why. An approach that looks at people and the changing conditions of the social environment at the same time can't easily be reduced to risk factor equations.[175] And, as we'll see in the chapter to follow, history and culture continue to influence our ideas about what causes illness and whose responsibility it is to maintain health.[176]

CHAPTER 3

Stress and the Biopolitics
of American Society

Merely fact-minded sciences make merely fact-minded people.
                                        —Edmund Husserl[1]

*It is clear to me that what is at stake in our understanding of "health" are the broadest
issues of the survival and death of the social order itself.*
                                        —Emily Martin[2]

Scientific ideas and terms like stress have such a broad—though often indirect and unacknowledged—influence on our day-to-day ideas about ourselves and the world that many of us have come to view ourselves, to describe ourselves, in light of those ideas and in those terms; they have become part of our very makeup.[3] We often don't feel the need to look under the skin of what passes for science, because it is assumed that science is natural and objective, that it "speaks for itself."[4] Once an idea is established as scientific fact, even evidence that flies squarely in the face of it often can't dislodge it. We've certainly seen this with a variety of food scares that have come along (scares about the dangers of coffee and eggs spring to mind). Since we tend to absorb whatever reinforces the knowledge and beliefs we already have, what we find is often what we had hoped and expected to find in the first place, leading to what biologist Ludwik Fleck has called a "harmony of illusions." What's more, once questions have been asked and answered in predictable ways, future explorations of a problem tend to travel along well-worn "thought tracks" that have already been laid down.[5] The harmony of illusions about health and health risks determines the questions that are asked—and answered—about the relationship between stress and illness, and those questions train our gaze on the person and the body rather than on society and its institutions.

In this chapter I'll be looking at how the stress concept helps conceal the social causes of many of the risks we face and spares us the turmoil of social change by keeping us focused on personal health and health maintenance. I'll look at how both academic and popular discussions of stress overemphasize individual psychological and physiological factors (judgments, emotions, hormones), highlighting the links between stress and health and underemphasizing the direct effects of stressful social conditions (poverty, inequality, discrimination) on health.

The following example from an article in the 2005 *Annual Review of Clinical Psychology* includes many elements common to academic discussions of stress. In this excerpt, the authors explain why they think it's important to understand the connection between stress and health:

> Our future as individuals and as a species depends on our ability to adapt to potent stressors. At a societal level, we face a lack of institutional resources (e.g., inadequate health insurance), pestilence (e.g., HIV/AIDS), war, and international terrorism.... At an *individual* level, we live with the insecurities of our daily existence including job stress, marital stress, and unsafe schools and neighborhoods.... It is clear that all of us are exposed to stressful situations at the societal, community, and interpersonal level. How we meet these challenges will tell us about the health of our society and ourselves...if stressors are too strong and too persistent in individuals who are biologically vulnerable..., stressors may lead to disease. This is particularly the case if the person has few psychosocial resources and poor coping skills.... There is much we do not yet know about the relationship between stress and health, but scientific findings being made in the areas of *cognitive-emotional psychology, molecular biology, neuroscience, clinical psychology, and medicine will undoubtedly lead to improved health outcomes* (italics added).[6]

Here the authors talk about the "societal level," but when they say that people need to adapt to stressful conditions, they're not advocating changing those conditions. They're saying that people have a clear choice: either adapt to stressful conditions and environments or accept biomedical or psychological interventions in order to ease the stress that these conditions and/or environments may create. When the authors talk about people *having* "psychosocial resources," resources that include social support, they give the impression that those resources belong to individuals rather than to the environments in which they live. This is why the researchers' division of "stressors" into two categories, individual stressors and stressors outside the individual, is so confusing. De facto segregation, crumbling schools, and neighborhood-threatening violence are not personal problems. So describing unsafe neighborhoods as "individual" stressors removes the element of social responsibility from the equation.

Scores of researchers who have examined the relationship between stress and disease have begun and ended their work by examining individuals—their hormones, their psyches, their personalities, their social networks, their lifestyles. But the association between stress and ill health is tied to social, cultural, economic, and political processes in ways that many contemporary perspectives rarely touch. This failure has a great deal to do with our society's long-standing faith in science and medicine, as well as our belief in the notion that people can, in the end, surmount all obstacles; what stands in our way we can prevent or fix. Medical science finds the causes and cures of illnesses inside the body and then looks to treat the *effects* of environmental conditions—or our perceptions of them—on the body. It is no surprise, then, to find that funding for disease prevention research that focuses on individuals is much more plentiful than funding for research focusing on society and its institutions.[7]

Many of the problems we used to consider social or moral are now considered medical problems. Some children who might have been labeled "bad kids" not very long ago are now diagnosed with Attention Deficit Hyperactivity Disorder. Criminals may be thought of as bad men or women, but they may also be diagnosed as having Antisocial Personality Disorder. The boundary between what belongs in the medical domain and what doesn't has become more and more elastic. Sociologists refer to this kind of transformation of social problems into disease as *medicalization*.[8] And now, in the twenty-first century, by virtue of technological advancements, we can say that *bio*medicalization that has further extended medicine's reach. As we've seen, the connection between stress and illness has a long history; the list of things that are considered "stressful" often seems unending; and researchers insist ever more forcefully that they can explain how a diverse array of stressors affects the immune system. The medicalization of stress has been underway for a long time.

HEALTHISM AND THE MORALITY OF HEALTH MAINTENANCE

In the 1960s, belief in the universal right to health spurred on movements to develop a medical infrastructure and reduce inequalities in access to healthcare. But, by the 1980s, the right to health had changed; it was now transformed into a mandate that people take responsibility for their health and modify their behavior and habits in line with scientific ideas about what was healthy—exercising, eating "right," not smoking.[9] In 1980, Robert Crawford, with some prescience, as it turns out, termed this kind of medicalization *healthism*: the "preoccupation with personal health as a primary—often the primary—focus for the definition and achievement of well-being."[10] Healthism assumes that solutions to health problems are matters of choice. Crawford argued that healthism comes with its own brand of insistent moralism: to consider *health* the outgrowth of personal choices is to consider *illness* a personal failing. These days, health is defined not only in terms of individual responsibility but also in terms of accountability to others.[11] People protect the health of society by protecting themselves from disease,[12] managing potential health risks, and remaining healthy through discipline and vigilance. To choose a lifestyle that *allows* illness is to violate a social contract. In the context of healthism, then, people who don't take adequate responsibility for their health become problems themselves. Healthism leaves little room for considering social and political change as significant pathways to improve the health of citizens.

Biological Citizenship in the Age of Susceptibility

The business of health promotion has thoroughly penetrated the fabric of American life.[13] We now live in a society in which medicine's lookout includes not just the sick person, but the person who *may* become sick; not just sickness itself, but behavior that is deemed unhealthy. In this climate, health is not merely a means to an end, but an end in itself. The good life, in Crawford's words, has been "reduced to a health problem, just as health is expanded to include all that is good in life."[14] Medicine has had an expanding role in creating pre-disease states such as high blood pressure and low bone density. For better or for worse, we are all "biological citizens" in the new political and economic health market economy, and as such we think and talk about ourselves in particular ways. We may describe ourselves as being easily "stressed out," as having high blood sugar, or as having a genetic predisposition to some form of cancer or mental illness. We use these descriptions and what comes with them to tell us how to act, what to be afraid of and worry about, and what kind of life we can expect or hope for.[15]

Over 30 years ago, Lewis Thomas, physician, etymologist, and essayist, made these observations:

> The new consensus is that we are badly designed, intrinsically fallible, vulnerable to a host of hostile influences inside and around us, and only precariously alive. We live in danger of falling apart any moment, and are therefore always in need of surveillance and propping up. Without the professional attention of a health-care system, we would fall in our tracks.
>
> … The television and radio industry, no small part of the national economy, feeds on Health, or, more precisely, on disease, for a large part of its sustenance… [A]lmost all the commercial announcements, in an average evening, are pitches for items to restore failed health: things for stomach gas, constipation, headaches, nervousness, sleeplessness or sleepiness, arthritis,… dandruff… The food industry plays the role of surrogate physician, advertising breakfast cereals as though they were tonics.… Chewing gum is sold as a tooth cleanser. Vitamins have taken the place of prayer.[16]

And all of this is going on, Thomas remarked, "while just outside, the whole of society is coming undone."

In the brave new middle-class world of body- and health-perfecting—in *Somatopia*, as Marc Chrysanthou calls it—many of us dream that information will enable us to achieve perfect health and the perfect body. The many mysteries of the workings of the body whet our appetite for yet more knowledge—more digitized views of our insides, more scientific "facts." We diagnose ourselves; we talk about our brains as if we are having a relationship with them ("My brain is telling me..."). In Somatopia we can prevent illness and stay young forever.

Health as Work

As biological citizens we have new ways of relating to scientific knowledge and the medical professionals who dispense it. We're no longer merely expected to sit—or lie—back and let the diagnosers diagnose, but to educate ourselves so that we can work on ourselves in a variety of ways and ask the "right" questions of our healthcare providers. Working on ourselves to achieve improved health may mean increasing our self-esteem, journaling, or meditating, and these activities require a different level of involvement with our "selves" than taking a pill. As Crawford points out, some of the cultural mandates surrounding health and fitness are in conflict with each other in particularly American ways. Middle- and upper-class Americans need to achieve and produce, but they also need to consume. Work out and *then* have a chocolate gelato.[17] It's confusing. We're counseled to budget and save—to discipline ourselves in a new environment of austerity—while at the same time we're encouraged to keep spending, lest the economy come to a screeching halt.

Doing "work" to better oneself is an ingrained liberal democratic idea, so, as an ethical matter, we shouldn't accept our biological future as preordained; we have to shape it through our actions. Part of the work is to cope better with stress in order to stay healthy. In the fight against stress, healthism meets capitalism in the form of "retail therapy" (e.g., purchasing health-giving foods, relaxation-inducing products, exercise machines—and, of course, psychotropic medications, courtesy of Big Pharma). And in the marketplace, health itself has become a commodity, something we can "have" or achieve if only we work for it. As medical anthropologist Charlie Davison reminds us, health consciousness is a sign of social class; it's just as elitist as fashion consciousness.[18]

A POPULATION ON THE VERGE OF SOMETHING:
RISK AND RESPONSIBILITY

Health consciousness begins with the awareness of risk. In the United States, we're continually bombarded with messages of all kinds about health risks—external and internal. From industrial pollution to trans fats to stress itself, the news of potential risks to our health is everywhere, and many constituencies have a stake in broadcasting that news: reporters, scientists, government officials.[19] Even though what a given society judges to be a risk may not be a "real" danger, the importance society ascribes to risks drives us to take action. "Risk" sounds less emotionally loaded than "danger," and certainly more scientific.[20] Danger doesn't need scientific or medical intervention; it calls for personal, community, or institutional action. But the job of determining which people are "at risk" and what aspects of human behavior put people at risk requires professional assessment and intervention.

The new medicine (David Armstrong has called it "Surveillance Medicine") is concerned with a fragile and transient state of "normal" health and the threat of illness. In this new medicine, symptoms are important not so much as indicators of disease, but as risk factors. "One illness becomes a risk factor for another," Armstrong says, creating an unending risk chain: "A headache may be a risk factor for high blood pressure (hypertension), but high blood pressure is simply a risk factor for another illness (stroke)."[21] The original illness is now considered less troublesome than the "pre-illness" risk status it points to.[22]

Going on the assumption that we're all in a state of potential illness, health researchers try to root out ever more specific risk factors,[23] often departing from sound scientific method, treating risk factors as though they were proven causes.[24] Of course, people are not all exposed to risk to the same extent. Many factors—race, socioeconomic status, geographical location—influence people's exposure to risk (more on this later). At the same time, because nothing is risky until it is judged to be so, culture has a great deal to do with the *perception* of risk.[25] If the public (or one particular segment of it) doesn't "buy" the potential for risk inherent in a given situation or behavior, public health officials often conclude that "they" ought to be further educated to make lifestyle changes.[26] Education or encouragement targets specific groups and is frequently handed down like used clothing from the rich to the poor.

Risk and Lifestyle

As something outside the body that influences what goes on inside the body, "lifestyle" is implicated in discussions of disease risk. A lifestyle that includes a fatty diet, for example, becomes a risk factor for cardiac disease on a par with conditions like angina or diabetes. In its "Healthy People" position paper of 2000, the Department of Health and Human Services noted the significant "impact of personal lifestyle choices on the health destiny of individual Americans and the future of the nation." "Medicine," it went on to say, has "taught us much about actions that each of us can take to control our risks for disease or disability. We have learned that a fuller measure of health, a better quality of life, is within our personal grasp."[27] But the business of changing a lifestyle is complicated. We learn health habits from our families, our friends, and from powerful social agents like advertisers. This makes our habits resistant to change.[28] Prevention and intervention at the level of the individual may not work when social institutions (advertisers, for instance) reproduce and reinforce poor health.[29] We can see the inevitable question "Want fries with that?" as part of a capitalist push/pull in which an ad for Merck's cholesterol-lowering drug Zocor asks: "What are you doing to protect your heart?"

Political decisions can also influence health outcomes, as they might have when the House Appropriations Committee proposed to cut $500 million from the WIC program (Special Supplemental Nutrition Program for Women, Infants and Children), a program that has provided nutritional support to women and infants for decades.[30] It can be threatening to acknowledge that political and socioeconomic forces can contribute to disease. Tackling discrimination, poverty, healthcare inequality, and other socio-structural problems implies change beyond the individual level—change, as Marshall Becker puts it, that is "not likely to be achieved by lowering the public's cholesterol levels."[31] In most cases, cholesterol levels can be fairly easily reduced; poverty cannot. But judging something as risky may help us manage uncertainty.[32] At least we feel like we're doing *something*. Don't we have to take some risks in life? As John-Arne Skolbekken points out, "Since life itself is a universally fatal sexually transmitted disease, living it to the full demands a balance between reasonable and unreasonable risk."[33]

Just as the sense of Manifest Destiny fueled Americans' zeal to conquer the West in the nineteenth century, it seems that it's our collective "health destiny" to conquer the body through our lifestyle choices so thoroughly that it can no longer be threatened by illness. A piece in *USA Today* entitled "9 Factors That Affect Your Heart's Health" tells readers that "lifestyle, not heredity, is the biggest culprit" in heart disease. In the article, an expert described as a "global heart specialist" says that 90 percent of heart disease "in every population on Earth" is accounted for by risk factors that include stress, obesity, diabetes, smoking, high blood pressure, "a desk-bound job," and "a diet rich in processed foods, low in fruit and fiber and missing [*sic*] a daily thimbleful of alcohol."[34] Just as George Beard theorized that nervous diseases were related to the advent of the telegraph, the railway system, and other artifacts of modern civilization,[35] the "health expert" cited in the article views clogged arteries a "societal disease ... brought on by cities built for automobiles and ease, featuring urban sprawl, high-pressure sedentary work, passive entertainment and lots of cheap, tasty processed food."[36] But although he may have called the disease "societal," the expert's recommended cures—individual changes in lifestyle—are not. In a paradoxical twist, it seems that the lifestyle-engineering approach to preventing heart disease doesn't help most of the people it is intended to help. "Heart health" campaigns screen entire swaths of the population, with the result that people who never before imagined themselves candidates for heart disease begin to think of themselves as at risk, even though most people who die from heart attacks are outside the "risk group."[37]

We are exposed to health information from every quarter, and yet the information is often of doubtful quality. The rush by researchers to see their studies in print and the eagerness of experts to get people to modify their lifestyles often comes before data from larger studies and/or from replication studies can produce persuasive cumulative evidence, and we, the public (certainly the middle-class public), are primed to worry about what each new risk means for us.[38] In addition, research evidence often enters the public domain lacking information such as sample size that would help us understand whether or not a study's conclusions can be generalized. But the glut of health information that's available now almost guarantees that people will pick and choose their "evidence" for health risks just as some politicians cherry-pick their "facts."

As we have seen, stress is often cited as a risk factor for disease. But, in fact, stress encompasses a vast set of risk factors, given the multiplicity of situations that are deemed stressful today. Talk of lifestyle and the need for changes in lifestyle brings stress to the fore as a menace to health, and people are often advised to free themselves of "stress" in order to maintain good health—to steer clear of too-stressful situations, to monitor their bodies for signs of tension, and to purchase products that promise stress relief—as if the stress itself were the problem that needed to be avoided, rather than the situations or conditions that evoke it.

THE GREAT DIVIDE: MIND, BODY, AND THE ENVIRONMENT

Well-publicized findings from the rapidly expanding field of cognitive neuroscience, whether substantiated or not, find a ready audience.[39] Today's biological psychiatry focuses on the gene-brain-behavior connection, reducing mind to body by explaining psychological processes in terms of neurons, a process that cultural anthropologist Emily Martin calls "neuro-reductionism."[40] As Martin points out, neuropsychologists often talk about brain functioning as if it were not embedded in history and culture, and this makes it harder for us to "see" the contexts that give human behavior meaning.[41] But we can no more reduce everything to the physiological than we can reduce everything to the psychological; they are flip sides of the same coin.[42] The widespread idea that body and mind are broken parts of a whole that need only be re-glued like a china cup erroneously implies that we can separate what is acquired from what is innate—that body and mind don't influence each other.[43]

Charles Rosenberg, who has studied the history of nineteenth-century Americans' dependence on medical men and scientists for moral truths about how to live, thinks that today's Americans look for more social and moral explanations for disease than genetics and neurobiology can possibly provide.[44] For quite a while now, I've been thinking about how the concept of stress provides those explanations. After all, stress is a prime player in the universe of healthism, linking health and morality through the pervasive idea that we can have ultimate control over how we cope with the circumstances in which find ourselves and how by controlling ourselves we can improve our health. In relation to stress, neurobiology and morality come together in ways that satisfy a social need. The concept of stress explains how we can manage social and environmental forces in terms of the body and its internal processes. It maintains our faith in science and medicine, even as it allays our anxiety about what those forces can do to us or might mean for us, by suggesting that we can have control over them. But while the stress concept could conceivably forge a necessary, inseparable connection among body, mind, and the environment, in practice it fails to do this in its present incarnation, because it is the somatic—the bodily—side of things that is consistently elaborated. And this is where the immune system comes in: current explanations of the relationship between stress and disease foreground the workings of the body by linking stress to the functioning of the immune system.

Health and the Immune System

Given today's easy chatter about clogged arteries, high cholesterol, and the like, it's surprising to consider that as recently as the 1950s there were virtually no descriptions in periodicals of what was going on inside the body. In the 1940s and 1950s, the major public health focus was on the surface cleanliness of home and body, with the goal of protecting the body against invading microbes, just as the housewife protected her family by wiping germs off the counter with *Lysol*. This was the era that introduced the metaphor of the body as a machine with parts that could break down. People's resistance in the face of disease was looked on as a passive rather than an active phenomenon; people were seen as standing up to a force that might or might not defeat them,[45] a far more fatalistic view than we would ever accept today.

During the 1960s and 1970s, new ideas emerged about the mechanisms that connected the body with the outside world. Scientists hypothesized that the immune response was affected by a system located completely within the body, linking the body and the external environment. The period of the late 1970s saw an increase in research on the relationship between the immune system and other systems, particularly the nervous system. By the 1980s, when the AIDS epidemic brought new attention to the immune system, Robert Ader named the study of these relationships *psychoneuroimmunology*. The media began to take notice of the immune system, and both academic and popular publications ever since have reflected a fascination with immune system functioning.[46]

The Language of the Immune System

By the late twentieth century, immunologists portrayed the relationship between the body and the world outside it as an active one. The new, flexible body could choose from a smorgasbord of health-promoting new antibodies that would permit it successfully to encounter any new threat. No longer was it commonly believed that resistance to disease lay outside a person's control—that the healthy person was lucky. Now the common assumption was that resistance could be altered—that immunity could be "built up" from inside the body.[47] Health has been virtually reimagined in light of new ideas about the immune system disseminated in books, magazines, newspapers, and other media, leading many people to connect aspects of their lives with the functioning of their immune systems. Smoking, fatigue, happiness, and, of course, stress, as well as many other factors believed to affect health, are understood in terms of the immune system.[48] Relational experiences, too—both positive (e.g., helping others) and negative (e.g., death of a loved one)—are viewed in terms of their influence on the immune system.

In her study of the role immunity plays in American culture, Emily Martin interviewed both scientists and nonscientists. Her interviewees commonly accepted the idea that thoughts or actions necessarily influence health, and that, by extension, they affect the immune system, for good or (literally) for ill. They also expressed the belief that people can train their immune systems, a notion that harmonizes well with American ideals of self-reliance and individual achievement. A biology professor Martin interviewed offered a perspective on the immune system as a sort of superhero of our age:

> In terms of personal empowerment, the idea that we have this thing [the immune system], we don't even know it's working...it's always taking care of us.... I think it's very empowering to think about the immune system, like we are strong. We are powerful. We are protected. We have

almost like the scientific version of thinking about an angel or a protector or something that they probably did in the Middle Ages. And it's us, and we're really strong....[49]

The people Martin interviewed generally had a profound faith in the immune system's ability to fend off constant threats to their health and strongly endorsed the idea that they need to keep their immune systems in good working order.

Although the immune system is often central to explanations of how social ills affect health, it offers an almost context-free prism through which to look at social problems. For example, a *Frontline* television program on PBS, "Hunger in America," explained the deaths of malnourished American children in terms of the adverse impact of malnutrition on the immune system, leaving the viewer to conclude that because malnourished children fall prey to other diseases, they don't actually die of starvation.[50] Of course, although this conclusion isn't inaccurate, the emphasis on immune system response softens an otherwise stark association between poverty and mortality.

Stress and the Immune System

In the 1980s, the stress and coping model devised by Richard Lazarus and Susan Folkman brought to the fore the idea that stress resulted from circumstances that overwhelmed a person's ability to cope,[51] and researchers began to hypothesize that people's coping ability depended to a large extent on their appraisal of what was overwhelming. The business of judging situations or circumstances, they thought, must be the bridge between stress and health outcomes. In the latter half of the 1990s, researchers worked on making more and more connections between the immune system and what people judge as stressful.

The link between stress and the immune system is now so well established that the label on Dannon's *DanActive* probiotic flavored yogurt drinks reads:

Helps
Strengthen
Your body's

Defenses
IMMUNITY

If you visit *DanActive*'s website (http://www.danactive.com), you will see an animated sequence accompanied by the following patter: "Unbalanced diet, stress, fatigue, cold weather—our body is often tested to the limit and it's our digestive system that plays a central role defending it.... The digestive system and your intestines...are intelligent: they help your body help protect itself against several challenges." One of the three defense systems named on the website is an "intestinal immune system" that produces "defense cells." The site offers proof, in the form of "scientific studies," that a "hygienic way of life and balanced diet that includes the consumption of fermented products" contributes to health. Although the purpose of the *DanActive* website is to sell yogurt, not to underscore the role of stress, it speaks succinctly to how stress has been reinterpreted in terms of the immune system.[52] The website offers the prospect of a stress-free, self-engineered adaptation to life through the achievement of balance.

The immune system is often portrayed as a system of relationships inside the body—helpful, friendly, and nonthreatening comrades engaged in a war with a hostile outer environment. There is a lot of talk of teamwork and "communication" between and among chemicals, cells, and the like. We hear of "chemical intermediaries" and "signaling" or "communicatory" molecules. "Invaders" come from outside to attack the immune system, and the immune system must "fight" in defense of itself. Cells, "the first line of defense," occupy "battle stations." A body under siege is rescued by natural "killer cells." Stress, on the other hand, is capable of wrecking everything. It is stress that pulls the "trigger," flooding the body with stress hormones,[53] and it can allegedly cause a breakdown in communication among cells and chemicals through its effects on the immune system.[54]

Only Adapt

In contemporary thinking, fighting stress means striving for homeostasis. Homeostatic mechanisms keep systems in a steady state when forces outside the system threaten disruption, just as thermostats keep a house at the same temperature regardless of how cold or hot it is out-doors. So adaptation to stress often implies achieving balance (a steady state). In 1953 Hans Selye told a large crowd that much chronic disease was traceable to failures in adaptation.[55] In his rendering of the General Adaptation Syndrome, the linchpin of his theory of stress, he said that "life is largely a process of adaptation to the circumstances in which we exist. ... The secret of health and happiness lies in successful adjust-ment to the ever-changing conditions on this globe; the penalties for failure in this great process of adaptation are disease and unhappiness."[56] Schneiderman and his colleagues, quoted earlier in this chapter, rein-force this idea in the present. They insist that responses are maladaptive if they don't help humans maintain homeostasis:

> Stress is a central concept for understanding both life and evolution. All creatures face threats to homeostasis, which must be met with adaptive responses. Our future as individuals and as a species depends on our ability to adapt to potent stressors.... Global threats...do provide the backdrop for our consideration of the relationship between stress and health.[57]

If the goal is to maintain a steady state, not only is stress a risk factor with respect to the biological systems of the body or the systems of the body politic, but the world itself is a risk factor for stress. In these terms, fighting stress has both a biological and a sociopolitical function.

Must threats to homeostasis in the form of stress always be met with "adaptive" responses? On the one hand, there is no doubt that adaptation to stressful conditions can be useful in some instances. Constantine and Sue have argued that people of color who suffer discrimination develop adaptive strengths as a result of their struggles.[58] On the other hand, as economist Amartya Sen pointed out in his 1998 Nobel Prize acceptance speech, adaptation to injustice, violence, and/or poverty doesn't necessarily improve the human condition:

> A hopeless destitute with much poverty, or a downtrodden laborer living under exploitative economic arrangements, or a subjugated housewife in a society with entrenched gender inequality, or a tyrannized citizen under brutal authoritarianism, may come to terms with her deprivation. She may take whatever pleasure she can from small achievements,

and adjust her desires to take note of feasibility (thereby helping the fulfillment of her adjusted desires). But her success in such adjustment would not make her deprivation go away.[59]

The idea that we can achieve a balance between inner and outer forces may also conceal differences between and among groups in relation to resources and power. A critical problem with Western ideas about balance and adaptation is that these are presented as something that anyone can and should achieve.[60] But we know that the deck is stacked in favor of people who have greater access to resources and greater power—and of course, access to resources *is* power, in many instances.

THE "SCIENCE" OF STRESS

To many scientists, the nervous system is key in explaining how stress can produce ill health through its presumed effects on immune system functioning. In the very close connection between stress and disease that researchers currently hypothesize, a number of hormone systems in the body (often referred to as neuroendocrine systems because of their association with the central nervous system [CNS]) are understood to interact with each other.[61] And researchers increasingly refer to certain hormones, such as cortisol, as "stress hormones." They typically make a distinction between two types of stress responses: acute and chronic. In the acute stress response:

> Stress hormones are produced by the SNS [sympathetic nervous system] and hypothalamic-pituitary adrenocortical [HPA] axis. The SNS stimulates the adrenal medulla to produce catecholamines (e.g., epinephrine). In parallel, the . . . hypothalamus produces corticotropin releasing factor, which in turn stimulates the pituitary to produce adrenocorticotropin [adrenalin]. Adenocorticotropin then stimulates the adrenal cortex to secrete cortisol.[62]

An increase in energy supplied to organs increases blood pressure, activating the immune system. The metaphorical "first line of defense" are cells called macrophages and natural killer (NK) cells that come into play immediately to increase the number of circulating immune cells. These cells move into tissues such as the skin and promote healing by managing microbes that might enter through wounds. In contrast, researchers hypothesize that when people experience chronic stress, stress hormone levels increase, and this can influence immune function by affecting the molecules called cytokines produced by immune cells.[63]

What evidence is there for this relationship between stress and immune system functioning? Scientific conclusions about this relationship have undergone multiple transformations even since the 1990s, and I'll offer only a brief summary here.[64] Building upon the work of Hans Selye, researchers long believed—and this idea still has currency in some quarters—that stress could globally suppress the immune system. But a model has been developed recently that proposes that the immune response is actually enhanced by acute stress and suppressed by chronic stress.[65] Suzanne Segerstrom and Gregory Miller compared over 300 empirical studies in order to examine the state of the science with regard to psychological stress and immune system functioning in humans.[66] Acknowledging that researchers have yet to agree on a single definition of stress, Segerstrom and Miller categorized stress studies according to the type of stressor examined in the studies: acute, time-limited stressors such as performing mental arithmetic or speaking in public; brief naturalistic stressors such as taking an examination; stressful event sequences such as natural disasters; chronic stressors such as caring for a spouse with Alzheimer's disease; and distant stressors such as past traumatic experiences.

Of the 300 studies Segerstrom and Miller analyzed, most looked at the effects of *acute time-limited stressors*. These are easier to study than chronic and traumatic stressors, because researchers can control and manipulate time-limited stressors in the laboratory. They can set up arguments between couples and then test them for levels of certain hormones after the fight,[67] or they can—and do—purposely give someone a small wound or injection[68] in order to see how it heals under stressful conditions they create in the laboratory. They control conditions, code biological responses, and correlate those responses with immune system functioning.[69] And, as we saw in Chapter 1, laboratory researchers are not shy about applying their results to human life—and death— in the broadest ways when they are interviewed. At the American

Psychological Association's Annual Convention, Janice Kiecolt-Glaser was reported to have said "If stress doesn't kill you, it will at least make you wheeze."[70]

Controlled laboratory experiments have had their critics, perhaps none more vocal than psychologist Urie Bronfenbrenner, who argued decades ago against substituting laboratory conditions for "real life" environments. Checklists and surveys that ask people to report on the nature and extent of their own stressful experiences have also been extensively used—and extensively critiqued, as we'll see in the next chapter. There *have* been naturalistic studies performed in participants' daily environments, studies in which people report on their stress levels in daily diaries and researchers test their saliva for levels of cortisol[71] at various times during the day, among other techniques.[72] But although salivary cortisol is a commonly used marker of psychological stress, this type of testing only measures stress indirectly.[73]

Although Segerstrom and Miller found a fair amount of evidence that when animals' immune systems are suppressed animals become more vulnerable to disease, they reported finding no "evidence linking stress-related immune change in healthy humans to disease vulnerability."[74] Even large stress-induced immune system changes can have very small consequences, either because the immune system has built-in redundancy or because immune system changes don't persist long enough make a person susceptible to disease. What Segerstrom's and Miller's review showed was that immune system changes seem to be related to the *types of events* that occur; that age and disease can influence the immune system adversely; and that chronic stressors influence the *effectiveness* of the immune response. This latter finding jibes with popular accounts emphasizing how the immediate physiological "fight or flight" response (see Chapter 2) that enabled cave dwellers to flee saber-tooth tigers isn't adaptive for "stressed out" citizens of the global economy.

Segerstrom and Miller said that their review showed just how flexible the immune system is and how much it can change without compromising the health of an otherwise healthy person. So, although they found a reliable association between stressful situations and changes in the immune system, they stood firm in their conclusion that changes in immune system response to stress are just that— *changes*, not cause-and-effect relationships. They made the far from sweeping assertion that as stress becomes more chronic "the potential adaptiveness" of immune changes decreases.[75] Their conclusions might be summed up in psychologist Howard Friedman's statement that "there is shockingly little evidence for a straightforward model of psychological dysfunction, consequent immune disruption, and subsequent disease."[76] Contrast these conclusions with the Public Affairs Office of the American Psychological Association's (APA) media release that followed Segerstrom's and Miller's analysis, stating that "psychologists have long known that stress affects our ability to fight infection, but ... major findings ... powerfully confirm the core fact that stress alters immunity."[77] Technically, this wasn't a misstatement. No facts were altered in the media release, and the researchers were accurately, albeit selectively, quoted. But the rather lengthy piece gave an overall impression of a much stronger association between stress and immune response than the researchers themselves had conveyed. Absent was the equivocal language used by Segerstrom and Miller; absent was any mention of their conclusion that there is "little or no evidence linking stress-related immune change in healthy humans to disease vulnerability." But there were good reasons for professional psychology to ramp up the rhetoric. Proof of a strong relationship among the immune system, stress, and disease is highly adaptive for the business of today's psychology, whose "hot" (funded) research projects are in the area of neuroscience.

Asking (and Answering) the Right Questions about Stress and Disease

It is one thing to appreciate the problems that arise for researchers when they try to answer questions about the relationship between stress and disease and quite another to determine whether the right questions about stress are being asked in the first place. Now that researchers understand that stressful experiences don't affect everyone's immune system in the same way— that individuals differ in the ways they respond to stress behaviorally, affectively, and cognitively, far from abandoning the search for cause-and-effect relationships among the myriad variables that are believed to influence immune system functioning, they are trying to discover *which* variables actually affect *what* immune system functions at a cellular level. In order to achieve the high level of specificity they seek, researchers are asking questions like: "Which psychological processes play a critical mediating role between stressor exposure…and immune alteration?"[78] The way these kinds of questions are framed speaks volumes about research priorities. What's important here, from the researcher's perspective, is to understand the subjective experience of people in order to explain the relationship between stressful conditions and illness. In theory, changing the individual psychology of the person will improve the outlook for his or her health. As one psychoneuroimmunologist, Margaret Kemeny, put it:

> The human brain allows for a great degree of latitude in the psychological response to stressors as well as more benign contexts. It is critically important to understand how cognitive processes and resulting emotional states influence peripheral biology, including the immune system, to map the neural substrates of these relations and to develop methods for intervening at the psychological level to improve physiological functioning and health.[79]

Applying research on primate social status hierarchies to humans, Kemeny asserts that continual exposure to "status threats" such as poverty or racial discrimination can "create a biological vulnerability with health consequences."[80] According to her, this happens when some people judge social conditions as threatening, given their own fears and sensitivities (read: personalities).

I confess, as a nonscientist, to being more than a little uneasy assailing the bastions of a specialty as unpronounceable and complex as psychoneuroimmunology, but I must protest the limitations of the questions being asked. I'm reminded of Fleck's dictum that by the time a problem is posed, it often "already contains half its solution."[81] When researchers like Kemeny place a premium on intervening "at the psychological level to improve physiological functioning and health," they are asking us to look first at how a person appraises a situation and *then* to consider how this appraisal influences her or his physiological response, rather than looking *first* at the situation or conditions at hand.[82] This, it seems to me, seduces us into focusing on personality over context.

Some researchers believe that it will be impossible to formulate a model that links personality, immunity, and disease, simply because it's so difficult to take into account all the complex factors that make up any relationship between human personality and health.[83] But I'm not so sure that the goal of finding a causal connection between personality and disease is what we should be aiming for, especially if the attempt is to nail down differences among people in terms of how they are drawn to "unhealthy situations."[84] This road can only lead to elitist moralizing at best and blaming the victim at worst.

TURNING THE ENVIRONMENT OUTSIDE/IN
Psychologizing Context

Increasingly, in their quest for professional credibility through scientific validity, psychologists have allowed biology to threaten to take over the field, as Susan Oyama has said, "with every flexing of [its] reductionist muscle."[85] Over the years, psychologists have regularly been accused of having "physics envy," and that envy is closer than ever to being quenched. Now there are a number of biologically oriented subspecialties in psychology, and the field of behavioral medicine is booming. The American Psychological Association (APA) Press recently published a book entitled *Contributions Toward Evidence-based Psychocardiology*. In its usual sweeping style, the APA's house organ, *Monitor on Psychology*, describes how researchers in the new field of psychocardiology are "uncovering how psychosocial factors such as low socioeconomic status, depression and hostility contribute to cardiovascular disease."[86] This is how Robert M. Carney, director of the Behavioral Medicine Center at Washington University School of Medicine in St. Louis, interviewed here by a reporter from the *Monitor*, describes the association between depression and heart disease:

> It's not just that depressed people often don't exercise, eat right or take their medications, says Carney. There may be physiological mechanisms at work too.... for example, Carney and co-authors note that medically well but mentally depressed people had high levels of stress hormones and that depressed heart patients had elevated heart rates, exaggerated responses to physical stressors and other indicators of dysfunction....

Other psychologists are exploring the role of the external environment. (italics added)[87]

Notice how Carney divides research psychologists into two groups: one group that explores the psychological and physiological side of depression and one group that explores the contribution of "the external environment." In a rather egregious instance of context-stripping,[88] the environment is talked about as if it were a single entity, just one among many factors that affect health and mental health, rather than as an aggregate of systems and institutions—social, economic, institutional, and political—that can influence these outcomes for better or for worse.

Setting aside for the moment the question of whether we can—or should—separate what we call the psychosocial world into its constituent parts, it is plain that psychological researchers who set out to explore the psychosocial world often give more weight to the *psyche* than to the *social*. Linda Gallo and Karen Matthews, featured in the *Monitor* article on psychocardiology as psychologists who tackle the "environmental" side of things, asked the following research question: Do "negative emotions play a role" in "understanding the association between socioeconomic status [SES] and physical health?"[89] In a move reminiscent of psychoneuroimmunologist Kemeny's thinking, they proceeded to frame the "environmental" question in terms of the role played by "negative emotions." As Gallo and Matthews explain it: "If cognitive-emotional factors play a role in connecting SES with health, a key question becomes how the environments that people with low SES inhabit lead them to experience negative emotions and cognitions, which, in turn engender early morbidity and mortality."[90] In the researchers' view, it is the individual-level factors ("cognitive-emotional factors") that bring on illness or death. These are what capture their attention and permit them to psychologize poverty.[91] But sociologists Angus Forbes and Steven Wainwright believe that psychosocial factors don't have much to say about health inequalities. They ask: "Even supposing there is a strong relationship between psychological distress and social status, what does that reveal? except [*sic*] that...social status...[is] important, together with how an individual or community conceptualizes that status."[92]

Gallo and Matthews have hypothesized that people of lower income are "more reactive to stress" than their higher earning counterparts because they "maintain a smaller *bank* of resources...to deal with stressful events"[93] (italics added). Here, from a high perch, the researchers issue pronouncements on "unhealthy behavioral coping strategies" that can create susceptibility to disease in poor people, as well as the "low self-esteem" that "lack of education" causes.[94] It's hard to believe that we should worry more about low self-esteem than about the origins of those educational deficits. Both educational deficits and educational opportunities are tied to a person's social position, but we don't spend much time talking about how well the middle and upper classes are coping with the good fortune of safe neighborhoods, well-equipped schools, and stable teaching staffs.

Sociologists have used the concept of *social capital* to explain how social conditions can result in the chronic stress that can lead to disease. They argue that lower socioeconomic status may be accompanied by a reduction in social capital, often defined as the reciprocal exchanges, norms, and trust that lead to cooperation.[95] Unlike Gallo's "reserve capacity" model, the idea of social capital has the virtue of locating the "resource bank" within the community rather than inside the individual. But critics of the idea of social capital have argued that overemphasizing social cohesiveness can lead to blaming communities for social problems rather than holding larger social institutions accountable. They maintain that social capital theory doesn't fully acknowledge political processes that strongly influence the health of populations,[96] and that the theory is too middle class in its unfailingly positive definitions of commitment and engagement, when not all social networks (consider drug-using communities, for example) are necessarily supportive or health-promoting.[97]

John Lynch uses the term *social connectedness* to refer both to (horizontal) interpersonal linkages as well as to (vertical) linkages between people and larger social structures such as political and economic systems. He suggests that perhaps less emphasis should be placed on the interpersonal bonds that the theory of social capital emphasizes and more on the ties between groups of people and the institutions that regulate their circumstances. Rather than paying so much attention to kinship and friendship networks, then, we would look at how much access generations of marginalized groups have had to institutions such as the medical system.[98] R. Jay Turner and William Avison have concluded, after studying differences in people's exposure to different types of *social stress*, that researchers should be paying at least as much attention to differences in people's *exposure* to stress as they have been paying to people's *vulnerability* to stress.[99]

The Truth about Washing Machines

While it is true that both personal mastery and social support are terrifically helpful to people as they face adversity, it is also true that the kinds of chronic problems that poverty brings with it can make these personal and relational resources less available over time to people at the bottom of the economic heap.[100] These chronic problems (researchers often lump such problems together under the umbrella of "chronic stress") lay the groundwork for more material losses, and these losses further reduce both personal and material resources that could otherwise help people cope with difficult circumstances.[101] This is not merely a matter of negative cognitive states or subjective appraisals of a situation. Nicole Ennis and her colleagues found that material losses that might appear to the non-poor to be relatively minor can have a particularly acute impact on people living in poverty. For instance, many of the low-income inner-city women they studied could be plunged into a full-blown crisis by something like the washing machine's breaking down.[102] For the poor, when the chips are down, family and friends don't always offer the kind of help that buffers adversity[103]—what social scientists generally mean when they refer to "social support." When Deborah Belle studied mothers in poverty, she found that they hardly experienced the kind of "help" that comes with a price tag of repayment of money or favors down the road as a boon.[104] Too, there are instances when the type of support offered doesn't fit the needs of the person asking for assistance.[105]

The stress concept enables a kind of outside-in thinking that makes what's outside the person important mainly because of its effects on the inside of the person. The natural sequelae of this way of thinking are prescriptions for individual change as the "cures" for external stressors. A lengthy piece in the *New York Times* Sunday magazine by Andrew Solomon entitled "A Cure for Poverty" illustrates just how far outside-in thinking can go.[106] Solomon's central argument is that the stress of poverty leads to depression and it's the *depression* that has to be treated:

> Poverty is depressing and depression…is impoverishing.… The poor tend to have a passive relationship to fate: their lack of self-determination makes them far more likely to accommodate problems than to solve them.… They can be saved only by pressing insight onto them, often through muscular exhortation.[107]

Using stress as a stand-in for a whole range of emotional reactions to social conditions makes for an interventionist perspective that encourages us to think in terms of psychological solutions to a host of socio-structural problems.

Thinking like Solomon's leads to the logical conclusion that we need to change the poor and how they function. But it may be, as Sendhil Mullainathan and Eldar Shafir argue, that the poor don't need behavioral fixing any more than anyone else does. The poor are

> just as susceptible to…the impulses and idiosyncrasies as those who live in comfort, but whereas people who are better off function in the midst of a system…that is increasingly designed to facilitate their decisions and improve their outcomes, people who are less well off typically find themselves without easy recourse to…[economic] "aids" [e.g., helpful employers] and often are confronted by obstacles…that render their economic choices all the more overwhelming and their economic conduct all the more fallible.[108]

Sandro Galea and his colleagues recently published a study in the *American Journal of Public Health* analyzing research done between 1980 and 2007 that linked social conditions directly to adult mortality.[109] The social conditions represented included racial segregation, income inequality, and poverty. They found 176,000 deaths attributable to racial segregation in 2000 and 133,000 to personal poverty (as compared with 119,000 deaths attributable to accidents and 156,000 to lung cancer every year). Galea questions why—since the connection between poverty and heart disease has already been well established—we don't look at poverty as a direct cause of death. He wants us to focus on poverty itself, not on the negative thoughts and emotions of those who experience it.

How Can We Know the Dancer (the Stress of Poverty) from the Dance (the Stress of Inequality)?

Some critics say that too many researchers have been looking only at poverty when they should be looking at various forms of inequality to explain the connection between income and health.[110] Studying inequality forces researchers to look beyond the characteristics of those who live in poverty to social factors that can affect health. Discrimination, for example, can lead to reduced educational and employment opportunities, and decreased access to quality healthcare.[111] Low self-esteem and discrimination don't exist on the same plane, just as depression and "the environment" don't, nor are they correctable by the same means. The difference in problem definition, naturally, leads to a difference in "cure." Psychotherapy for "self-esteem issues" differs vastly in scope and effectiveness from political action to combat discrimination. In societies that perpetuate inequality, people's responses can't always be attributed to their own incompetence, insecurity, or fear. There are social norms that affect people beyond their psyches. If there is a strong norm in a school against aggressive behavior, for instance, children are less likely to be the perpetrators or victims of violence than they are in a school where there are no such norms.[112] Social workers and community psychologists have consistently argued that changing individual psyches is not the answer to ensuring community "health."

Sociologist Richard Wilkinson has questioned why it is that as a society we "expect to make a substantial impact on health inequalities without reducing disadvantage."[113] He worries that if we imply that we can do this when we can't, we may weaken the political will to do anything to reduce actual deprivation. Trying to reduce the *effects* of disadvantage (e.g., stress) without reducing disadvantage itself would mean needing more services—more rehab programs, more police, more psychotherapy—and all this with little potential effect. Looking at real deprivation by focusing on the material conditions of people's lives, such as housing and transportation, not just on the psychological consequences of stress, can lead to social change.

Amartya Sen, in the Nobel Prize acceptance speech I referred to earlier, spoke about how we can't rely only on psychological well-being as an indicator of advantage. He talked about how people living under conditions of inequality or tyranny may take whatever small pleasures they have, adjusting their wants to the stringent limits of what is possible, and not seeing themselves as deprived or disadvantaged.[114] But just because a person doesn't experience a condition as stressful does not mean that it isn't unjust or harmful in the long run. In the United States, for example, many slave owners tried to justify slavery on the basis that some slaves who had benevolent owners were singing in their chains. Stress is not simply in the eye—or the cognitions or emotions—of the beholder.

Stress, as it is currently viewed, has deep roots in the biomedical universe. It is often defined as a psychological or emotional factor. This means that the "stressor," or the social/environmental situation or condition, carries less weight than the person's emotional response to it. And, as Mildred Blaxter maintains, even when the emphasis is on the "stressor" rather than the "stress," even when we acknowledge the social causes of health problems, we don't define those social causes as poor health itself.[115] Stress clearly has a political use in helping us maintain a view of the individual as *ill from* society rather than acknowledging the need to tackle the *ills of* society.

CHAPTER 4

Mars and Venus Stress Out, Naturally

The currents of home-life are so many, so diverse, so contradictory, that they are only maintained by using the woman as a sort of *universal solvent*; and this position of holding many diverse elements in solution is not compatible with the orderly crystallisation of any of them, or with much peace of mind to the unhappy solvent.

—Charlotte Perkins Gilman, *1903 (italics added)*[1]

SELF-MADE MAN AND HIS "UNIVERSAL SOLVENT"

My mother liked to say, half-jokingly, that she never felt such love for me as when she saw me at the kitchen sink washing the dishes. This is easy to understand. My mother did everything that needed to be done for our family with little help from my sister or me and without much overt appreciation from either of us (it went without saying that my father offered no help on the domestic end of things). Nineteenth-century Americans generally gave more praise to women than anyone in our family gave to our mother.[2] The lavishness of their praise, as we have discussed, placed middle-class women on a moral pedestal, their long skirts well clear of the filth of the city streets and their minds free of the muck of daily commerce.

The business of self-making belonged to the men, as the realities of a white-collar world put men behind desks and under bosses.[3] But in a dramatic transformation that took place over decades, not centuries, old-style *manhood* was transformed into new-style *masculinity*—two very different things. As cultural historian Michael Kimmel has pointed out, whereas manhood referred to qualities of character, masculinity is not bred in the bone; it can only be defined in relation to femininity. Men have to demonstrate their masculinity over and over again if they are not to be considered—perish the thought!—too feminine. And this means that differences between men and women have to be staunchly asserted and proven. It is no wonder, then, that the question of women's place in the modern world (the so-called Woman Question) became a hotly debated topic during a period when men, already in some sense compromised by the business of self-making, confronted the possibility of changes in women's status (e.g., acquisition of the vote, public activity, higher level employment opportunities) and came face to face with what these changes might mean for them.[4] As it turned out, of course, women's entrance into the public arena did indeed make it more difficult for men to prove they were men, and fears that society was fast becoming feminized have been aroused regularly ever since.[5] John Gray, originator of the Mars/ Venus distinction, seems to be expressing a new-millennium version of these fears when he says:

> Being equals does not mean that we have to be the same. Given their hours working outside the home or the increased demand on them as mothers and homemakers, women undeniably need more help at home, but that need should not require men to change their nature.... When women today return home from work, they often wish a loving and supportive wife was there waiting for them ... in various ways and to different degrees, women want men to become like women.[6]

As I'll discuss further in the next chapter, middle-class women's movement into paid employment hasn't been matched by an equivalent transformation in the amount of men's caregiving and household labor. Our attachment to the idea of "natural" differences between men and women gives the impression that there has been little change over the decades in the structure of our society, when in fact there has been a profound—indeed, a tectonic—shift. No matter how much similarity there is between men's and women's roles in the world, we continue to insist that men and women are essentially different in their very natures, because, as Deborah Cameron succinctly puts it, "culture change is hard."[7]

Stress and the Status Quo

In the twenty-first century, the question is not whether women should have an education, vote, or work outside the home; it's not even whether they can "have it all" (that question has been asked and answered). Now the question is whether women can and should *do* it all. Consider media coverage of the "mommy wars" that are allegedly being waged by employed and stay-at-home moms, mothers who are portrayed as lunging at each others' throats. Determining whether these wars are or are not really happening is far less important than attending to the message that mothers shouldn't abandon their traditional posts on the home front (how convenient that men no longer have to sustain that argument!). And if reports on the mommy wars don't do the job, the stress concept can help perform the chastening. Women, who are getting incredibly "stressed out" as they attempt to manage their lives in the workplace and in the home, should perhaps stop trying to do it all and stay where they belong, not just for their families' sake, but in their own interest, for the sake of their physical and mental health.

Consider how much media attention has been devoted to the fact that more women than men are graduating from college, as if this is a desperate situation for boys and men, even though throughout the world men continue to exert more power and control than women. And while some have called the recession that began in 2008 a "mancession,"[8] it is *women's* earnings that dropped by 2 percent in 2008 and women who are much more likely—a third more—than men to have held subprime mortgages.[9] Although as Michael Kimmel points out, "gender relations are [not] a zero-sum game [in which] if girls and women gain, boys and men lose,"[10] it often seems like it.

For well over a century, the mere prospect of changes in women's status was enough to unleash a media uproar over the damage those changes would wreak. According to Caryl Rivers, in her book *Selling Anxiety: How the News Media Scare Women*, women are always the "early warning systems of change."[11] When women change, so it goes, social bedlam will ensue and women will be miserable. There are times these days when it seems that all the news about women's lives is bad news:

> If you believed the press, you'd assume that modern women were psychological wrecks, miserable in personal relations, joyless at work while causing great damage to their children, desperate in midlife unless they were housewives, filled with regret if their choices had involved ambition.... The media no longer tells women...that we can't achieve.... The new message is that the price of achievement is too high.... At least with the former [message], the solution was clear: *Just do it.* Today, it's more subtle: *Poor dears, the price for your accomplishment will be unhappiness, regret, failed marriages, wretched children.*[12]

For the past 30 years or so, the stress concept has become a vehicle for explaining women's struggles to have/do "it all." The popular message is that women need to calm themselves down so that they can continue with business as usual. The stress concept papers over our collective failure to act on the idea that care is both men's and women's work, and this makes discussions about caregiving work rough going for lots of couples—for some women because they're afraid of being seen as nags or sounding like whiners or because they fear starting a fight they think they'll lose, and for some men because it's disturbing to think about what a change in the status quo might entail. If we can't deal with this stuff at the family level, it's hardly surprising that it seems nearly impossible to elevate caregiving to a national priority at the policy level. If a woman can keep thinking that too much stress is her central problem, she's a lot less likely to put her energies into demanding that that the Family and Medical Leave Act do more than give *unpaid* leave from work for caregiving. And she's less likely to demand more cooperation from her mate with the laundry or organizing their child's birthday party or to suggest to him that sending a Mother's Day card to his own mother is his responsibility.

Who's responsible for holding women primarily accountable for caregiving work in our society? Men? Women themselves? The media? In my view, these aren't the questions we should be asking. If we look at the dilemma through a postmodern lens, it is clear that we all drink from the same well. We absorb and act on knowledge available to us, and it's impossible to pin responsibility on one particular institution or group, since none has cornered the market on that knowledge.[13] So, if I believe it is my responsibility, based on what I've come to understand about what's expected of me as a woman, to plan the birthday party or send the Mother's Day card, this understanding is difficult to change. There's an emotional investment in "doing gender" in certain ways: we claim our maleness or femaleness through our conduct[14] and we're motivated by what Barbara Risman calls "the moral necessity of being a man or woman" to demonstrate to ourselves and other people that we are *good* women or *good* men.[15] What we understand about how we are supposed to think about and deal with stress is entangled with what we understand about being a good woman or a good man; stress, as we'll see, comes in gendered packages. The discourse of stress—what is "in the air" about stress—is shaped by our ideas about who should be helping whom, whose job it is to nurture the young; whose job it is to handle household responsibilities. But in the public forum, discussions of stress are dominated by talk of the differences between men and women: Who has more stress, men or women? Who handles stress better, men or women?

Silas Weir Mitchell's advice to his nerve-wracked middle-class patients to "eat regularly and exercise freely" now seems oddly contemporary.[16] But men are no longer the primary recipients of advice on how to manage stress. Although the progress-and-pathology story still hammers home the message that modern life is dangerous for *everyone's* health, these days it is the challenges white middle-class women face (and the solutions to those challenges) that are at the heart of popular discussions about stress. This is true despite the fact that poverty, inequality, and racism are arguably the most critical stressors that women face in the United States.[17] Yes, stress certainly does continue to be talked about in relation to men, particularly in relation to employment and joblessness; but although stress is seen as a problem that affects both men and women, it is more often viewed as a woman's problem to solve. For this reason, you'd think that when I performed a Google News search for "men and stress" and "women and stress" the search would have yielded many more links for "women and stress." So imagine my confusion (not to say horror) when more links—millions more—appeared for "men and stress." There goes my central thesis that stress has taken on a female face, I thought. But a closer (and calmer) look revealed a story the numbers didn't tell. Random viewing of a great many "men and stress" links showed that the majority of them centered on the subject of men's and women's *differences* in relation to stress. Almost none of these appeared in the "women and stress" search. "Women and stress" was a subject unto itself: all women, all the time.

My rather unscientific Googling supports much of the evidence I have uncovered elsewhere showing that stress has fallen into the male/ female "difference" bin, whose contents we'll pick through shortly. And if the sheer quantity of references to women's stress in the media didn't demand that we look at popular discussions of gender and stress carefully, the way the stress concept is differentially applied to men and women would compel us to do so. For example, warnings about the dangers of stress take on special meaning for women as the perennial guardians of the family's health. The pervasive message to women is that they must find ways to deal with the elusive entity called stress in order to remain the linchpins of family life. "Let mothers be educated in all that concerns life and health," intoned Mrs. Eliza de La Vergue, M.D., back in the mid-1800s. And there were other cautions: "Woman was neither made a toy nor a slave, but a help-meet to man, and as such devolves upon her very many important duties and obligations which cannot be met so long as she is the puny, sickly, aching, weakly, dying creature that we find her to be";[18] and "Some sick women grow selfish and forget that, in a partnership..., others suffer when they suffer. Every true husband has but half a life who has a sick wife."[19] Women are still the "universal solvent" for family life, as Charlotte Perkins Gilman wrote back in 1903.

The following piece from the Associated Press, published in the *Newark Star Ledger,* reflects several contemporary themes that often emerge in relation to the subject of women and stress:

Holiday Stress Hits Women Hardest

The holiday season is the *most emotional time* of the year for many Americans, particularly for women who often *feel pressured* to make it special for those they care about, said Sharon Gordetsky, a psychologist who specializes in children, families, and issues of female development.

Even in families where fathers play a bigger role in parenting, child caring, and household work, "women tend to often still do more of the nurturing, do more of the social and family organization" for the holidays, said

Gordetsky.... "*Women have to take care of themselves if they are to be able to take care of others,*" Gordetsky said. Among the healthier methods experts recommend to cope with the holiday stress are *opting for* less elaborate festivities and *saying no* to that serving of delicious...lasagna (italics added).[20]

Naturally, "emotional times" are more stressful for women. After all, we know, don't we, that women are "more emotional" than men? And there is no actual pressure on women; women only "feel" pressured. They can "opt" to do things differently, and this will reduce the stress that threatens their health. When under stress, women should eat less, drink less (the piece emphasizes this), and exercise more. The takeaway message? Women have to take care of themselves if they are to be able to take care of others.

At the same time that women are being peppered with advice on managing stress, they are increasingly being praised for their superiority in dealing with it. In the previous chapter, we saw how, paradoxically, women were defined by their fragility and yet extolled for their strength as mothers. Now, instead of holding women up as paragons of moral virtue, we're seeing them as frazzled husks on the one hand and, on the other, as sturdy, stress-bearing vessels (or is it vassals?). Praise or no praise, women still seem to "need" expert guidance in order to remain strong—and extolling their strength is in the service of their continued caregiving work, just as it has been for 150 years.

Emotion as Women's Disease

At least part of the reason that advice on stress management is so often geared to women has to do with the belief that women's emotionality makes them less well equipped than men to deal with stress. In our society, emotion has never been gender-neutral; the experience and expression of emotion are thought to be among the "natural" male-female differences. The mainstream American idea that emotion is irrational and chaotic has combined with a traditional association of women and emotionality to legitimate the need for women either to control themselves or be controlled by men.[21] There's a great deal on the line for women in terms of how they handle stress, because how women handle stress conveys a message to others about whether they're in charge of themselves and their lives.

Psychologist Stephanie Shields conducted an experiment in which she had both men and women answer questions after reading a brief story about a person whose car had just been stolen. There were two forms of the story. Although identical in all other respects, the car owner was named "Karen" in one version and "Brian" in the other. Some subjects (men and women) in the study read the "Karen" and some the "Brian" version of the story. Those who read the "Karen" story responded very differently from those who read the "Brian" scenario. Here are a couple of typical reactions by the subjects of the study to the way "Karen" and "Brian" responded to the theft of a car:

[About "Karen"] Karen's car got ripped off and she flipped!! Started screaming and crying[;] no one could calm her down.

[About "Brian"] I assume Brian's initial response was shock but then weigh[ing] out the consequences he realized life goes on. There is probably disappointment but he can live with it.

Remember: the stories were identical, apart from the names of the protagonists. But to the subjects, whereas Brian was acting emotional, Karen *was* emotional. Karen's emotionality was more ingrained than Brian's—more a *part* of her.[22] This is not unexpected; ideas about emotional expression still form a bright line separating men and women in the public imagination. And, as we'll soon see, it's no accident that these emotional differences are a touchstone of the popular Mars/Venus distinction.

In the nineteenth century, women were thought to be weak, flighty, and sentimental—prone to "mere emotionality." Manly emotion, on the other hand, was not sentimental; if controlled, male passion could guide decisive action. Since women were considered to have only a limited capacity to manage emotion, the *emotion itself* was seen to be the problem. This was not the case for men. Some might fail to control their emotions, but this was deemed a failure of rational thought and will.[23] Men's and women's strengths and weaknesses were seen to complement each other.[24] *He* could channel his passions into mastery of the world of commerce, thereby creating a career and a fortune; *she* could help soften him and smooth his rough edges, restraining any tendencies he might have toward harshness at home. The idea of complementarity, however, did a real disservice to women, appearing to make equal what was inherently unequal.[25] *He* could rule *her* "rationally," but *she* could only try to temper *his* moods. Men and women did not have equal power, nor were their emotions equally valued. Now in the dominant culture, women are expected to show a kind of emotional openness that Shields calls *extravagant expressiveness*.[26] What has not changed are the associations between feminine emotion and nurturant selflessness and between manly emotion and rationality. And the cultural perception that women's emotion can career out of control at any time certainly hasn't changed: "Karen's" emotion derives from her "nature"; "Brian's" is provoked by the situation in which he finds himself.

When Catherine Lutz, a cultural anthropologist, interviewed men and women about how they express emotions, all her interviewees— male and female—subscribed to the view that women are the "emotional" ones. But beyond this, the women themselves perceived their emotionality as dangerous and felt they needed to have better control over their emotions and the situations that evoked them. The women Lutz interviewed conceived of a metaphorical boundary over which what was inside (uncontrolled emotion) might spill out.[27] Emotion was either in or out of bounds, a distinction that mirrors the age-old division between the (inside) "women's" sphere of the home, where emotionality is permitted, and the (outside) world of men, where rationality allegedly prevails.

Side by side with the continuing denigration of women as "too emotional" by both men and women, there is a fairly widespread vaunting of women's "natural" emotional gifts. The same access to their emotions that seems to make women dangerous and in need of control is also what gives women their cherished ability to accommodate to and empathize with others. Arlie Hochschild defines "emotion work" not only as the attempt to change an emotion, but also as "the work of affirming, enhancing, and celebrating the well-being and status of others."[28] In the latter sense, emotion work is, literally, "social" work, and I would argue that it is women who are the prime emotion managers in our society. When a woman tells herself "I shouldn't have flown off the handle like that; I'll be more understanding next time. I better help him calm down," she is *working on* her own and others' emotions in ways I would construe as emotion work. When she asks a friend or partner who is looking angry or glum, "What's wrong? Is there something the matter?" she is doing emotion work. This work is necessary in the service of caregiving and nurturing,[29] and the skills needed to perform it don't come "naturally"; they are essential survival skills that most people of subordinate status must learn.[30]

Openness to thinking, learning, and talking about their emotions can make many women especially receptive to what experts have to say about how they should manage their out-of-control emotions and the stress that "causes" them. Women's responsibility for managing stressors (outside) is strongly related to the need to manage their emotions (inside).[31] As the contemporary discourse of stress would have it, women need to find ways to reduce their stress so they can remain healthy and free of undue anger. The stress concept has become a vehicle for messages to women about the perils of out-of-control emotion—warnings that stress could cause them to experience emotions that will hurt those in their care. On the ABC special "S-T-R-E-S-S H-U-R-T-S,"[32] "Maria," an overburdened single parent, describes her mornings this way:

> I would say I get angry from stress a lot. [The children's] misbehaving sets off my anger. It's the only way I get through my morning—is to yell. I sometimes feel a little trapped because of the fact I can't go places and do things like I would be able to if I had, you know, some help sometimes with the kids, and things like that.

Here Maria explains, using the language of stress, what she believes causes her anger: she gets "angry from stress a lot." If the stress causes her anger, that anger surely won't be directed toward the kinds of social problems that might merit her wrath, such as the lack of affordable day care, flexible workplace policies, or the gendered nature of caregiving.[33]

Stress and Depression

For years, psychologists have tried to figure out why so many more women—twice as many[34]—are diagnosed with depression than men. Because the evidence for men's and women's biological and personality differences is pretty slim,[35] researchers have begun to try to answer this question by looking at differences in the amount of stress in women's lives and in women's response to stress. What follows is a posting on *iVillage*'s message board, "Women and Stress," entitled "Everything Gets to Me":

from: lissa91

Mar-15 11:22 am

I don't get it. I have everything I want. 2 beautiful, smart kids who adore me, a man who is supportive and loving and just amazing, a great home to live in that I keep clean, food on the table every night, wonderful friends, a big family and plus an extended family on my BF's side who think I hung the moon. What else could I need? Yet I get so irritated.

My son decided a little over a year ago to go live with his dad. My daughter lives with me. I've been divorced twice and a child resulted from each marriage. My son will be 11 and my daughter will be 5. I'm living with my BF of almost 2 years since February and we are blissfully in love and honestly, don't get on each other's nerves. We both work and take care of things well together. This is not a problem at all and I don't get irritated with anything in our relationship. I do get overwhelmed at work quite a bit because I've been there a while and have gotten no raises and keep getting more added to my workload which can be quite stressful on me. My BF was working nights so I was rushing home to cook before he'd have to leave and I'd be alone with my 4 year old til the next morning and trying to get housework done and tend to her when she's bouncing off the walls from having to be quiet at pre-Kindergarten is quite difficult. Having to juggle quality time with her and other things I have to do each night are not easy. And I find myself losing my temper with her which is not a good thing. Then there is a cousin of mine who I love dearly.... Anyway, my cousin calls me and is always wanting me to do something and trying to plan stuff for me and gets aggravated with me if I say no. It's almost as if I owe her for things. And if I don't answer the phone, she calls over and over. Then texts me to call her ... or calls J's phone. And it's always over something that is not near as important as she makes it out to be. Then there is my mother who still sees me as 10 years old. I'm 37 and have yet to be able to get her to cut the cord.... If I tell my mom how she's hovering and how it irritates me, she will play the martyr and hang up and go cry to daddy who will then call me to tell me what a big horrible piece of crap I am for making mom feel bad. SO I can't even tell them how I feel about their hovering.... I just let everything get to me and I am too nice to tell people how I feel. J [boyfriend] told me I was just too sweet for my own good and needed to get in people's faces every so often if they irritated me and let them know it was unacceptable to treat me like they do. Anyway, I'm scared I'm heading back into my old depression and will need to go back on meds which I hadn't had to since postpartum days. I know J will understand and know it isn't him that is triggering this but gosh I'm worried that I'll end up a basket case.

Stressed,
Melissa[36]

In her post, Melissa makes what has become a common connection among stress, irritability, and depression. When Melissa wonders why she feels so terrible despite having "everything," or when she blames herself for being too nice, is she ruminating in a way that is common to depressed women? Are the chronic stresses that Melissa describes— low pay and little power at work; "juggling" employment and 24/7 childcare—responsible for why she feels so bad? Have the family problems to which she refers made her more vulnerable to depression when stressful situations present themselves? Research on stress and depression suggests these possibilities and more. What most research on stress and depression doesn't measure, however, is *chronic* stress,[37] even though day-to-day burdens like Melissa's may well have a stronger connection to depression than single, acutely stressful events.[38]

Susan Nolen-Hoeksema, who has researched women's depression over a period of more than 20 years, believes that the greater incidence of depression in women than men may be related to their tendency to ruminate about their life situations.[39] She sees a connection between this tendency and what she calls the "chronic strain" women experience when they don't have a sense of control over their circumstances, when they are not being affirmed or supported in their close relationships, or when they are faced with inequities in housework and childcare. Nolen-Hoeksema believes that the rumination, mainly centered on women's sense of responsibility for the circumstances in which they find themselves, might represent a woman's fruitless attempt to achieve control, a belief that "there must be something I can do/should do about this." Women who don't believe they can control their circumstances may feel helpless and dejected, and these feelings can engender more difficulties down the road. But there are women who *do* believe they have the ability to manage their lives, and yet are actually *unable* to control their situations. Battered women with children, for instance, may not be able to leave their abusive partners because they can't support their children on their own. Nolen-Hoeksema's view of Melissa's distress would probably center on Melissa's ruminating on how people often take advantage of her; how little control she has over her parents' rejecting behavior and the escalating, uncompensated demands at work; and the burden of full-time housekeeping and child-care responsibilities.

Nolen-Hoeksema and other researchers may well pay attention to the social and cultural underpinnings of women's depression in their research, but this is not what others—or even they themselves—ultimately focus on when their work is publicized or popularized. Yes, there are plenty of discussions in the media about how stressful women's lives are and plenty of questions raised about whether men or women are better at handling stress. But there's little interest in looking at what social forces may underlie these differences. Consider what happened when the American Psychological Association's monthly magazine, the *Monitor on Psychology*, reported on Nolen-Hoeksema's research. In an interview for the *Monitor*, Nolen-Hoeksema was cited as saying that the reason women tend to ruminate more than men in response to sad feelings has primarily to do with culture. She said that "there are differences between what it's OK for women versus men to focus on emotionally." But instead of exploring these cultural differences, the reporter blithered on: "Gender aside, ruminators share some common characteristics ... ," and the cultural context remained terra incognita.[40]

Pressure to focus on quick solutions had Nolen-Hoeksema herself giving tips to readers of *Working Mother* magazine about how to use exercise or a community college class to divert the "ruminating cycle" so they could "stop a brewing depression before it starts" and feel more in control so that they wouldn't "blow little things out of proportion."[41] And when Nolen-Hoeksema's book *Women Who Think Too Much: How to Break Free of Overthinking and Reclaim Your Life* came out, her talk of "toxic thoughts" and "morbid meditation" pointed up how her research had been ground up and mixed with self-help pap for a media market aimed at middle-class women.[42] Paradoxically, popular advice to women about managing stress reinforces just the sort of ruminating that Nolen-Hoeksema decries. Women are often asked to take responsibility for how much stress they are bringing on themselves, while at the same time they are charged to change themselves or their circumstances in order to reduce stress.

Does "Melissa" fit the morbid ruminator mold? She seems to. And yet I don't think that's really the right question to be asking. To my mind, the question should look more like the one that Nolen-Hoeksema has been tackling for years in her research: What does it mean in terms of women's depression that more women than men are prey to chronic strain and feel both responsible for their circumstances and powerless to change them? That the burden of care in our society falls squarely onto the backs of women clearly is related, in many cases, to the development of depression in women. It's certainly no accident that depression often strikes women in their childbearing and child-rearing years.[43]

Literally hundreds of studies have been performed with the goal of teasing out the relationship between stress and women's depression, and many use checklists of life events. Checklists are widely used because they are easy to administer. They generally contain a circumscribed number of life events (e.g., deaths, divorce, domestic violence, rape, teen pregnancy). Most of the studies that use checklists don't take into account the particular meanings and judgments that color particular events and can lead to wide differences in how people experience them, nor do they examine the timing of events and the contexts in which they occur. Critics of the checklist method have pointed out that checklists often confound the stressful event or circumstance (stressor) itself with its outcome. For example, in one checklist, fighting among partners may be listed as a stressor; in another, it may be listed as an outcome of stressful events.[44]

Few checklists explore events in relation to individual and social transitions and dislocations.[45] Separation from a partner, for example, can be quite different for the one doing the leaving than for the one being left,[46] and at this particular time in history, leaving a partner will have different meanings than it did 40 years ago. The meaning of a life event will depend on the person's age, ethnicity, race, gender, and social class, among other factors. Because checklists look only at recent life events, they tell us very little about how these factors affect people over a lifetime, particularly when they encounter major obstacles or chronically stressful conditions such as poverty or discrimination.[47]

It's not just life event checklists that have substantively removed life events from their social and environmental contexts; research on genes and depression also performs this sort of decontextualization. There are a couple of theories about how genes influence depression. According to the "genetic control" argument, genes influence whether people will seek out higher- or lower-risk environments.[48] Effectively, this means that a low-income mother of three who lives in a dangerous neighborhood with a drug-abusing partner has "selected herself" into this particular set of circumstances. The "genetic sensitivity" hypothesis, on the other hand, holds that this mother's genes determine her vulnerability to the same set of stressful circumstances. She may or may not become depressed, depending on how the genes are aligned. Without denying that there are individuals who are genetically vulnerable to developing depression or that a genetic propensity for depression can lead to the selection of environments conducive only to more depression, one can still ask why it is necessary to hold genes centrally responsible when there are social and environmental factors aplenty that contribute to women's depression.

This is the question Kristine Siefert and her colleagues have chosen to examine. In studying depressed and nondepressed mothers who had received welfare or were on welfare, they found that the depressed mothers were much more likely than the nondepressed mothers not to have enough food in the house, to live in dangerous neighborhoods, and to have endured domestic violence and racial and sex discrimination.[49] Not unpredictably, the depressed mothers were much more anxious, had higher rates of posttraumatic stress disorder (PTSD), and were more dependent on drugs and alcohol than their nondepressed counter-parts. But instead of recommending individual-level interventions like psychotherapy and medication, the researchers suggested prevention in the form of changes in social policy. More food for the household, they advised, would be "cost effective relative to maintenance pharma-cotherapy." On the face of it, these recommendations are obvious—so obvious, perhaps, as not to have been worth the study's funding by the National Institute of Mental Health. After all, we know that the majority of those who live in poverty are women. Isn't it self-evident that reduc-ing poverty, racial discrimination, neighborhood violence, and other social ills would help keep many women from becoming depressed?[50] Apparently not.

In Chapter 3, I referred to Andrew Solomon's article, "A Cure for Poverty: What If You Could Help End People's Economic Problems by Treating Their Depression?" Solomon's perspective is about as far from Siefert's thinking as you can get. Indeed, his ideas are much more in tune with the contemporary trend toward individualizing social problems like poverty. This trend has been responsible for creating the idea of the welfare "queen" and has led to representing the need for welfare as an individual, medical problem.[51] Recall Solomon's statement that "poverty is depressing, and depression . . . is impover-ishing. The poor tend to have a passive relationship to fate. . . . They can be saved only by pressing insight onto them, often through mus-cular exhortation."[52] In his article, Solomon told the story of "Wendy," an African American woman who had been sexually abused at age 6, physically and verbally abused by her first boyfriend at age 17, raped by a family friend not long after this, and subsequently abused by the man who fathered her three children. In addition to caring for her own children, Wendy also took care of her sister's children. By age 18, she was parenting 11 children. Eventually she had to quit her job because she was in the throes of a major depression and had begun to use painkillers to get to sleep. Solomon endorses the idea of antidepressants as an antidote to a predicament like Wendy's: it is "reasonable to treat the depression itself so that these people can alter their own lives," and cheaper than "the social services that the indigent require."[53] No one could argue that it would be helpful to use any and all tools to help mitigate Wendy's depression, but the idea of "pressing" treatment for depression "onto" Wendy as the primary solution to her problems is particularly disturbing. Are we not to consider how Wendy's situation came to be? Where is the place for social policies and practices that might have prevented her circumstances from becoming so dire? There seems no tipping point at which the convergence of severe and chronic stressors or their inexorable, cumulative effects call for a different response to the circmstances of Wendy and others like her.

When sociologists and psychologists consider a social phenomenon like poverty as one among many "stressors," they lump poverty together with stressful situations that are hardly comparable. Poverty cannot be equated with wedding preparations or even chronically stressful work situations; it is a set of *conditions* that brings with it high-crime neighborhoods, poor schools, and, for some, compromised social networks. So Wendy, unlike Brenda the bride who is preparing for her wedding or Paula the worker on the factory floor who is maltreated by her authoritarian boss, cannot benefit from typical recommendations on stress management from helpguide.org, which prescribes these "cures" for stress under the title "Dealing with Stressful Situations: The Four As":

Change the situation	Change your reaction
• Avoid the stressor.	• Adapt to the stressor.
• Alter the stressor.	• Accept the stressor.

A couple years after Solomon's piece came out, the *New York Times Sunday Magazine* featured another lengthy article that could have been its twin: "There's a killer haunting America's inner cities. Not drugs. Not handguns. But...stress?"[54] It told the stories of several African American women who were suffering from diabetes, asthma, and cancer, among other diseases. The article's author, Helen Epstein, put forward two "schools of thought" about the relationship between difficult environments and high rates of disease with which the poor must contend: according to her, one school maintains "that the problem has mainly to do with stress (e.g., pressures of "family responsibilities," racism, discrimination) and the other school sees the problem as having to do with actual deprivation." Epstein insisted that it's of supreme importance to determine whether the "emphasis" belongs on stress *or* on deprivation, and she wasn't averse to sharing her own thoughts on the subject:

> If stress is a major cause of ill health, interventions to alleviate it—counseling, antidepressants, even yoga—might be beneficial. A recent article in The [sic] *British Medical Journal* suggested that building self-esteem actually helped a group of Native Americans manage their obesity and diabetes.... On the other hand, if material disadvantage is a major cause of ill health among the poor, then extensive changes in the environment in which the poor live.... are needed.[55]

Epstein's distinction depends, illogically, on a separation of person from environment. According to her, "stress is subjective, a feeling, and it means different things to different people."[56] In defining stress as "feeling," though, the relationship of stress to an environmental condition or situation disappears. One might well ask: What happens when the "feeling" of stress is *caused* by the condition of deprivation?

Mrs. Moody, one of Epstein's interviewees, changed her diet from fatty to healthy, and Epstein points out how the fact that fat cells can interfere with the production of hormones that reduce stressful "feelings" can "explain how the stress of poverty creates a biological urge to overeat,... putting poor people at risk of obesity and its consequences—diabetes, heart disease, stroke, and certain types of cancer."[57] (More about this later, when we discuss scary stories about stress.) What Epstein doesn't talk about is the high ratio of Dunkin' Donuts shops and their ilk to stores selling fresh fruits and vegetables in many inner-city neighborhoods, now referred to as "food deserts." Nor does Epstein account for the plethora of fast food advertisments specifically targeted at the low-income African American population. And there are other things she doesn't talk about: gender, class, ethnicity, and race, to name a few. Epstein and Solomon, both of whom featured only women in their articles, never even mentioned the relationship between women and poverty. And the exclusive representation of African Americans in their discussions of poverty leads to a consistent confounding of class and race.

It's not just Epstein who is influenced by current ideas about stress and depression; her interviewee, Mrs. Moody, talks the talk of depression rather than anger; stress rather than rats, racism, slum landlords, or preoccupied politicians:

> ...it was stressful just to walk out of that place [her old apartment]. You were always scared for the kids.... You wake up stressed, go to sleep stressed, you see all the garbage and the dealers. That is depressing. In a bad environment like that you say, "What's the use of doing anything?"[58]

There is mounting evidence that the gender/stress/depression association will not be unraveled unless more researchers address the complexities of the reciprocal relationship between people and their environments that occurs against a backdrop of changing mores and social conditions. But as everyday life is increasingly translated into psychological terms through a process that Nikolas Rose calls the "psychologization of the mundane," this seems less and less likely.[59]

COPING

Since the late 1970s, there has been an incredible amount of research centered on how people cope with stress—perhaps more research than on any other single topic in psychology. In light of this fact, it's particularly disconcerting to find that many experts in the field believe most of that research is poorly conceived and pretty useless.[60] Researchers have vainly put a great deal of time and energy into trying to nail down differences in the ways men and women cope with stress. In some cases, it seems that any difference will do. Back in 1980, even though Lazarus and Folkman found very few differences in men's and women's styles of coping with stress, when they wrote up their research they focused on those very few differences, concluding that men just might "persevere" longer when solving problems and "be disposed to think more about the problem than women,"[61] promoting a vision of men as better problem-solvers than women under stressful conditions.

Examining the literature on women's coping in the early 1990s, Victoria Banyard and a colleague noticed that when questions about coping were posed in terms of differences in men's and women's coping styles, women invariably came out badly. They strongly felt that this wouldn't be the case if researchers were to examine the influence of the entire context of people's lives on their coping strategies, rather than looking principally at how people cope with single events and situations.[62] For instance, if an employed woman encounters a health crisis, how she appraises the situation and how she copes with it are going to depend heavily on what effect taking time off from work will have on her financial situation and the degree of access she has to the healthcare system. As the largest proportion of part-time workers in the United States, women have more limited access to healthcare and paid time off from work than men. But resources and power are not usually examined in stress and coping research.

Although racial and ethnic differences may well affect women's ways of coping, the effects of race and ethnicity on coping are rarely a research agenda. In studying African American and European American women living in inner-city Detroit, Nicole Ennis and her colleagues found that the African American women depended more on networks of support to cope with extreme stress, whereas, consistent with the tenets of European American individualism, the European American women depended more on their sense of mastery.[63] When we consider the kinds of advice given to women about how to cope with stress (e.g., make to-do lists and take scented baths), as we will shortly, we have to consider not only the fact that this mastery-oriented advice is rooted in middle-class mores, but that it is rooted in whiteness as well.

Although very recent research still focuses on male-female differences both in coping style and vulnerability to stress, these differences are likely to be studied by analyzing the influence of the neurological and endocrine systems on stress and coping. Today's academics talk of differences in terms of the "biobehavioral impact" of stress on health and mental health.[64] Gender differences in managing stress are frequently buttressed with science—often questionable—on brain and hormonal differences between men and women, and research on genes, brains, and hormones feeds a wellspring of advice about how to handle stress that women are showered with on a daily basis (and yes, by the way, there *are* shower products designed to reduce stress). These are the subjects I'll tackle next.

SELLING STRESS: ADVISE AND CONSENT

> Be it that immediate, knot-in-stomach feeling or a broader sense of discomfort, long-term stress is at an all-time high, according to the American Psychological Association. It's especially pervasive among women: Over 80 percent report feeling prolonged stress about money and the economy, and 70 percent say they're often worried about health problems affecting themselves and their families.
>
> *AOL* website[65]

Stress Kills: Scary Stories

In the following excerpts, taken from the ABC special "S-T-R-E-S-S Hurts: A Wake-up Call for Women," stress is described as a "destructive force." It is "toxic," "lethal"—a saboteur and a "killer"—and, if that were not enough to scare a woman, there's the constant refrain about stress making women fat. The narrator of the special, Nancy Snyderman, M.D., introduced the program this way:

> Good evening. Tonight you'll meet some women you'll probably recognize. They're very much like you or your friends, trying to juggle a career, children, aging parents. Women say there are not enough hours in the day, and certainly no time for themselves. Are they under stress? You bet they are—like never before; and it *hurts*, not only putting us at risk for serious illness, but affecting us in everyday ways, increasing our weight, fueling our tempers, ruining our sex lives, *and* our sleep.

Against pictures of clocks, sounds of ticking and hurry-up music:

> FEMALE VOICEOVER [THE NARRATOR, NANCY SNYDERMAN, M.D.]: "Listen to the voices of women under the influence—of a very common, very destructive force—stress. They feel pressure to do it all—the job, the house, the kids."
>
> VOICEOVER OF MALE AUTHORITY: "We're talking about stress levels that approach those you see in combat."
>
> FEMALE VOICEOVER: "Tonight, a life-changing hour for every woman, and the men who care about them. What does stress do to a woman's body?

Her mind? Her sex life?"

NARRATOR [SITTING BEFORE A GROUP OF WOMEN]: "Does stress interfere with having a normal sex life?" [*Women, as a group, laugh uproariously in response.*]

FEMALE VOICEOVER: " … Did you know that constant stress packs on the kind of fat that can kill?" [*Camera zooms in on a storefront with a neon sign advertising sundaes and chicken wings.*]

VOICE OF PAMELA PEEKE, M.D.: "How you *think* ends up at your waistline." [Narrator adds] "…and triggers explosive, damaging anger." [*Cut to an African America mother in bathrobe standing in a somewhat messy room, calling back angrily over her shoulder to her child; cut to White, male, bearded expert*] "It's actually causing little nicks and tears in the inner lining of the arteries that feed our heart."

NARRATOR "If you often feel overwhelmed, the next hour is for you" [*Cut to women looking distressed, wrinkling their brows as if from headaches*].

Fear-inducing rhetoric often accompanies advice to women about how to handle stress. Psychotherapists, academic researchers, and authors of popular psychology books are recruited by various media outlets to issue dire warnings, often couched in blood-curdling language, about the havoc stress can wreak on body and mind. Frightening women in order to get them to behave in certain ways is not a new cultural pastime, of course; we need only think back to nineteenth-century doctors' insistence that higher education could prove the ruination of young women.

Close behind the "stress-is-dangerous" message lurks the more insidious idea that woman themselves are responsible for the negative impact of stress on their health and appearance. According to Dr. Pamela Peeke, author of *Fight Fat over Forty,* we're "sitting around obsessing, worrying, complaining and back and forth about stress, and then *allowing* the cortisol to rise, driving us to carbs and fats" (italics added). If it's not yet crystal clear that dealing with stress is an individual responsibility (e.g., women can and should control our hormones [cortisol]), Dr. Peeke, on the program "S-T-R-E-S-S Hurts," makes sure we know that stress is purely subjective—"that stress is any stress that you see in your life—it's all individual—that is associated with hopelessness, helplessness, and defeat. If you don't *perceive* something as being completely out of control, hopeless and helpless, your cortisol doesn't rise. How you *think* ends up at your waistline."

From *Self* magazine comes this bit of wisdom: "Being chronically frazzled might contribute to high blood pressure, which can lead to a stroke. Blow off steam at least weekly with a tension tamer such as yoga or meditation." And later in the same issue: "Yes, we know stress takes a serious toll on our health, but it can also harm our teeth. Turns out, the hormone cortisol, released during times of anxiety, can worsen gum disease, the *Journal of Periodontology* indicates. Next time you feel frazzled, take a deep breath to save your sanity and your pearly whites."[66] (Note the use of the word "frazzled" twice in a matter of a handful of pages).

Bad Habits, Blameworthy Women

There's plenty of fear and blame to go around. If women allow themselves to be "stressed" and fail to take appropriate action, they are morally reprehensible. But if women "work on" themselves, they can prevent everything from weight gain to premature death. According to Rebecca Lee, M.D., author of *The SuperStress Solution*, "SuperStress," which seems to exist somewhere between "jangled nerves" and PTSD, is "a new pandemic, as deadly as any public health crisis we have ever faced." This, Dr. Lee soberly intones, "is not your grandmother's stress." SuperStress is created when we sit in traffic jams, eat junk food "on the run," and tether ourselves to "addictive devices" like iPhones that give us "screen sickness."[67] According to Dr. Lee and her "stress-is-anything-that's-bad-for-you" school of thought, behaving in certain ways and putting ourselves in certain situations lead to "macro stresses," and the solution for women is to stop doing things and/or putting themselves in the way of situations that are bad for them. There is quite a bit of talk in Dr. Lee's and other advice books about the need to "detox" from stress.[68] Here stress is perceived as but one bad habit in a long line of women's "addictions," from food to relationships, as anyone familiar with women's self-help books knows. The notion that women are in some way addicted to stress's "high" is evident in a *Harper's Bazaar's* piece, "How to Reduce Your Stress":

In this new no-leisure age, we take a perverse pride in being the busiest woman on the block.... our sense of self-worth has somehow become wrapped up in our impossibly exacting schedules.... Can't we live without the heart-thumping rush of stress hormones coursing through our veins? Can we let go of our pathological perfectionism?[69]

Although the author says that women are "culturally programmed" to overschedule themselves, she makes no mention of the societal expectations that may play a part in the "programming." But she *does* recommend "a change of attitude, rather than a change of life" as "the solution to stress." It is assumed that women can make these changes themselves. As two obstetrician/gynecologists insist in their book *So Stressed*, "the good news is that you can change your set point to become more stress-resistant."[70] Remember Melissa's post on *iVillage*'s website? When the "community leader" of the message board responded to Melissa, she never referred to Melissa's worries about static pay, her increased workload, or the effect of shift work on childcare arrangements. Instead, her remarks reflect the tenor of popular advice to women as to how they should deal with difficult life circumstances: Take a "couple of hours a week ... to unwind and release some stress," she said. Take a bubble bath, have a manicure; make a trip to the park to read a good book.[71]

Many advice-givers recommend that women analyze their "stress type" so that they can tailor stress-relieving strategies to their personalities. These stress types are defined by patterns of emotional responsiveness, and it can be difficult to distinguish them from frank accusatory labels. For example, in Dr. Lee's book, one type is "Agitated, Overwhelmed by Life"; another is "Explosive, Can't Slow Down"; and yet another is "Driven, Controlling."[72] This way of categorizing stress types or stress personalities reinforces a perception of stress as an individual, subjective phenomenon rooted in the emotions. It leaves no room to imagine that there might be some external stressors that could affect almost anyone, regardless of "stress type."

The Commodification of Stress: Venus Takes a Scented Bath

Freud famously asked, "Was will das Weib?" ("What does a woman want?"). Little did he anticipate when he asked that question that one of his nephews, Edward Bernays, would use his uncle's ideas to answer it in a way Freud would have found more than a little objectionable:

women want to smoke. In the interest of testing his theory that people's behavior could be influenced outside of their awareness, Bernays, now the acknowledged father of public relations, launched a PR campaign to persuade women to smoke.[73] Asked by the president of the American Tobacco Company to try to break through the taboo on women's smoking, Bernays went off to consult his uncle's disciple, the well-known psychoanalyst A. A. Brill. Apparently, a cigarette was not just a cigarette; according to Brill, a cigarette symbolized male power. Brill's notion was later carried forward to spectacular effect in Phillip Morris's popular 1968 campaign for Virginia Slims, "You've come a long way baby."[74] Women have always been the natural audience for advertising. Early on, advertisers discovered how to employ the art—and commerce—of suggestion to get women to use the products they were selling. Historian Ann Douglas has said that advertisers "knew that... women would operate as the subconscious of capitalist culture which they must tap, that the feminine occupation of shopping would constitute the dream-life of a nation."[75]

Advertisers haven't failed to notice that the number of women visiting female-oriented websites—from sites that feature makeup and fashion products and tips to "mommy blogs"—has almost doubled since 2006. Large media companies and venture capitalists have begun investing substantially in women's sites, which are infinitely better financial bets than sites specifically targeted at men. They are not particularly interested in websites that offer a serious take on subjects like politics or, heaven forefend, those that offer a feminist perspective on "women's issues," with the result that many of the most visited websites for women bear a striking resemblance to glossy women's magazines.[76] Stress is a frequent topic on these websites. *iVillage*, the second most popular women's site on the web, has a "stress" message board that, when I last checked, had 13,821 posted messages.[77]

Today, advertisers underwrite a great deal of the "expert" advice dispensed in women's magazines. That capitalism shapes consumption is self-evident; that capitalism "shapes biology in its own image," as sociologist Ellen Annandale has pointed out, is not quite as obvious.[78] Stress sells. In article on the new "field" of psychodermatology, an *Elle* magazine article speaks to the dangerous connection between stress and a haggard face:

Unchecked, [stress] spikes cortisol, causes inflammation, and increases cellular oxidation, all of which contribute to wrinkles, sagging skin, and gray hair.... researchers continue to mine the relationship between stress and the signs of aging.... Psychodermatology ...is based on the premise that body and mind are inextricably linked—if you're happy, your skin is happy.[79]

Certain products are engineered to make your skin very, very happy. Only a month after this piece appeared, *Harper's Bazaar* Beauty News was shilling for a product called *The Antidote Quenching Daily Lotion* that contained kelp from the "laid-back land" of Iceland and promised to "give your face the break it needs." Although products have changed over the decades, much advertising still promises to bring the woman who buys them power and/or freedom. Freedom from stress gives women the power to attract men through a youthful appearance, unmarked by the signs of aging that stress, allegedly, can etch on her face.

An ad for *Hormel Always Tender* pork loin filet features a woman in a meditative pose—eyes closed, fingers on temples and legs in a quasi-lotus position, with the tag lines "Stress-free day. It's a day to clear your mind. A day to free your soul." Neutrogena's *Acne Stress Control Power-Clear Scrub* "makes acne one less stress in your life." Products that promise stress relief and "expert" advice about how to deal with stress coalesce around the idea that women must fight stress and its attendant dangers through their behaviors, their attitudes, and purchasing power. The nineteenth-century rest cure has its twenty-first century correlates in the form of face creams, scented candles, and pastel yoga mats. At the heart of the message to women about stress? *Handle those pesky emotions that can lead you to feel overwhelmed day to day.*

NEUROENCHANTMENT: FOR THE LOVE OF DIFFERENCE

PARIS RELIEVES PAIN?
Researchers noted that male mice licked their wounds less (indicative of higher stress levels) when a scientist was present. To determine whether the sight or smell of a human was to blame, they showed mice a card-

board cutout of Paris Hilton. With fake Paris in sight, male mice—but not females—still spent less time licking their wounds, supporting research that indicates the sexes react differently to stress.

Time Magazine, November 16, 2007[80]

Differences Sought and Differences Found

It was no accident that John Gray's *Men Are from Mars, Women Are from Venus* was the best-selling book of the 1990s. The news media are full of reports of research studies designed to uncover evidence of differences between men and women, and questions about alleged differences in men's and women's exposure to stress are a part of the "difference" debates. Why the intense fascination with difference? Why is it so important to know whether men or women are more capable of bearing the brunt of life's vicissitudes under today's conditions? One premise is that investigators are simply interested in the differences in health outcomes for men and women related to their differential exposure to stress.[81] But, whereas it is true that this question shapes research agendas, it doesn't speak to the social engine that drives the enormous interest in those differences. Since the nineteenth century, establishing gender differences and showing them to be stable and enduring has been important for the maintenance of social stability. Judith Lorber has argued that unless we can see difference we can't rationalize inequality.[82] If we stick with the difference paradigm, then nothing really has to change. Whereas in the nineteenth century, scientists declared their biases on the "Woman Question" boldly, contemporary biases are less overt. But the emphasis on difference itself has not changed much. Differences between men and women continue to be used to ensure that middle-class women keep to their "place" as family caregivers, although what we used to call hearth and home may now be called good parenting or family responsibilities.

As we saw in Chapter 2, nineteenth-century middle-class men were viewed as being under a great deal more pressure than women. More recently, a 1999 analysis of 36 years of research on sex differences in life events concluded quite differently that "life is indeed more difficult on Venus."[83] But establishing a clear answer to the question of whether men or women are under more stress has been difficult for a variety of reasons.[84] What and how many differences are captured by researchers depends on the diversity of the sample under study and the method of investigation, and perhaps even more on the social conditions under which people live.[85] What is true in relation to the research on women and depression is true in relation to research on gender differences in general: in order for their conclusions to mean anything, researchers must use methods that will reveal differences in power—gender differences, yes, but also differences in social class and race, among other factors.

When they've asked the question about difference in the standard way ("How do men and women differ in their exposure to stress?"), some researchers have concluded that men are under more stress than women, at least in part because of the pressure they face in our culture to compete and achieve and the self-blame and social opprobrium they may experience as a result of failure. Others contend that women's overall reduced power and control, coupled with what has been termed the "cost of caring," leads to greater stress. Yet another view is that stress is comparable for men and women, but that stressful *events* differ in relation to gender roles.[86] Research on the way men and women respond to stress shows that there are differences in the ways men and women subjectively perceive stressful situations, the ways in which they respond to stress biologically and behaviorally, and what stress means for their physical and mental health.[87] But—and this is a big "but"—there is no conclusive evidence that men or women are either more vulnerable or more resilient across the board.

Stress on the Brain—and Genes—and Hormones

As we have just seen, questions about difference are pervasive in discussions about stress. But how much evidence is there for so-called "natural" differences between men and women? "Hormones, Not Environment, Make Women Different from Men,"[88] blares a *Chicago Tribune* headline, suggesting a zero-sum relationship between hormones and the environment. In her book *Sexing the Brain*,[89] neuroscientist Lesley Rogers takes both fellow scientists and nonscientists to task for their persistence in giving genetic explanations for sex differences in brain structure or function with barely a nod to human experience or learning. "Something," she says, "seems to drive us to assume that these have genetic or hormonal causes. We might just as inaccurately assume that sex differences are caused entirely by environmental influences, but this has been a far less popular view."[90] Scientists want to deal with what is tangible, and biological differences can be measured, whereas *environment* is vague. Like psychologists (see Chapter 3), biologists, too, often refer to the environment as if it were a single entity—*the* environment—rather than a host of influences (e.g., social systems, geographical location).[91] Fascination with gender differences[92] reflects the long-standing splitting of nature from nurture that we have already discussed. Rogers warns against interpreting biological differences as evidence of genetic "hardwiring." The reciprocal influence of biology and experience is undeniable; biology is as much a part of experience as it is of genes, and for this reason the fact of male-female biological differences does not imply that genes alone are responsible for those differences. It is often taken for granted that genes influence cognitive and behavioral differences via sex hormones. But this chain of influence—genes to hormones to brain to behavior—isn't rooted in men's and women's biological differences alone; there are sources of influence outside the individual that are just as potent. And, as Rogers points out, discovering a biological difference between men and women doesn't say "anything about what caused it."[93] What we assume to be the causes of male-female differences are more a function of historically driven attitudes than anything else. We can assert that the "evidence" that speaks to innate ("natural") differences between men and women has nothing to do with values (and many do), but this simply isn't so.[94]

Two recent books have added fuel to popular discussions of differences in men's and women's "hardwiring:" Simon Baron-Cohen's *Essential Differences: The Truth About the Male and Female Brain*,[95] and Louann Brizendine's books *The Female Brain* and its more recent companion, *The Male Brain*.[96] Baron-Cohen, an expert on autism, entered the "pop psych" universe of Mars and Venus with his theory that the brain has two types of hardwiring: one for systematizing and one for empathizing. In what he calls this his "E-S theory," a woman *can* have an empathizing brain and a man *can* have a systematizing brain, and most brains are handed out that way, but Baron-Cohen insists he's not talking gender differences here.[97] Nonsense. He refers to a "female advantage in empathizing" and brings much allegedly scientific—and a great deal of anecdotal—evidence to bear on this subject that puts women squarely in the "empathizing" and men in the "systematizing" camps. It isn't my job to carry on at length about the "science" behind Baron-Cohen's assertions, but, suffice it to say, it is very shaky.[98] Baron-Cohen clearly did not heed Rogers's warning about the dangers of slavishly following the genes-hormones-brain-behavior causal chain, and this is nowhere more painfully obvious than when he asserts: "An obvious biological factor that might be causing sex differences in the mind is the hormone (or endocrine) system," and when he talks of "the genetics of... systematizing and empathizing."

Brizendine's and Baron-Cohen's assertions often rely on results from the kind of animal studies that some researchers are loathe to generalize to humans. For example, in support of his connection between "male" hormones and the "systematizing" brain, Baron-Cohen cites evidence that female rats injected with testosterone at birth learn how to negotiate a maze faster than their sister rats who have not been dosed with male hormone.[99] Diane Halpern, who has made exhaustive studies of the literature on sex differences in cognitive abilities, has not only found very few such differences, but has concluded that even if we were to find structural differences in men's and women's brains, we wouldn't know whether to attribute them to biological processes or to the social environment, or both.[100] And in her analysis of 46 studies on psychological sex differences, Janet Shibley Hyde found a tendency among researchers grossly to inflate these gender differences when, in fact, there's no basis on which to conclude that they are large and consistent over time. Men and women are far more similar than different, psychologically speaking—so similar, in fact, that on the strength of her findings Hyde formulated a "gender *similarities* hypothesis" (italics added).[101]

What is truly lethal in the popular writing on men's and women's brains is its retrograde rehash of the "separate spheres" distinction that reinforces gender stereotypes. Baron-Cohen, of course, vehemently claims *not* to be doing this, but in his formulation, the "male brain" makes those who possess it good at leading, at getting power and keeping it, and at using aggression, among other things. The "female brain" is awash in emotion, particularly in empathy for others (this shouldn't surprise us because, according to Brizendine, the female brain "marinates" in estrogen).

Anyone reading the popular male brain–female brain literature is quickly brought back to evolutionary theories about the differences between hunter-gatherers and nurturers, leading to the inevitable conclusion that power and leadership are clearly "male brain" functions. Although Baron-Cohen is not so crass as to say that women should moulder by the hearth, the division of labor he lays out points to just such a conclusion.[102] With a scant nine pages out of his entire book devoted to culture, he's clearly not preoccupied with the social and historical context of men's and women's lives.

Hardwired for Softness? Stress and Shaky Science

In his latest affirmation of the difference paradigm, *Why Mars and Venus Collide: Improving Relationships by Understanding How Men and Women Cope Differently with Stress*, John Gray uses the hunter-gatherer/nurturer distinction to justify his position that "our brains developed with gender differences to ensure our survival."[103] On the basis of a perilously few studies and some sketchy information from Internet sites, Gray draws dramatic conclusions about male and female brains in which the hemispheres of the brain might as well be the "separate spheres" so well delineated in the nineteenth century. He insists that managing stress depends on men's and women's awareness of their "natural" (read: biological) differences:

> … When you learn to cope more effectively with stress and remember the *gender differences that are hardwired into our brains*, you will blame stress, rather than your partner, for your problems. Men are from Mars and women are from Venus, and *our differences are intensified by stress*.[104]

Gray goes on to say that men are hardwired to do only one thing at a time, which leaves them open to forgetting about their partner's needs.[105] The structure of a man's brain allegedly makes it possible for him to reduce his stress more effortlessly than his female partner can: "He can more easily disengage from his serious, responsible left brain and allow it to rest and regenerate. When a man is stressed, he can simply change his focus to a hobby or watching TV and he begins to relax." Women can't do this, Gray insists, because "the connective tissue between the two hemispheres...won't allow her to disengage so easily."[106] (Ah, the ties that bind! Who knew they were made of connective tissue?)

Gray insists that managing stress depends on men's and women's awareness of their "natural" differences. Rather than shouldering an equal load, a husband can "help" his wife handle what Gray clearly sees as her burden to bear. Prop her up and she will tote her load with a smile, because, as Gray says, "When women have plenty of energy, they take great pleasure from their responsibilities." And a woman *should* have plenty of energy, because according to Gray, "her body is designed for endurance. Recent research reveals that a woman's body has almost twice the endurance of a man's."[107] These kinds of assertions about men's and women's differences may make good fodder for the media, but they have nary a basis in fact.

Gray, Baron-Cohen, Brizendine, and their like make no acknowledgement of power differences between men and women. Indeed, the fantasy of gender equality lives on in both popular and professional discussions of difference, such that we are seduced into viewing men and women as absolutely equal, but merely different. Deborah Cameron holds an alternate view. She says that "rather than being treated unequally because they are different, men and women may become different because they are treated unequally."[108]

Whereas hormonal differences between women and men certainly do exist, the effects of hormones on brain development and social behavior have not been definitively proven. This lack of evidence hasn't prevented Gray from declaring that women and men have a responsibility to manage their stress by managing their hormones—testosterone in the first instance, and oxytocin in the second. Indeed, Gray has flung himself onto the second-millennium bandwagon of those who tout the influence of hormones on brain and behavior.

A note here about oxytocin: oxytocin is a hormone produced in the brain (in the hypothalamus, to be exact) that is responsible for uterine contractions during childbirth and the "letdown reflex" that permits breast milk to flow. It has been associated with bonding and pair bonding in nonprimate mothers. Although both males and females secrete oxytocin, it is understood by neuroscientists that in females estrogen amplifies oxytocin's effects. However, most of the information on oxytocin comes from studies on rats, voles, and nonhuman primates. Gray, who seems to have read few of these studies and whose primary sources on hormones derive from a website called oxytocin.org, has put a morsel of knowledge to his own dangerous uses. He and the folks at oxytocin.org have taken to calling oxytocin the "cuddle hormone," and Gray himself calls testosterone "the king of hormones."[109]

Gray explains the effects of hormones on men and women in ways that would make even the most devout psychoneuroimmunologist cringe. Nonetheless, these explanations serve the retrograde logic of his Mars and Venus paradigm. A man depletes his testosterone while at work such that in order to build it back up at the end of the day, he has to go into "recovery mode . . . free from his innate need to be responsible." To his mate, this might look like laziness, but it's not, Gray maintains; rather, men have a "biological imperative to rest."[110] According to Gray, "oxytocin creates a feeling of attachment," rising when a woman feels loved and supported and falling in relation to the disappointment that follows upon inflated expectations of help from her partner. Since that male partner absolutely *needs* to disappoint her in order to rest, she must find other sources of support. Her partner can't do everything: "By expecting her partner to be the main source of stimulation to produce oxytocin, she is setting [him] up to fail."[111] In the end, Gray's message is clear: men should hug and talk to their mates, and even help them out with chores, but they must be able to relax and replenish their testosterone in order to manage their work stress. On the other hand, women, who produce testosterone in the workplace, according to Gray, have to make sure they counter this buildup of male hormone by producing plenty of oxytocin through connecting with other women and through taking care of their children.

In a move that elevates personal responsibility for body regulation to a new low—or high, depending on what sort of scale you're using—Gray has 100 tips for women on how to increase their oxytocin. It is important to do this, according to Gray, because "if . . . oxytocin levels are optimal, the resulting lowered stress produces an endless source of energy as well as an ability to enjoy sex,"[112] and we certainly wouldn't want any tired, grumpy women rebuffing their mates' advances, now, would we? Gray includes the following activities in the list as if they are equally relaxing: taking a yoga class, having a facial, preparing meals for sick friends, taking care of children, and having a picnic (guess who's doing the cooking?). By Jove—or Mars—if doing yoga and taking care of children are equally stress-reducing, I'll eat the plates on which I served the dinner I prepared for my sick friends. According to Gray, chores like doing the laundry, cooking, and cleaning are "oxytocin-producing" for women, but they are energy-sapping and boring—for men. But Gray has answers for us, as any good self-help author should. Here is Gray's explanation of his "90/10 solution" for women and their partners:

> The man has always been a provider and protector. Though men still hold that role, it is not as significant, because women can provide for and protect themselves.... Imagine a woman's need for oxytocin to be a well that needs to be filled; a man can only fill about 10 percent. The rest of the well is her responsibility to fill. When a woman is already almost full, a man is naturally highly motivated to bring her to the top.... By taking 90 percent responsibility for their own happiness and only expecting 10 percent from men, women can set up themselves and their partners for much greater success in the relationship.[113]

I will (with some difficulty, I confess) forbear commenting, as the "solution," I think, speaks for its unendurable self. One can only ask: How many young women today, if promised a "90/10" partnership, would say "I do"?

Although Gray acknowledges how stressful dual-career partnerships can be, his explanations of what men and women need echo historical arguments about the fulfilling nature of motherhood and housekeeping: "Women seek social contact, especially with other women, and spend time nurturing their children to cope with stress."[114] This last remark, I believe, is a reference (although Gray doesn't cite one) to research studies conducted by Rena Repetti, who found that children observed their fathers and mothers responding differently when they returned home after a stressful workday. The children said that their fathers went off to be by themselves or "picked at" everyone, whereas their mothers were even more affectionate than usual.[115] Repetti never suggested, however, that nurturing their children *in itself* helped the mothers cope with stress. In fact, Repetti's work makes it clear that a withdrawal from the hustle and bustle of home life benefits both partners. Contrary to Gray's conclusions, there is research showing that when their spouses have a stressful day at work, women work harder at home out of a need to compensate for the decrease in their partners' domestic contribution.[116]

The association Gray makes between oxytocin and women's care-giving behaviors also bears a distant relation to the research, based primarily on evolutionary theory and animal studies, that Shelley Taylor and her colleagues have undertaken in order to show that when under stress the female of the species shows a "tend and befriend" rather than the "fight or flight" response historically attributed to both males *and* females. Oxytocin is credited with a major role in this tend-and-befriend response.[117] Taylor, a psychologist, not an endocrinologist, maintains that the tend-and-befriend response biologically predisposes women toward nurturing and protecting their children and leaning on social supports rather than fighting and running from danger, actions that could jeopardize the survival or well-being of their young. From an evolutionary perspective, for females to flee with progeny in tow or to stand and fight in the face of a threat doesn't make good sense, Taylor argues. "Tending" refers specifically to nurturing actions that decrease distress and enhance the safety of the young; "befriending" refers to a mother's developing and preserving social networks that support nurturing.

Beyond evolutionary theorizing to support their hypothesis, Taylor and her colleagues cite animal studies (and a very few human studies) that suggest the possible behavioral and hormonal origins of tending and befriending. Early on, she and her crew made it clear that they were not drawing a direct connection between what they found in animal studies and human behavior. Although they believed that oxytocin played a significant role in female stress responses, they assured readers that tending and befriending had a good deal to do with social and other processes. They also strenuously insisted that they were not trying to prescribe women's place in the social order, nor were they saying that biology is destiny. Taylor carefully pointed to the reciprocal relationships among biology and society, culture, cognition, and emotion.[118] But the media went wild, declaring that now there was hard evidence of differences in men's and women's responses to stress. And Taylor, as it turned out, didn't hold fast to her early, moderate pronouncements.

In 2000, Taylor had described tending as a "response." By 2002, she was calling tending an "instinct" and titling the book based on her research *The Tending Instinct*.[119] Earlier, Taylor had made it clear that the nature of the threat determined the neuroendocrine response to stress, such that in some cases the tend-and-befriend response to stress and oxytocin might "be involved in some kinds of stressful events and not others."[120] And, fair to say, in her book Taylor tried to cover her bases (or something else) when using the conditional form of the verb to say that "oxytocin *may play* a role in tending neurocircuitry" (italics added).[121] But page upon page of information on oxytocin's effects on women made her hypotheses sound more like facts. Taylor's statement that "the exact role that oxytocin plays in maternal behavior, including human maternal behavior, is not yet known," is buried in a footnote.[122]

In her book, Taylor somewhat confusedly supported her "befriend-ing" theory by giving examples like the one below:

[When they are asked] what they do when they're feeling stressed, women say they talk to their friends, share their problems, or call some-one on the phone; men say they do this only rarely. Women ask for directions when they're lost ....

When you listen to men and women talk about the different ways they cope with stress, as I have done for over two decades, it doesn't take long to realize that women's responses are profoundly more social.[123]

Taylor justified these sorts of examples on the basis of "scientific evidence." But the scientific evidence she marshaled in support of the example above—the 30 studies she mentions that "show that women draw on their friends, neighbors, and relatives more than men do"[124] may not be valid. In statistics, the fact that certain phenomena are con-sistently observed (reliable) doesn't mean that the observations them-selves are accurate (valid). Taylor's use of the argument that 30 studies can't be wrong is reminiscent of her story about the way she quelled her rising worry about challenging the universally held theory of the "fight or flight" response to stress. It was the glut of e-mail and letters she received from women that did the trick, she says, as exemplified in one woman's statement: "I've been reading popular accounts of science for years, and finally, here is something I recognize."[125] Caregiving and social proclivi-ties long associated with women may be entirely rooted, not in biologi-cal sex differences, but in the ways that women and men learn how to "do" gender. What we are already primed to know certainly has an intui-tive appeal, and we're well prepared to embrace traditional explanations of male-female differences. The women who "recognized" themselves in Taylor's science found what we might expect them to find.

There is a good deal more with which to take issue in Taylor's work. For example, who is to say that back in the Stone Age, "befriending" other females who were in a vulnerable position was necessarily a good strategy for dealing with threat? From an evolutionary perspective, it might make more sense for females to associate with stronger, more powerful males of the species if protection was required.[126] Taylor's insistence that women's desire to affiliate themselves with other women is an evolutionary phenomenon, based on research on the "befriending" tendencies of rats and prairie voles, disregards the well-grounded historical fact that in nineteenth-century United States and Britain, middle-class women's strong bond with each other originally sprang from a need for mutual assistance and support under the frequently oppressive conditions that kept them close to home.

Criticism of the tend-and-befriend hypothesis has come from research endocrinologists like Sarah Knox, a stress researcher at the National Heart, Lung, and Blood Institute, who has remarked: "It's one thing to say that women behave differently than men—there's a whole body of literature on that, but to say that women don't have the same neuroendocrine stress response as men is not supported by the literature." "When a woman experiences chronic stress...she has the same neuroendocrine dysfunction as a man."[127] The practice of calling oxytocin the "social" hormone, as Taylor does[128] and as other neuroscientists have taken to doing (some neuroscientists have even taken to referring to oxytocin as "affiliative circuitry"), has a strong whiff of what psychologist Cordelia Fine has termed *neurosexism* clinging to it.[129]

Tending and Befriending: The Sequel

By 2006, research literature on the human tend-and-befriend response to stress and the role of oxytocin was still, by Taylor's own account, "modest." By then, Taylor and her research team had made a finding that seemed to challenge their previous idea: they had discovered high levels of oxytocin in women who were having *decreased* contact with family and friends or were not feeling understood or cared for by their mates. When detachment was greater, oxytocin levels were up. Taylor acknowledged the inconsistency between this and her previous findings, offering several explanations, but in the end she was forced to conclude that "significant paradoxes remain" and that more research would need to be done in order to pin down oxytocin's role in the processes of affiliation.[130] A couple of years later, Taylor was still manufacturing hypotheses, among them the notion that perhaps oxytocin rises under socially stressful or painful conditions in order to "lead people to seek out more and better social contacts."[131]

To Taylor's credit, she *has* looked at the social context of stress and the stress response and has discussed how important caregiving is for both men and women. And she has generally been more careful in interpreting the results of her research than are many who refer to her work. When linguist Mark Liberman doggedly searched out the source for an assertion attributed to Taylor (in *The American Spectator*) to the effect that "when women chit-chat, their oxytocin level...rises," he finally found it—or thinks he did—in a paragraph in Brizendine's book *The Female Brain*, where Brizendine makes the unsubstantiated claim that teenage girls' oxytocin rises when they talk to each other on the telephone.[132]

For all her disclaimers, attempts at clarification, and her acknowledgment that there is more work to be done, however, Taylor's insistence on the evolutionary roots of the male and female stress response have helped shore up traditional views of men's and women's "natural" propensities and responsibilities that the media are only too happy to dine out on. It's still hard to find a newspaper or magazine article or a website discussing women and stress that doesn't put forward the tend-and-befriend theory as established fact. The website www.the-heart-of-motherhood.com tells its visitors that "our modern life frequently prevents our ability to Tend and Befriend [*sic*], so we may be cut off from our natural sources of stress relief. We are often away from our children long hours.... This makes it difficult to engage in the type of "tending" that produces oxytocin." What to do? Well, one of the bits of advice on the website takes a page out of John Gray's playbook: "Don't expect your husband to meet all of your emotional needs, especially during times of stress. Demands for closeness during times of stress may actually create more anxiety for men. Your husband's body responds differently than yours ["fight or flight"], because historically, his function has been different from yours."[133] In the next chapter, we'll see what happens when the stress concept is applied to the world of the employed middle-class mother and meets the brave new metaphors of juggling and work/life balance.

CHAPTER 5

The Other Mommy War: Stress and the Working Mother

When husband and wife are away from home during business hours, joint housekeeping or sharing household tasks night and morning is rarely successful. Yet if the wife has regular hours in business, it is manifestly unfair that at home she should bear alone the burden of such household tasks as must be done. And so in this home supported by the double salary one of two conditions exists: With open or secret unwillingness the husband shares the household tasks, or the wife bears the entire burden to her physical and nervous undoing. And neither is content.

—Anna Richardson Steese, *Woman's Home Companion*, 1920[1]

It's strange, but in 1982, when I was a full-time working single mother of a five-year-old and a part-time doctoral student living paycheck to paycheck, dependent on a very loose safety net of emergency helpers (principally friends), I don't remember thinking or hearing about stress. This was not because the term *stress* hadn't been coined yet; as we've seen, by then it had had long and varied history. The reason I wasn't using the term *stressful* to describe my life is because back then it wasn't as commonly applied to the conditions of daily life as it is now. But even though women's lives weren't being regularly characterized as *stressful*, this didn't mean that no one was talking about the changes that were taking place as more and more white middle-class American mothers were joining the paid workforce.[2] To many women in the 1960s and 1970s, "wanting it all" had implied a revolutionary and energetic embrace of a specific, progressive social agenda. But by the 1980s, journalists were remarking on the sour taste of some of the fruits harvested in first wave of the women's liberation movement. It didn't take long for a discouraging perspective on combining work and family to emerge, as the following excerpt from a 1982 *New York Times* article demonstrates:

> Many women are discovering the difficulties of trying to negotiate the demands of a full-time career and motherhood.... They fear and suspect that the sacrifices such a juggling act entails are costly to their careers, to their children and to their marriages. They are beginning to re-evaluate their goals and to question their ability to "do it all."[3]

Maybe we'll never know whether large numbers of women were actually "re-evaluating" their goals; in fact, this may never have been the case. But this kind of rhetoric clearly pulled the threads of an old story through the fabric of the present, with an old warning to mothers: Beware, mothers; your decision to enter the public world may have dire consequences. The message that trying to "have it all" might have profound implications for women's health was coming, soon to be taken up in discussions of working women and stress. A sturdy bridge connecting women's choices, the stress those choices might bring, and the negative health effects that might follow upon them made a case for women's staying at home that was much more potent than any wan conjecture about working mothers' unhappiness with their decisions could be. We've already looked at the culture's mandate to women to manage themselves so that they can adjust optimally to the stressful conditions of modern life. We've also seen how important this sort of expression of individualism has been to the popularity of the stress concept. As good health has become a moral imperative (see Chapter 3), the idea that too many responsibilities can break down a woman's health has had real staying power, creating yet one more way station on the journey from progress to pathology. The self-management/adjustment scenario has particular meaning for women these days, as they struggle to accommodate to social conditions that have pitted the claims of work against the claims of family life.

Framing the stress "problem" in individual terms doesn't take into account the extent to which the ideology of the separate spheres (see Chapter 2) still dominates American society. But the old public/private arrangement has become more and more fragile in the wake of the explosion in the number of dual-earner families over the past

40 years or more. Popular discussions about stress have helped contain many of the tensions created by our continuing reliance on old structures to support new conditions. Without that container, there might be a need for massive social and political change that, as I've already argued, we seem reluctant to undertake. So, as they've done for a very long time, women continue to make an adjustment on behalf of a society loathe make a public commitment to the work of care. And the longer society's commitment to change is deferred, the more anger, tension, and frustration employed mothers and fathers face.

WORKING MOTHERS: THEMES AND VARIATIONS

On the cover of the December 2009 edition of *The Economist,* Rosie the Riveter, that iconic World War II representative of the American working woman, is flexing a bicep. "We Did It!" the cover emphatically announces, the "it" being women's attainment of majority status in the American workforce.[4] "Women's economic empowerment" is "the biggest social change of our times," the article bleats; "millions of women have been given more control over their own lives." And all of this has occurred "with only a modicum of friction," although there are a couple of itty-bitty "stings" that have attended this development. For one thing, as the *Economist* points out, "juggling work and child-rearing is difficult" because women are forced to choose between career and children. On the other hand, "men have, by and large, welcomed women's invasion of the workplace" (an odd turn of phrase, considering that invasions are not generally welcomed by the party whose territory has been overrun).

The Economist makes the common assumption that women will continue as the primary caretakers of children for the foreseeable future. It insists that "motherhood, not sexism, is the issue" that underlies the substantially lower earning power of mothers as compared with women who don't have children. But increasing flexibility in the workplace should help take care of this problem, and "new technology is making it easier to redesign work in all sorts of family-friendly ways." "Let the market do the work," the *Economist* advises. No "massive intervention" should be attempted. There are "cheaper, subtler ways" through which government can improve women's lot. Greater investment in public day care and a longer school day and year could solve what they term these "nagging problems."

The same issue of the *Economist* also reported on a study of graduates of the University of Chicago business school showing that almost half the women who had had children in the 10 to 15 years following graduation were not working full-time, and that almost a quarter had dropped out of the workforce completely.[5] The pay gap between the graduates who were mothers and those who hadn't had children was substantial. Marianne Bertrand, who headed the study, insisted that this was a "good news" story, because her data didn't show discrimination as the cause of the pay gap. "Looking at the data," she said, "this is not a story of women knocking on a door they can't open. It is more a story about a set of mothers who, given the structure of the jobs available, make a choice with their spouses that they would rather slow down than stay on that fast track."[6] Shortly I'll explain just how constrained that choice can be.

The popular stress concept supports many of the assumptions about women, motherhood, and paid work implicit in the *Economist* article, and these are some of the assumptions I'll be exploring in relation to the stress concept in this chapter:

1. Women will continue as the primary caretakers of children for the foreseeable future.
2. Only a "modicum of friction" has resulted from the vast increases in women's paid employment over the past 40 years or so.
3. "Juggling" work and family is a woman's problem.
4. It is women who must "choose" between outside employment and family.
5. No "massive intervention" is required or should be attempted.
6. The "working motherhood" problem has nothing to do with sexism, because it doesn't involve workplace discrimination.

ASSUMPTION #1: WOMEN WILL CONTINUE AS THE PRIMARY CARETAKERS OF CHILDREN FOR THE FORESEEABLE FUTURE

In the United States, we don't refer to "working" fathers; we talk about working mothers. As Anita Garey points out, "it is the mother who works, not the worker who has children."[7] When Virginia Schein interviewed 30 employed single mothers, she found that what they had in common was that they identified themselves as mothers before everything else. For these women, Schein says, "work and all decisions related to it [were] placed within the context of their role and responsibility as a mother. They [did] not see themselves as providers, struggling to parent in that context. Rather, they view[ed] themselves as mothers, and struggle[d] to be providers within that context."[8] Some women dislike the "working mother" label. One 36-year-old clerical worker told Garey: "I have a real problem with that phrase [i.e., working mother], because it implies that women who are at home don't work."[9] The idea that working outside the home is an *activity* and that mothering is a *state of being* reinforces the invisibility of the work that mothers actually do. The fact that women who work outside the home are underemployed compared to men and earn less also means that the "symbolic responsibility" for earning money still rests with men.[10]

We have seen how women's elevation to the position of angel of the hearth in the late nineteenth century served larger social purposes. This elevation did not come with a corresponding increase in the perceived economic worth of women's work,[11] although there was a time in our history when women *did* have greater economic value as providers of goods and services. In the eighteenth century, growing food, making clothing—even making furniture—were considered women's work, and women's work ran parallel to men's labor, which during that period usually took place in or near the home. But in the new market economy, when middle-class men left home to work, men and women no longer shared the same types of labor, and women's family work was classed as economically unproductive. In the U.S. Census of 1878, work was defined as *paid* work for the first time, effectively distinguishing it from "women's work," which, despite Elizabeth Cady Stanton's characterization of it as "unpaid, unsocialized, and unrelenting,"[12] was generally touted as a labor of love. Moral responsibility, of course, is not the same as economically significant activity. By 1900, it was considered a settled matter that mothers who weren't gainfully employed outside the home were "dependents," and that women who did paid work would naturally be paid less than men because, since they were supported by their husbands, they didn't "need a living wage."[13] Although in most cases it was his wife who *made* the self-made man[14] by handling all duties on the domestic front and enabling him to focus solely on his work, this new way of looking at women's work consigned it to a shadow world,[15] and this has had lasting implications for women, men, and families.

The mythology of the "male provider" not only obscures the contributions women have long made to men's ability to provide; it overlooks how men's work has influenced the way employment itself has been structured in our society.[16] The obsolescent "ideal worker" upon whom the U.S. economy now depends is a male full-time worker capable of putting in the hours a job requires, no matter how long, relocating if necessary, and performing any and all duties required whenever they are needed.[17] This worker has classically had "backstage support" from a wife who took care of family business at home.[18] In heterosexual two-parent families, this arrangement has legitimized fathers' absence and mothers' ultimate sway over child rearing. Today, that backstage support is often given by women who are working outside the home. Individual employers are still getting a free ride, and so is the global economy. As Ann Crittenden points out, "unpaid female caregiving is not only the life blood of families, it is the very heart of the economy. A spate of new studies reveals that the amount of work involved in unpaid caregiving...rivals in size the largest industries of the visible economy.... Up to 80 percent of this unpaid labor is contributed by women."[19] The disappearance of mothering from the category of visible labor has made mothers economically and politically vulnerable, and because of our society's dependence upon their labor, mothers have had few champions.[20]

There has been a great deal of talk these days about how we're returning to "traditional" notions of women's work, though, in fact, in some respects we've really never departed from those notions and in other respects we've departed from them radically. On one hand, the mere substitution of the word *parenting* for *mothering* does not make a departure from tradition,[21] and "tradition" has always included paid work outside the home for low-income women (see Chapter 2). On the other hand, there's nothing traditional about associating masculinity and the provider role with individual success, since until very late into the eighteenth century the middle-class man was principally a domestic animal not governed by the need for professional achievement.[22] Moreover, the phenomenon of the "stay-at-home mom" doesn't actually represent a full-scale return to traditionalism, despite what the press has often suggested, because both work and family—the two "separate spheres"—have altered dramatically. As Joan Williams and her colleagues have observed, women are now "caught between new, more time-consuming versions of what it means to be a good mother and a good worker."[23]

Time and Housework Wait for No One

From 1979 to 2000, the time married couples with children spent in paid work increased about 500 hours a year.[24] Over that span, more than half the employed men and women in the United States had no control over the beginnings or ends of their workdays, and over half of all employed parents said they had no way to take time off to care for a sick child without either losing pay or vacation time or having to invent a pretext for missing work.[25] Although women and men had roughly equal amounts of free time in 1975, by 1998 women showed a daily 30-minute leisure gap as a result of increased time spent in paid work, a gap that wasn't offset by a decrease in time spent in family labor.[26] Although a 30-minute difference between women and men's leisure time may seem unremarkable, it doesn't tell the whole story. Today, even women who have the same amount of free time as men are saying they feel rushed. Paid employment, kids, and marriage cut more deeply into women's free time than men's, and women's free time is more entangled with caregiving and domestic labor than men's.[27] Many middle-class mothers manage to spend as much time with their children as mothers did in the 1960s, but they often manage to do this by sleeping less and taking less time for themselves.[28] Another way women manage is by multitasking, spending their "free time," say, shopping for themselves with the kids along. Women also spend a substantial amount of time organizing tasks, something researchers rarely account for in time allocation studies.[29]

If time spent in paid and unpaid work is added up, men and women's total hours come out about the same. So why is it that study after study shows that women feel more rushed and pressured (read: "stressed") than men? Women are doing much less housework—almost half as much—now as they were in the 1960s, and men are doing more housework *and* childcare than ever before.[30] But these changes are relative. Overall, men are still doing more paid work than women, and women are performing more of the (unpaid) housework and childcare than men.[31] Mothers spend at least twice as much time doing domestic chores as fathers.[32] When an employed woman becomes a mother, this significantly increases her unpaid family labor, but not her partner's.[33]

When it comes to the relationship between stress and family work, we need to look beyond statistics on time allocation. Differences in the types of tasks that men and women take on play a part in whether people experience family labor as stressful or depressing. Chores like preparing meals, cleaning up after meals, and buying groceries have to be done on a reasonable schedule (and frequently), permitting the person who performs them little control over timing, whereas tasks like washing the car or raking leaves allow for greater flexibility. And—you guessed it—the low-control tasks, the ones that people find most annoying, are most often performed by women.[34]

In order to be considered acceptable mothers, many middle-class employed mothers are expected to be available to their families and not to work evenings or weekends.[35] This means, for example, that a businesswoman is not as free as a businessman to attend an evening sports event with clients, and a man is not as free as a woman to take family leave to care for a sick child. These gendered time constraints keep women and men in their historical "places." Jerry Jacobs and Kathleen Gerson, who have studied changes in Americans' working lives, view *time* as the newest type of inequality that divides social groups—the excessively hardworking from the underemployed, women from men, parents from couples without children.[36] They argue that women pay a "family penalty" because they experience more pressure to combine family work with paid work than men. Women pay this penalty in a variety of ways. For one thing, they have less freedom and flexibility at work and more pressure to reduce their hours or forgo advancement in order to manage changing family circumstances.[37]

Unsurprisingly, flexibility in the workplace is even less available to economically disadvantaged women than it is to middle-class women. Poor women, particularly single mothers, operate in an environment that is dauntingly unforgiving. In many cases, the loyalty employers require of poor mothers (e.g., to be at work no matter what childcare problems they encounter on a given day) is not met with commensurate loyalty on the part of the employers.[38] As this union representative for nurses' aides and hospital janitorial workers reported:

> You can say, "I'm only interested in days," or "Because I have a kid, I want [evenings] to make sure they're home from school" or whatever...but I think that because you're new and coming in, they say "Well, we have an on-call, that means you work all shifts. And people—you know, they want the job.... Now I had a person who said she had a problem with child care and she talked to the manager...and it was no problem, but later on I don't think she ever finished her probation.... So they have to be very careful, so they don't complain.[39]

In the retail industry, not only are nonstandard hours the norm, but schedules can be changed by the employers with little notice. Aneya, a part-time worker at a discount store, explains how she wasn't allowed to turn down extra hours, even when it meant she couldn't properly take care of her child:

> At nights, um, we'd have to stay late and clean up the store and they schedule you to 11:00 and I feel that if they schedule you to a certain time, you, I mean, I would say, I don't have no problem with it [staying late] but after 2, 3 hours go past...that, I think that that's too much because I have a child to go home to, and so does everybody else. They have family to go home to. And...they [employers] don't care. It was just, whenever we're done, we're done.[40]

Mothers are four times more likely than fathers to say that child-care responsibilities account for their working nonstandard—evening and weekend—hours.[41]

Harried and Hurried? Superwoman, Meet Supermom

By the early 1980s, the *superwoman syndrome* and the *myth of superwoman* were firmly implanted in the American psyche, and by the end of the 1980s, stress was increasingly being paired with the superwoman label. *Supermom* was out there as well, but it wasn't until the 1990s that this term began to reach its present popularity, seeming even to eclipse *superwoman.* Susan Douglas and Meredith Michaels have revived the term *momism* from the dustbin of the 1940s and 1950s, when it was a pejorative label attached to the practice of overprotecting and smothering children.[42] They define the new *momism* as a type of contemporary middle-class mothering that demands utter fealty to the principle that parents must be involved in every aspect of their children's lives and consciousness. Sharon Hays, who calls this style of parenting *intensive mothering,* believes that some women have been drawn to it because the family has become increasingly captive to capitalism.[43] The more consuming the world of market relations, the more powerful the need for parents, principally mothers, to prepare children to meet it. The separation of private from public has drawn boundaries tightly around the family (the private sphere) in the service of the market economy (the public sphere). And in our society, gender- and class-based associations are made between motherly care and children's social and economic success.[44] The idea that it is mothers' job to prepare children to be the next generation of capitalist achievers has been around for a very long time. But more recently, expectations about what constitutes good parenting—at least good upper- and middle-class parenting—have grown exponentially as a counterweight to fears about whether children are going to be able to make it in a brutally competitive job market.[45]

When supermom works outside the home, she is increasingly represented by the media as a person who can have it all but can't *do* it all: to wit, this example from the *Anchorage Daily News*: ["Lorrie] Montgomery looked around at friends who, one by one, had fallen into the supermom trap. Sure, they juggled jobs and children, some heroically so. But they were exhausted."[46] Some of the middle- and upper-class mothers Judith Warner interviewed for her book *Perfect Madness: Motherhood in the Age of Anxiety* found that the new intensive parenting wasn't quite what they had signed on for when they'd married. A 39-year-old working mother had this to say: "It [intensive mothering] just does not look healthy or normal to me, especially with the mothers typically on the edge and stressed all the time. How much of this stress will be reflected on the kids?"[47] In a study of 1,600 married women (stay-at-home mothers and mothers working outside the home) Katrina Leupp found that the stay-at-home mothers had more symptoms of depression— and she found that the paid working mothers who had a "supermom" standard for parenting had a higher risk for depression than the ones who didn't.[48]

Warner had expected the mothers she interviewed to be more angry about the pressures upon them than they were, but she found that most were not asking more of their spouses. In fact, some of the women sounded a lot like disciples of John Gray when they insisted that everything boiled down to accepting the differences between men and women. In the words of one of Warner's interviewees, women's managing their responsibilities meant "accepting the strengths or weaknesses of your spouse or the good and bad in your relationship."[49]

ASSUMPTION #2: ONLY A "MODICUM OF FRICTION" HAS RESULTED FROM THE VAST INCREASES IN WOMEN'S PAID EMPLOYMENT OVER THE PAST 40 YEARS OR SO

Warner's research sadly reinforces this assumption. The seeming "naturalness" of unequal domestic arrangements produces less protest and more acceptance on the part of women than one might imagine. Many women, it seems, view the division of household labor as unequal but not unfair.[50] Sabrina Asker and her colleagues found that whereas young unmarried men and women both wanted and expected equity in household chores and childcare after marriage, the young women, unlike their male counterparts, anticipated that they would be doing more domestic work than their husbands after marriage.[51] These expectations may well play a role in tamping down anger when the reality hits the fan. Many husbands are, unsurprisingly, quite accepting of a lopsided status quo, as was this husband who, when interviewed for the ABC special "S-T-R-E-S-S H-U-R-T-S," described what happens when his wife comes home from work:

> HUSBAND: "It's just amazing to watch her; she'll just flow into the kitchen and the kids are really hungry, so they want to eat really fast, so they're tugging on the pant legs, and after we eat she runs up to give them a bath. That's really my down time."
> INTERVIEWER: "When does she get her down time?"
> HUSBAND: "She kind of doesn't *make that time for herself*, I guess. But you know, it just flows the way it does right now, and...." [wife

interjects] "He's O.K. with that." [Wife smiles slightly and raises an eyebrow. Husband laughs, and continues], "But, uh, it just seems to flow right now" (italics added).

In Lara Descartes's study of families in Dexter, Michigan, a small township heavily populated by white, middle-class dual-earner couples with children, both husbands and wives frequently described the man as taking on family chores in order to "help" the woman. The following conversation took place in a focus group of women that was part of the larger study:

JOELLE: "My husband...will help, but I always have to ask him.... He'll do anything I ask. But it's like, one time it'd be nice not to have to be the one."

SHIRLEY: "Is it unanimous? We all feel that we are in charge?"

HANNAH: "It's true. Every woman I know, whether or not she's working, feels that it is her responsibility, and it's the number one complaint...."

TAMI: "And we just can't let it go. Even if you are at your job, you're thinking, 'Brownies. Is he going to get her there or not? I'd better call.' And I'm grocery shopping on my lunch hour to get something for dinner.... Men don't have to do that...."

MARCI: "They're just totally different from women.... He doesn't think...about what's for dinner, he doesn't think about the dirty laundry.... Bless his heart, he's very good, he'll help, but like Joelle said, you have to ask."[52]

This situation doesn't seem much different for white working-class families. After a large number of steelworkers who were the main breadwinners for their families were laid off from a big U.S. steel manufacturing plant in 2001, two researchers decided to find out who was doing most of the housework after the layoffs. They discovered that the women were still doing most of the family work. But even though many of the women conceded that this arrangement was unequal, over a third of them vouched for the fairness of the division of labor. Many said that their husbands were "helping out" more, but it turned out that the help often took the form of barbecuing or heating up frozen foods. The husbands didn't "cook-cook," according to their wives. And they straightened things up, but they didn't "clean-clean."[53] The women said they wheedled and yelled at their husbands sometimes, but in general they tried to avoid fighting. They didn't press hard, they reported, because they viewed their husbands' sense of masculinity as having already been compromised by the layoffs.

It seems, then, that the reasons women are not upsetting the domestic applecart with angry complaints and demands for more help from their mates are deep-rooted. Women's sense of responsibility for caregiving and other unpaid family work is consistent with society's ideas about what it means to be a good woman and a good mother. Family work, then, is not, in Liana Sayers's terms, "a gender-neutral bundle of chores," but a gendered allocation of time that sustains and reproduces differences in power between men and women.[54] Remember the husband on that ABC special saying, "It just seems to flow right now"? Sociologist Myra Ferree says that when women experience family work as something that "flows out of their 'natural' desire to care for their families, women may feel guilty about every unmet 'need'" and construe men's contributions as favors.[55] Friction is certainly reduced when couples view their individual roles and circumstances as inevitable.

Even when couples try to split chores and childcare 50/50 they are on their own without a road map and with few social supports. Francine Deutsch, who made a study of couples trying to share family work equally, concluded that when they depart in any way from their parents' scripts, couples often believe their sharing is closer to 50/50 than it actually is.[56] In Knudson-Martin's and Mahoney's study of couples who wanted to "halve it all," the man's work situation (he generally made more money) was usually the shaper of the division of labor and other family decisions and arrangements.[57] These couples didn't seem to have a clear idea of what equality on the home front should look like and how differences in men's and women's access to power and resources in the wider world came to shape what happened inside their relationships. Remember Melissa from Chapter 4, who said, "We both work and take care of things well together," even though she was home alone after working at her outside job all day, doing housework and taking care of her five-year-old while her boyfriend worked the night shift? We can't forget that couples make decisions within a social context that often constrains their choices. Deutsch has noticed how many people, when meeting a pregnant woman and her husband, ask "her if she is going to go back to work after the baby." But, she remarks, "How many have asked *him*?" (italics added).[58]

So there *has* been only a "modicum of friction" resulting from changes in middle-class women's work status over the past 40 years or more. Ferree believes that if there actually were more conflict over family labor than there seems to be, it might be a healthy indicator that women are feeling empowered rather than feeling that they're trying hard and still failing to adapt well to difficult conditions.[59] The cultural message seems to be: Ask not what your spouse can do for you; ask how you can fix yourself.

ASSUMPTION #3: "JUGGLING" WORK AND FAMILY IS A WOMAN'S PROBLEM
Balance and Juggling: Two Metaphors in Search of a Meaning

The assumption that juggling work and family is a woman's problem relates to Assumption #2, that women and men have made a virtually frictionless adjustment to conditions as they are. It is certainly true that if juggling is a woman's problem, tensions between men and women are kept to a minimum, because it's *her* job to resolve so-called "work-family conflict" by achieving the ever-elusive "work-family" or "work-life" balance. But is it?

Juggling is a dangerous business. Something can fall. In *Working Mother* magazine's "25 Stories of Stellar Moms," Hollywood stars and high-powered professionals talk about their "balancing secrets." A few examples: "You'll never strike the right balance every single day, and that's okay.... We're all juggling... every day."[60] Of course, for Reese Witherspoon, the Hollywood star who was one of the "stellar moms" interviewed, balancing may be quite a bit easier than it is for Lillian Alvarado, detective and divorced mother, featured in the "How She Does It" column of *Working Mother*. This is how Ms. Alvarado, mother and detective, allegedly "does it":

> Between the demands of work and home, she stakes out time for herself. She wakes at 5:30 a.m. each day to lift weights or take a quick run before

the boys get out of bed. At the end of the workday, Lillian takes 15 minutes alone. She lights some scented candles, lies on her bed and thinks about her day.[61]

Beyond my amazement that 15 minutes at the end of the day was deemed sufficient for Ms. Alvarado's self-care, I note a familiar line of reasoning here: if the juggler takes care of herself, the work/family "conflict" will be reduced—or, in the words of another "stellar" mom: "If Mommy's okay, everyone else is okay."[62]

Today, particularly for women who are mothers and professionals, work and family are seen, not as compatible, but in competition with each other. Discussions of work-family balance suggest that imbalance leads to stress, and stress leads to imbalance. Moreover, the very idea of work-family or work-life balance assumes that the public and private spheres have equal weight—that they *can* be balanced. But work and family, public and private, are hardly equally weighted in a society that devalues caregiving.[63] Balance surely cannot be achieved when a thumb is placed squarely on the scale. In the words of yet another "stellar" mom, there is no such thing as "true balance" for women, because "family comes first."[64] Yes, family comes first for many women, but this doesn't mean that social policies and workplace policies actually put families first.

The hallmark of the new rhetoric of "work-life" or "work-family" balance is its vagueness. Is balance merely the absence of conflict,[65] or is it something else? What does the "life" part in "work-life balance" mean? The "work" part seems to refer only to *paid* employment, and when this is contrasted with "life," that freeing royal joyride to happiness, it seems alienating and limiting. What does it mean to undertake a "family" role? Does it mean caring for the children? Making money so the family can survive?[66] If "life" or "family" included wage-earning, and "work" included childcare and housework, there would be nothing to balance. Work and life/family would be one, with acrobatics kept to a minimum. But in the words of Lara Descartes and Conrad Kottak, the public discussion and media representations of the work-family debate "express an ongoing cultural tension about how far…role permeability should go."[67]

Although the term *role strain* had been around since at least the 1940s, in the 1970s it began to be applied frequently to women's experience. These days, although terms like *role strain* and *role overload* often poke out from under the ever expanding work-family conflict tent, it is still widely assumed that it is the *number* of burdens women carry that is stress-inducing. But some researchers have come to the conclusion that the *quantity* of roles women take on is not the problem. R. W. Connell points out, for instance, that the real burden for women is the responsibility "for managing the *relationship* between household and workplace" (italics added).[68]

Does Juggling Cause Stress?

The culture's focus on work and family conflict has sensitized many women to the idea that performing multiple roles is inherently stressful. When women were milking cows, killing and plucking chickens, minding children, sewing trousers, and making breakfast for the field hands, no one was talking about the downside of women assuming multiple roles. Nor was this the case when women were working as domestics or in sweatshops and running home to take care of their own families.[69] And today, not all women who perform multiple roles report work-life conflict. Actually, there's quite a bit of evidence that many women find combining roles very stimulating, that one role can compensate when problems crop up in another, that holding multiple roles expands the universe of people with whom one can share joys and pains—and more.[70] It's clear that what is stressful relates to much more than juggling per se—to work hours and conditions, to children's ages, to family size, to the quality of partner support and quality of marital relationships, to type and status of job, to race and social class.[71]

We can't think of each role a person assumes as having equal weight, and we can't always think of roles as just piling one upon the other. Becoming a paid worker, for example, doesn't mean just taking on an additional role. It means assuming a position in an economic culture that, as I've noted previously, often grants women and men different access to a variety of resources.[72] Researchers' emphasis on the relationship between women's social roles and their health has come at the expense of greater focus on women's socioeconomic position, even though both are equally important in determining health. In one of a handful of recent studies of stress and coronary heart disease (CHD) in working women (and this study took place in Sweden, where many consider paid work and family barely to be in competition with each other), women at the lower end of the occupational spectrum had a far greater risk of developing CHD than women in executive/professional jobs, not so much because they had less control on the job—although this *does* seem to be a predictor of CHD in men—but because there are many other aspects of life that exert pressure unequally on women, depending on their social class and race. The foremost among these are increased caregiving demands, including elder care and care of extended family.[73] It seems that high demands and low material resources are potent predictors of CHD among women but not among men.[74]

In comparison with professional women, women who do unskilled labor may be doubly hobbled because they don't have similar access to resources that might mitigate the effects of stressful work and family conditions on their heart health[75]—decreased work hours, domestic help, or easy access to transportation to and from work. The concept of balance is itself class-related. Nancy Moss argues convincingly that gender and socioeconomic inequalities go a long way toward explaining variations in health among women.[76] And the attempt to "balance," whether successful or not, seems to require stress-relieving strategies that take a lot of time or money and are virtually impossible for poor and working-class families to perform.[77]

As I discussed in the previous chapter, much of the advice literature suggests that juggling leads to stress, and stress leads to physical illness and psychological distress. But whereas juggling can lead women to feel pressured and time-starved, there is little research evidence that juggling roles causes mental and physical problems in and of itself.[78] Even so, juggling and stress are often paired in popular and academic writing in ways that make this appear to be so.

Faye Crosby has argued for years that it's not necessarily juggling that induces stress. She says we've fallen for a false syllogism that goes like this: Lots of women juggle home and work. Most of these women feel stressed; therefore, juggling causes stress. But, Crosby has argued, "the reasons for which [combining roles] benefits women [e.g., decreased depression, increased self-esteem, greater life satisfaction] are distinct from the reasons for which it causes stress."[79] Juggling different roles was *never* the source of the problem for women, she concluded after interviewing many "jugglers"; it's just that the issue of juggling has brought to light long-standing problems related to mothers' isolation and the hard work of mothering infants and very young children. Mothers and wives, she found, experience distress whether or not they are employed.

> The woman who tries to minimize the stresses of juggling by eliminating significant roles or by reducing her commitments is chasing an illusion.... society makes life unnecessarily depressing and stressful for wives and mothers, no matter what their participation in the labor force, and unjustifiably difficult for employed women, no matter what their domestic situations. Because stresses exist as potently for women within each role as between roles the hope of escaping harm by restricting one's involvement either to the labor market or to the family is misguided.[80]

In light of recently collected data from the Pew Research Center, Crosby may not be far off the mark: a recent Pew survey found that 86 percent of mothers engaged in paid work said that they felt stressed "sometimes or often." But so did 82 percent of mothers who didn't work outside the home.[81]

Crosby says that we've been so busy looking at how the mother and worker roles fit together that we're not looking at how well *marriage* and paid work fit together. In her conversations with women, she found that combining the paid worker and mother roles was not nearly as stressful as combining the *spouse* role with other roles. The women she interviewed were trying to hold in tensions and avoid fights to such an extent that they began to see the problems of day-to-day life as their own personal problems or failures—or as a sign of their husbands' failures.[82] John MacInness has questioned whether what we call "balance" is just the absence of out-and-out fighting.[83] Twenty years after the completion of Crosby's study of the phenomenon of juggling, women are still being distracted by all the talk about stress from looking at the social sources of the problems they face. As I see it, stress is assumed to be the price women pay for adjusting to the status quo, and stress management is the adjustment technology that has been invented to cure it.[84]

Is Balance Achievable?

Studies of work-family conflict often start out by accepting basic differences in men's and women's natures and responsibilities and end up making recommendations for individual change. Ideas about changing the gendered nature of current work-family arrangements are almost nonexistent in this body of research literature. What Jeffrey Greenhaus and Saroj Parasuraman recommend is that each member of a heterosexual couple manage "boundaries" between home and work not only by "juggling time commitments but also learning to avoid transferring stress from one role to another, engaging fully in a role rather than being preoccupied with another role, and learning to apply behaviors appropriately from one role to the other."[85] But if women bear the major responsibility for managing the relationship between work and family and their "free" time is more entangled with family responsibilities, as we have seen, this means they may well have a harder time maintaining boundaries between home and work. The assumption that men and women should both be able to maintain boundaries with equal ease does not take into account the fact that work life and home life are not created equal. Women may give men more leeway to be distracted by work responsibilities at home because they (women) are picking up more of the household slack, whereas few employers are granting women similar leeway to be distracted by household and family matters in the workplace.

Whereas work-family conflict and its negative effects on health are now heavily studied, the same can't be said for the beneficial effects of work and family on each other.[86] When researchers study work-family conflict, they generally examine the psychological effects of the stress that the alleged conflict is said to produce. Although the metaphor of work-family conflict implies that it is work and family that are doing battle, it is the stress concept that places the conflict *inside the person* of the juggler/balancer, often a woman, rather than against the backdrop of the social context in which that conflict occurs. It is the woman who is "stressed" and who must "de-stress" herself if she is to achieve balance. People seem to think that somehow balance is the antidote to stress. But in the physical sciences, stress is a measure of applied force. In theory, then, the fact that a load is balanced will not prevent what is underneath it from collapsing if the load is great enough. Many mothers who work outside the home doubt whether balance is achievable. When Joseph Gryzywacz and his colleagues studied over a thousand adults, they found that only about 9 percent had achieved work-family balance, defined as "high levels of work-family enrichment and low levels of work-family conflict."[87]

When Melissa Milkie and Pia Peltola surveyed men and women about their experiences trying to achieve balance, both men *and* women reported success in balancing work and family. But this didn't seem to square well with all the rhetoric about the troubling impact of "juggling" on women. One theory Milkie and Peltola proposed is that many married women believe they're doing a better job of balancing than other women they see who are in the same boat. Another is that doing less housework than their mothers did and seeing their husbands doing more than their fathers did makes them feel less overwhelmed; yet another is that the methods researchers use to measure success may not reveal the extent to which women are making major trade-offs, such as leaving the labor market altogether in order to keep things manageable at home.[88] Now that middle-class women are firmly entrenched in the world of paid employment, wide use of the work-family conflict metaphor hardly seems accidental. The idea of a conflict between work and life or family reinforces a sense of unease many women have about the effects of their paid work on their responsibilities at home. And this unease often fuels action. No one wants to be in the middle of a "conflict"; the best thing to do is to get out. But if a woman decides to cut back on or eliminate paid employment, does this actually contribute to "balance?" Or does balance necessarily refer to the *compatibility* of paid work and parenting? And if achieving balance is accomplished through individual change, then can we really say that it is actually work-family balance that is being achieved?

Pew Research polls revealed that from 1997 to 2007, working mothers' interest in working part- rather than full time increased substantially.[89] Over a third of professional women in the United States report that they've worked part-time at some point in order to balance work and "life," and a quarter say they've reduced their full-time hours. Thirty-eight percent report that in order to manage things on the home front, they've taken a job that paid less and had a lower level of responsibility than their expertise warranted.[90] But, according to the U.S. Bureau of Labor Statistics, although 60 percent of working mothers may now say they would prefer part-time jobs, only about a quarter of all working mothers have them.[91]

Not only are most women unable to work part-time; many of those who do, particularly mothers who are limited by education and socioeconomic status, do so involuntarily. Even though, as we'll soon see, more affluent women's decisions to work part-time may have less to do with choice than they think, there's a vast difference between electing to work part-time and being stuck working part-time. As Anita Garey says, for some mothers "part-time work is…a problem that prevents them from adequately providing for their families…. In this situation, the flexibility mothers seek is in their childcare arrangements."[92] Half of all women who work part-time work at only ten types of occupations, and most of these are low-paying service-sector jobs.[93] All mothers, regardless of class, whether employed full-time or not, pay a wage penalty for motherhood that increases with the number of children they have.[94] Lowered wages may be connected with an employer's perception that there will be work-family conflicts, and this perception results in discrimination[95] against mothers. Alternatively, the wage penalty may be related to job changes or downgrades made by women themselves when they become mothers.[96] In addition to a wage penalty, professional women who are mothers may also pay a time and flexibility penalty. Kathleen Gerson and Jerry Jacobs found that women who work 50-plus hours a week don't have as much flexibility in their work hours as men who work equivalent hours, giving women even less control and freedom than men. There's still that "glass ceiling" that prevents many women from achieving the status positions in the corporate hierarchy that would give them greater schedule flexibility and control.[97] And those who want the big jobs are often forced to consider hiring other women at relatively low wages—women who may be immigrants and who may have their own children—to pick up the slack.

No Nanny? No Problem

Newspaper and magazine stories often focus on "celebrity moms," emphasizing how they manage not to leave their kids behind even though they work hard outside the home. Actress Sarah Jessica Parker is quoted in *Parade* magazine as saying, "We've had two occasions recently when both

Matthew [her husband, actor Matthew Broderick] and I were working, and it was so hard on the kids, especially James Wilkie.... On the other hand, there are big chunks of time when we're home a lot more than conventionally working parents. So you hope to make up for it." The article makes a point of the fact that Parker and her husband don't have live-in help. Parker says, "It's such a good feeling to know that we're competent and capable.... I give the girls their bath every night. Matthew cooks amazing things...."[98] There's no mention of the help they can afford when they are both working, nor of the private nursery school or day care that probably offers just a bit of "help."

When the "balance" question comes up in relation to celebrities, a moral tale is often told about the wisdom of scaling back work in favor of motherhood. According to the *New York Times*, this is how motherhood transformed the life of champion swimmer Amanda Beard:

> In motherhood [Beard] is infused with a joy that was missing when she was breaking world records and gracing Olympic podiums. Before the birth last September of her first child,.... Beard's life was a blur of swimming pools and airports, red carpets and splashy headlines. In and out of the water, her eye was always on the clock. Now Beard is on her son's timetable. She trains for roughly half the hours she used to, then banishes swimming from her mind when she returns home.... Beard twice broke the world record in the 200-meter breaststroke.... Yet during that period, Beard said, "I was never really, really happy."[99]

Here we need to ask ourselves not whether Beard has the right to shape her life as she wishes (she certainly does), but how these kinds of stories—and they are legion—reinforce the message that motherhood is the key to happiness, while suggesting at the same time that any "conflict" between career and motherhood must be resolved in favor of motherhood.[100]

ASSUMPTION # 4: IT IS WOMEN WHO MUST "CHOOSE" BETWEEN OUTSIDE EMPLOYMENT AND FAMILY

This relates to the idea (assumption #3) that juggling work and family is a woman's problem. If it is a woman's problem to "juggle" and the juggling gets stressful, achieving balance inevitably suggests that the "choice" between work and family is the *woman's* choice. The question here is whether women in most instances freely choose to be mothers over being paid workers. The culture supports some so-called choices more fully than others, and men who choose to stay home with their children are much more stigmatized than women who choose not to be stay-at-home moms. Our society certainly favors the "choice" of motherhood[101] over paid work for women, and although there is broad recognition that for many women and their families, mothers' work outside the home is economically critical, the language of choice continues to pervade discussions about middle- and upper-class women in the workforce. As I've already noted, throughout our history poor women's entry into the workplace has rarely been a matter of choice. In fact, poor women have experienced the painful double bind of being disapproved of whether they work outside the home or stay home with their children: in the first instance, they are not good mothers; in the second, they are leeches on society.[102]

As Cynthia Epstein maintains, when women make more time for themselves by retreating from or delegating specific family responsibilities—that is, by using time-honored male-identified solutions—they often face social disapproval.[103] Women are expected to decrease so-called "work-family conflict" by making choices that favor the family, such as reducing paid work hours or eliminating paid employment altogether, despite the fact that this option is not available to most women and may have economically devastating ramifications down the road even for women who can afford to avail themselves of it. As Sylvia Ann Hewlett has pointed out, for professional women, it's far easier to take the "off-ramp" than to get back on the "on-ramp." One mother who worked in a high-level corporate job for many years describes her struggles to get back to work after time away:

> I was exhausted, worn out from twenty years of juggling twelve- to fourteen-hour workdays and three children, and burned out from the cumulative strain of "battling the corporate culture."... For a year I took full advantage of my freedom.... [Then] I hit the job market.... I went on a ton of interviews and received...some positive feedback.... So where am I? The hard fact is: it's twenty months later and I'm still

unemployed.... recruiters and employers are hugely suspicious of the fact that I've taken some time out, that I voluntarily left my last job.[104]

Women should take a book like *Time Off for Good Behavior: How Hardworking Women Can Take a Break and Change Their Lives* with a giant grain of salt.[105]

Choosing One's Choice

Stewart Friedman and Jeffrey Greenhaus say that "women are more likely than men to have family as their life role priority." Since they also believe that the life role priority influences "*choices*—about how we spend our time and where we invest our emotions," to them it seems obvious that women are exercising freedom of choice when they step away from their careers:[106]

> Many women have concluded the path to the executive suite is simply not worth pursuing, glass ceiling or no. Every accomplishment comes with a price, and a senior management position may simply demand more time and greater single-minded devotion to career than many women (and men, for that matter) are willing to devote, especially if status and power are not *important personal values*. Women face a lot more competing demands for their time than do men.... Many of these [dual-earner mothers] make a *choice* to limit career involvement, at least temporarily, to meet family needs. Less than 10 percent of these dual-earner women believe their careers have a higher priority than do their husband's [*sic*] careers. (italics added)[107]

It's disturbing to consider how these researchers construe status and power (two factors that any sociologist will tell you are purely social) as "personal values." Below, in a Mars and Venus moment, Friedman and Greenhaus seem set on defining difference and calling it choice:

> Generally, the process of establishing intimate relationships with other people is a central part of a woman's self-identity. Since the family is a *natural* arena in which to establish intimate relationships, it is no surprise that women commit more time to their families than do men. It

could even be that for women—having traditionally had responsibility for the family domain—involvement in the intimacies of family life becomes *second nature* (italics added).[108]

In the TV series *Sex and the City*, Charlotte, explaining to her friends why she's planning to leave her job when she becomes engaged to a wealthy man, protests a bit too vehemently, "I choose my choice! I choose my choice!"[109] As Americans, we understand our lives as the products of our choices,[110] and because of this there is hidden pressure on women to view their decisions as freely made, no matter how constrained the social circumstances that surround those decisions. If by doing things in a certain way people can show themselves to be good, moral creatures, then they will develop a "natural" investment in doing them that way. If that certain way is gendered, meaning that it is defined as a woman's or man's way, then women and men will solve their problems according to the logic of gender.[111] As we've seen, people know what it means to be a good husband or father and a good wife and mother in the terms their culture sets out, and when they act to satisfy these culturally ordained ways of being, they believe they've made a choice.[112]

When Diane Kobrynowicz and Monica Biernat analyzed how mothers and fathers evaluated themselves in their respective roles, they found that the mothers set the bar for good motherhood much higher than the fathers set it for good fatherhood. Even though the men and women in the study reported spending the identical amount of time away from their children, the men in the study described themselves as "very good fathers," whereas the women said they were only "all right" mothers. "Very good mothers" were mothers who were willing to do and give their all for their children.[113]

Stressing Out and Opting Out: Choice within Constraint

In 2003, widespread media coverage of the so-called "opt-out revolution" began with an article in the *New York Times* by journalist Lisa Belkin. It seemed that highly educated career women were leaving the workplace in droves in order to stay home and care for their families. This decision was viewed as a voluntary, natural solution to the pressures of trying to balance home and work. Stress once again figured as the villain in the battle to "balance" career and family life, and the gender- and class-specific nature of this retrograde "revolution" was ignored. As it turned out, census data never supported the idea that massive numbers of well-educated women (the "opt out" set) have left or are leaving the labor force. In fact, it is less well-off women—women with earnings under $40,000 a year—who more often end up staying home with their children. These women are often stuck in low-paying jobs with little chance of advancement[114] and fewer stable options for childcare than their better-off counterparts.

Although in Belkin's article opting out was framed as a choice, a number of the women whom Belkin interviewed talked about workplace policies that made life very difficult for them as mothers. Like them, "Judith," a senior executive in a telecommunications company, talking to Sylvia Ann Hewlett, gives a potent description of how traditional, male-influenced work culture contributed unnecessarily to an environment that was distinctly unfriendly to her as a mother:

> My boss, the CFO, could have been sent down from central casting. He was a conventional man with a nonworking wife and a traditional division of labor on the home front.... He had no idea what it was like to find—on short notice—weekend babysitting for three children....
> He just didn't have a clue as to the realities of my life. Core hours were 7:30 a.m. to 7:30 p.m. God help you if you weren't present and available between those times. It wasn't unusual for an e-mail to go out at 5:30 p.m. announcing a meeting at 7:00 p.m.—which could then drag on to 8:30 p.m.... Very little was covered that could not have been dealt with by e-mail—or in person the next morning. I always thought of these meetings as some kind of test—you needed to prove by your physical presence that you were single-mindedly devoted to your job. Women, of course, tend to fail this test.[115]

Arielle Kuperberg and Pamela Stone found that over and over again journalists emphasized mothering itself rather than workplace obstacles as the cause of women's leaving the workplace, even though academic research clearly shows that long work hours and rigid schedules are more often at the root of a mother's decision to quit, rather than her desire to be at home full time with her children.[116] There is incontrovertible evidence that the current policies at many workplaces are incompatible with the care of young children. Women do not "opt out;" as Joan Williams and her colleagues assert, they are "pushed out" of full-time jobs because of problematic workplace policies and are frequently marginalized in the working world. Hewlett has talked not only about the "push," but about the "pull" that propels women out of the workplace. Whereas the "push" has to do with less than desirable conditions in the workplace, the "pull" consists of family responsibilities. When job advancement is limited, Hewlett maintains, women who can afford to do so are much more likely to be lured by the "pull" of family.[117] In interviews with 54 career women who said they had "opted out" of the workplace, Stone discovered that the fact that husbands were not around much or were unwilling or unable to shoulder a portion of the caregiving was frequently responsible for their wives' decision to leave their jobs.[118] Over and over again, she heard women saying that their husbands were "supportive" of their decision to quit and had told them "it's your choice." Stone observed:

> Women and their husbands appeared to perceive the latter's responsibility as limited to providing the monetary support to make it possible for their wives to quit, not to helping wives shoulder family obligations that would facilitate the continuation of their careers. "It's your choice" was code for "It's your problem."[119]

Male-Female Difference Redux

Men who say that family work is naturally divided unequally because they have more demanding jobs or are making more money than their wives are (consciously or unconsciously) helping to safeguard the traditional division of labor that assumes a relatively unencumbered man in the workplace with a wife at home.[120] Explanations that rely on differences in wages and job demands between men and women fail to account for the reasons wage inequality exists and also fail to account for the demanding nature of professional men's jobs. The same culture that insists that caregiving is more compatible with femininity makes the male breadwinner the masculine ideal. Disdain for men who take on family obligations in a big way is common.[121] Caregiving has little cachet for men, whereas having a stay-at-home wife/caregiver confers status.[122] All this aside, it seems that men feel the tensions between work and family as acutely as women, and that both men and women want more time for themselves and their families than they currently have.[123]

For many upper-class men who, on average, spend 55 hours a week working and commuting, who come home late and work one weekend day at minimum,[124] not being able to spend time with their children is a stressor that gets much less mention than women's "juggling." Here an engineer in Silicon Valley talks about how work hours make the man:

> Guys try to out-macho each other, but in engineering…out-machoing somebody means being more of a nerd than the other person…. It's not like being a brave firefighter…. There's a lot of see how many hours I can work, whether or not you have a kid…. He's a real man; he works 90-hour weeks. He's a slacker; he works 50 hours a week.[125]

As Joan Williams has said, to the extent that masculinity needs to be demonstrated this way, women have less leverage to push for men's equal participation in family work.[126] The price fathers pay for the traditional arrangement is reduced involvement in family life, and the more tightly we cling to that arrangement and the ideology that supports it, the more elusive the brave new world of shared parenting and equal-opportunity family labor seems.

Who's Left Out of the Discussion: African American Women

For African American women, whose rate of participation in the labor force exceeds that of white women,[127] the so-called mommy wars and the opt-out discussions don't seem to have much resonance or relevance.[128] As one African American lawyer who is the mother of two put it when she was interviewed for a *New York Times* article on race and work-family conflict, "We don't generally have the time or luxury for the guilt and competition that some white mothers engage in."[129] And the owner of an executive search firm said that "as black women who still have a hard time moving up, there is a fear that opting out will be one more strike against you." Businesswoman Janet Hill, mother of NBA player Grant

Hill, is quoted in *Ebony* magazine as saying, "I do think that my advice to young women, all women, but especially African-American women is not to stress about any sense of guilt when they leave their children."[130] For one African American career woman who did become a stay-at-home mother, it was her own mother who had the harshest words about her decision. Thinking back on her trials as a single parent, the woman's mother said: "A lot of financial sacrifice when into helping her get two degrees. ... There are no guarantees in life, and I worry that if she just gives up her career, ... she will have nothing to fall back on."[131]

In magazines and newspapers with a primarily African American audience, advice to working mothers about how to handle stress isn't different in many respects from that in mainstream magazines like *Harper's Bazaar, Elle, Vogue,* and *Self:* take time for yourself, exercise, eat well, get more sleep.[132] But in other respects there are major differences. For one thing, there is more frequent mention of income level and of the multiple responsibilities African American women have to care for others—not only for children, but for other family members as well. Women who are under stress are encouraged to look for connections with others and to ask partners for help, as in this piece in the *Indianapolis Recorder* on relieving stress:

> African-American women are most likely to be taking care of older relatives in the home and are less likely to have access to health care.... Whatever their income level, many African-American women find that leisure time doesn't come easily.... Redistribute responsibilities with your partner if you are the only person caring for the children and tending to household needs.[133]

A major piece in *Ebony* centered on how women *could* integrate and *were integrating* work and family.[134] One woman interviewed for the article, a television actress, said "Superwoman is a lie. I am lucky because I have a terrific husband. He helps out around the house by cooking and picking up our daughter from her play group." A married paralegal with four children said she and her husband had support from family who babysat and drove the children to activities. A blue-collar divorced mother who was employed full time, has two children, and was working on her bachelor's degree in physical therapy said she hoped her example would encourage her children to set high educational goals. An editorial in *Black Enterprise*, even after recounting the tale of a married corporate executive with two children who had left her job when her mother became terminally ill, took the position that a stressful situation "doesn't mean you have to make changes as radical as leaving your job."[135]

ASSUMPTIONS #5 AND #6: NO "MASSIVE INTERVENTION" IS REQUIRED OR SHOULD BE ATTEMPTED; AND THE "WORKING MOTHERHOOD" PROBLEM HAS NOTHING TO DO WITH SEXISM, BECAUSE IT DOESN'T INVOLVE WORKPLACE DISCRIMINATION

When work-family conflict is viewed as women's problem to solve, it gives the impression that no "massive intervention" should be required, just as the *Economist* article suggested. Why change anything in the traditional arrangement when the costs of caring are borne by women? The "work-life balance" idea is a chimera that evaporates as soon as we consider the value American society places on home life relative to the value it places on the economy. As R. W. Connell has said, the idea of work-life balance is "a conservative expression of a radical impulse." That "[radical] impulse is for...gender equality, and for the fuller life made possible for everyone by just human relations." This impulse gets transformed into a need for "balance" because gender equality is impossible to achieve in a society that places the economy above home and family.[136] We shouldn't let anyone tell us that the "working motherhood" problem and the stress concept that accompanies it aren't political. Any process that reduces social problems to "private troubles" is political.[137]

Government attempts to relieve pressures on working parents have been seriously lacking. When the Family and Medical Leave Act (FMLA) was passed by Congress in 1993, it was hailed as a real advance for working families. Under its provisions, adults could take up to 12 weeks off from work to care for a newborn or newly adopted child or a very sick family member.[138] But for all its—and Bill Clinton's—good intentions, white middle-class women were the only group really helped by it. Under the FMLA, leave is *unpaid*, and many women—some middle-class women included—can't afford to take unpaid leave. In addition, the only employers covered by FMLA are those with 50 or more employees,[139] leaving over half the workforce (home health aides, cooks, and childcare providers, among others) uncovered by its provisions. In a survey by the National Partnership for Women and Families of low-income working women, over half the women said that the reluctance of employers to accommodate illness and other family-related scheduling problems made it hard for them to find or maintain a job.[140] Men, often stigmatized in the workplace when they act like members of families, don't use the leave provision nearly as often as women, largely because even men who can afford to take unpaid leave worry about how their absence from work will be perceived. And there's evidence that they are right to be concerned about workplace hostility toward paternal leave.[141] It's a troubling state of affairs, because fathers who can't spend much time with their infants often become fathers who are outsiders in their children's lives well beyond the period of infancy.[142]

As long as responsibility for work-life balance rests on the shoulders of women, we can talk about their stress and we can keep trying to help women find individual ways to manage it. In the absence of a larger public de-gendering of care and caregiving[143] as well as transformations in the old ideal (male) breadwinner system, even institutional efforts to achieve equality for working mothers can be stymied. For instance, despite very effective efforts by M.I.T. to curb discrimination against women professors through such measures as increasing the hiring of women and providing childcare on campus, the professors kept getting invitations to talk on panels about how they manage to achieve "work-life balance." They said it made them very uncomfortable to receive these kinds of invitations, because it signified to them that motherhood is still regarded as a "women's issue."[144]

CONCLUSION

> Most companies...have not formulated a policy to deal with the problems of working mothers. Many have yet to acknowledge that such problems exist.... Some corporations believe it is not their responsibility to provide such assistance, and others say that it is not feasible in the current, troubled economic climate.[145]

Although these sentences could have been written yesterday, they were published in the *New York Times* nearly 30 years ago. The framing of the issue has a familiar ring today: the "problems of working mothers" can be resolved by altering inflexible workplace policies. Not a bad thing. But the contemporary focus on the need to develop family-friendly workplace policies as a solution to the challenges facing working mothers and fathers shouldn't blind us to the static nature of gender arrangements inside the home and workplace that construe work-family tensions as a woman's "problem." As long as this interpretation persists, we'll keep talking about women's stress, and women will feel the need fix themselves by de-stressing, because, naturally, "if Mommy's okay, everyone else is okay."

Legal scholar Martha Albertson Fineman reminds us that, for all our posturing, universal equality is not really our national ambition. In America, society's obligation is "neutrally [to] provide opportunity or access." But opportunity and access don't have much meaning in the face of profound class and gender inequalities.[146] The United Nations 53rd Commission on the Status of Women, recognizing that gender norms around the world have burdened women with the exhausting, exclusive care of AIDs patients, has called for gender equity in caregiving.[147] Women may pay the price of care, but the wider society pays a price, too, in Fineman's words, "when things are structured in such a way that many families are doomed to struggle and some to fail in their assigned societal role."[148] When the problem we confront is defined as work-family conflict or work-life balance, the role economic and social forces have played in continually reproducing separate spheres of male breadwinning and female caregiving throughout our history are obscured. These are the forces that have not only supported gender inequalities in the workplace but have also caused women to favor motherhood over paid work.[149]

My first reaction on reading Arianna Huffington's statement that fatigue is the "next feminist issue"[150] was that it was an incredibly silly, superficial remark—and it is, if Huffington is suggesting that a long nap and soak in the tub are the answer to women's dilemmas. But if she means that women's fatigue is a social problem that must be tackled by all of us, she's got my attention. Fatigue—or stress—can't be the next feminist issue *unless* it mobilizes women, their partners, their employers, and the public-policy makers to do something about it beyond suggesting that women make another to-do list before bedtime.

There are some organizations that are trying to set out policy agendas that will bring change for mothers (and fathers); MomsRising (www. MomsRising.org) is one of them. And there are also programs designed to tackle the task of changing the corporate culture by making the "life" part of "work-life" balance more achievable for their employees. A fascinating initiative that was put into practice at the corporate headquarters of Best Buy, Inc., is called the Results-Only Work Environment (ROWE).[151] The process of instituting it highlights both the difficulties and promise of change in the entrenched "ideal worker" norm. Beyond working toward flexible schedules, ROWE actually tries to change that norm by altering employees' assumptions that a blind commitment to long hours, "visible busyness," and immediate responses to extra work that gets piled on at the last minute are company hallmarks of worker productivity. The program presents a competing view of the ideal worker as a person who combines work and personal life well. Workers are told that as long as they get their work done, they can arrange their work lives to suit themselves. As one might expect, when the program was introduced the women in the company were more enthusiastic about the program than the men. Researchers who studied ROWE as it was being implemented and sat in on the meetings with employees said that responses to it flowed along class and gender lines. For example, a male manager in his late thirties said that ROWE didn't fit his corporate life at that point because he had so many meetings:

> He also joked that some of things listed (as benefits) aren't relevant: "I'm not allowed to do laundry [at home]." A woman then explained that Monday was her first day back from maternity leave so laundry was a big part of her life right now, with a newborn and a two-year-old. She said that it would be great to do a few loads…at 9 a.m. rather than trying to do some every night.[152]

The researchers had this to say about the male manager and other men in the program who were tied to the ideal worker norm:

> By distancing himself from housework and expressing ambivalence about ROWE elsewhere…he lays claim to being an ideal worker and suggests the initiative is not relevant to men such as himself. The close ties between middle-class masculinity and business success point to the loss of status that might come if the work culture changed in ways that fit women's lives better.

Women who had lower-status jobs as administrative assistants were also worried about ROWE, but for vastly different reasons. They weren't afraid that it would hurt their careers; instead, they found it hard to believe that they could ever attain the flexibility the program promised. One woman administrative assistant asked, "What about when your boss or your boss's boss says, 'I'm meeting with so and so and I need these metrics, Can you pull them up?'"[153] A request like this meant to her that she had to do her boss's bidding right then, regardless of her schedule. The mostly female support staff felt they were making it possible for their bosses to have freedom, just as many of them were invisibly supporting the freedom of their spouses from extra demands at home.

These responses to the ROWE initiative point to how hard it is to make a dent in the ideal worker norm. While cautiously optimistic, the researchers began to worry that if most of the men didn't endorse the program, everything would return to square one: women who did embrace it would be penalized, in which case they would find themselves compared to the employees—mostly men—who accepted a status quo in which paid work trumps nonwork responsibilities.[154] This points up concerns researchers like Gerson and Jacobs have about "family friendly" policies in general: that if these policies focus on women and exact penalties from people who use them, they may "re-create earlier forms of gender inequality in a new form."[155] So policies that purport to be "gender neutral" can end up penalizing mothers *and* fathers for placing family over paid employment.[156]

In the United States, as the fiction of the ideal worker economy crumbles in the face of a dual-earner reality, it is the stress concept that helps cloak the sociopolitical context of women's daily struggles. The stress concept is an increasingly important obstacle to the public and private acknowledgement that the difficulties of working motherhood are not going to be resolved with to-do lists and bubble baths. As long as women are increasingly helped to view stress—and their own emotional reactions to it—as the enemy to be vanquished, possibilities for widespread social critique and social action will be stymied. We will need to throw out the bath oil with the bathwater if we are to find societal solutions to the work-family dilemma that favor women, men, and children.

CHAPTER 6

Posttraumatic Stress Disorder and the War for Mental Health

"Psychological pain" does not by itself seem to me to be a definite fact, but on the contrary only an interpretation—a causal interpretation—of a collection of phenomena that cannot be exactly formulated—it is really only a fat word standing in place of a skinny question mark.

—Friedrich Nietzsche, *1887*[1]

It is well that war is so terrible—otherwise we would grow too fond of it.

—Robert E. Lee, *1862*[2]

I've been through a lot and it was a pretty traumatic experience.

—Paris Hilton on *Larry King Live, June 28, 2007*[3]

Winthrop C., well dressed, with a military man's erect bearing, showed up at a psychiatrist's office at the urging of his wife and married daughter. What the psychiatrist knew from the wife and daughter was that Mr. C. was miserable and uncommunicative. His family believed he was desperately unhappy, but they couldn't get him to talk. Mr. C. told the psychiatrist that as an 18-year-old boy from a working-class family he had run away to join the Marines and gone to fight in the Pacific in World War II. Following the war, he had graduated from college and then from law school, eventually making partner at a West Coast law firm. By all outward measures of the American dream, he had achieved success. For years, Mr. C. had tamped down memories of the war and stayed away from veterans' gatherings. But now, in his sixties, he felt he had lost his ability to stave off memories of the killing he had done. He told the psychiatrist:

> I was made over into a killer. A proficient, remorseless killer. I probably killed dozens of enemy soldiers. Most at a distance, but several very close up.... But I did something so awful.... This is the thing I have hidden all these years.... The thing I did that can't, can never be undone. He must have been a military doctor. We overran his position. A small field hospital.... He raised his hands, dropping the stethoscope at his feet. He had been...treating a guy with a lot of blood on his chest.... His eyes were fixed on me. He just watched me. I can see him—so quiet, just waiting.... He didn't plead.... He just looked at me.... His face was drawn and sad, waiting. Oh, God! I shot him. I killed him. He slid to the ground still looking at me. And I...shot him again and again.[4]

By the end of his story, the man was sobbing. "There is no end to it, you know. No way to close it out,"[5] he said.

The psychiatrist did what he had learned to do: he prescribed medication; he saw Mr. C. every week for psychotherapy. After a couple of months, his patient looked much better. He went back to work, and his wife and daughter expressed gratitude to the psychiatrist for the changes they saw in their husband and father. But Mr. C. didn't thank the doctor. Yes, he was able to stow the memories away again and to eat and sleep, but, he said, "You know as well as I do that what's bothering me can't be treated or cured.... How all of us are capable of murder. In the midst of war when all hell breaks loose and you are empowered to act with impunity, you can do horror and be decorated for it.... Only the patriotic memories last. The killing is forgotten. The suffering [is] remembered, because it is legitimate to speak of it. What can't be said—I mean in public—is what I did. What does that tell you about the soul?"[6]

Twenty years later, the psychiatrist, Arthur Kleinman, now a professor of medical anthropology, reviewed his notes on the sessions with Mr. C. and judged them to be "disturbingly off the mark."[7] He had decided to re-read the notes because he became concerned that he had never really dealt with the ethical questions his patient had posed. Mr. C. had been trained to be a good soldier, a good killer, a protector of his small band of brothers. And he had done all these things very well. He had taken actions within his world's moral compass. But it was when Mr. C. saw himself taking what he viewed was a step too far that he questioned the world that had endorsed the morality of the patriotic soldier, the good comrade in arms. The Arthur Kleinman who had focused on treating the symptoms of psychopathology 20 years ago is the Arthur Kleinman who now sees what his patient had implied back then: that "moral experience... can lead a normal person toward murder. Normality, not pathology, was the problem. Normality could be abusive; it was dangerous."[8]

In his notes, the young Kleinman had written that dissociation might be at the root of his patient's problems—that Mr. C.'s thoughts might have been cut off from his emotions or his behavior from his moral awareness. At the time when he wrote those notes, psychologists and psychiatrists were talking more and more about how one of the ways humans escape events that are tremendously threatening is to disconnect the event(s) from present awareness and subsequently from memory (essentially, a different kind of fight-or-flight response), only to have memories of it break through later in symptoms of posttraumatic stress disorder (PTSD) or some other mental illness. Twenty years ago, Kleinman had diagnosed his patient as being depressed; today, his patient might be given the diagnosis of Posttraumatic Stress Disorder (PTSD), the fastest growing diagnostic category in the *Diagnostic and Statistical Manual of Mental Disorders* (*DSM*).

Did Mr. C. "have" PTSD, or was he suffering from a complex ailment whose symptoms are rooted in our culture—or both? As I hope to show in this chapter, PTSD has enshrined a certain way of thinking about traumatic stress that we take for granted today, particularly since the events of 9/11 and the return of American soldiers from Iraq and Afghanistan. But the way we look at traumatic stress now didn't just emerge full-blown from these events; that perception has been created over more than 30 years. And it has been made in America.

TRAUMA AS METAPHOR

In 1964, when my family moved again and I entered a new high school (my third in three years), I started coming home from school with headaches every day. The first day at my new school had not gone well. A fight had erupted in the cafeteria; trays were flying. I'd never seen anything like it. I didn't know where to sit because, of course, I didn't know anyone. I must have made some connection between my family's move and my headaches, because I remember slamming into the house one day in the first week or so of the term and unleashing a volley of blame at my mother for our move. She listened patiently until I ran out of gas. The headaches vanished after several weeks. I "adjusted," as they used to say, to the new school, made friends, and had a good year. That was what my parents and I expected. Nobody worried about my anxiety; some people were just worriers, some not. People didn't go around saying they "had" anxiety, and I didn't view myself as an anxious person. When I was worried about something, my father often reminded me of my resilience. He said I had a great capacity to bounce back, and I believed him.

Of course a new school, even an urban school, isn't an Iraqi war zone. I had educated, caring parents, a terrific big sister, food and shelter. I was fairly smart and very energetic. But today, despite all these "protective factors," as we now label them, my headaches and anxiety might well form the center of a trauma story ("Nine schools in 17 years? Uprooted so many times? How stressful! How traumatic!). I might be shuffled off to the school counselor, and from there to the family doctor for meds and/or a shrink for therapy. Back then, even if I had actually been hit by a flying tray in the cafeteria and had had nightmares about it afterward, there would have been no diagnosis of PTSD (the diagnosis didn't exist), no anti-anxiety or antidepressant medication (these were not routinely dispensed to children and adolescents), and, likely, no psychotherapy (rarely recommended for kids, and highly stigmatized in general).

I'm not saying that the lack of options for and the stigmatization of mental health treatment in that period were wonderful things or that we should return to a time when people had to be considered "loony" in order to get help. What I want to get at here is what it means when human suffering becomes trauma. As trauma and traumatic stress have become part of our common vocabulary, describing everything from the horrors of war to a broken fingernail, they have shaped the way we look at ourselves and the world. Throughout this book, we've seen how the way we learn to describe our experiences and emotions shapes the kinds of people we are and how any culture limits the ways available to people to describe their experience. Trauma and posttraumatic stress are relatively new ways of describing and categorizing experience that support some ways of being as "normal" and others as pathological.[9]

Earlier in our history, physicians used the term *trauma* to refer to a physical wound. Today, trauma is used as a metaphor. It is often called an invisible or psychological wound, and we talk about emotional scars or mental scars[10] that do or do not heal following traumatic events. In order to consider trauma in these kinds of psychological terms, we have to make at least two major inferences: first, that the "wound" is invisibly located in the psyche; and second, that there was some event that caused the wound in the first place.[11] But the analogy between physical and psychic wounds only goes so far. People don't respond to psychological "wounds" the same way they respond to stab wounds. As British psychiatrist Derek Summerfield reminds us, "suffering arises from, and is resolved in, a social context."[12]

Culture shapes the *meaning* of a person's experience of suffering and how he or she expresses it. But, as Laurence Kirmayer has said, when we try to come up with "a simple cause-and-effect relation between trauma events and specific symptoms, [this] ignores the social and cultural embedding of distress that ensures that trauma, loss, and restitution are inextricably intertwined."[13] And yet "psy" professionals continue to act as if symptoms and their meanings are the same from culture to culture. After the January 2010 earthquake in Haiti, psychologists fretted aloud that the disaster might have long-term effects on children, probably in the form of PTSD and depression.[14] Well-intentioned Western psychologists and psychiatrists have descended on countries like Rwanda, Indonesia, and Sri Lanka, prepared to help people "process" genocide or natural disasters in order to relieve their suffering.[15] In their efforts to export Western ideas about and treatment for psychological distress, these clinicians have found confusion at best and anger at worst, and only some of them come away with an appreciation of how *social* a process suffering really is. People do, of course, suffer in ways that are unique to them as individuals, but, as historians and anthropologists remind us, history, culture, and politics determine whether and/or how war, genocide, and natural disasters get transformed into disease and individual misery.[16]

Once upon a time in the Western world, people were expected to be pretty resilient when confronted with adversity,[17] but the way we think about trauma today makes the vicissitudes of life seem unduly risky, creating a sense of our own vulnerability in a menacing world.[18] No one would deny the global uncertainties and the local risks of human life today, but when a culture places an inordinate value on people's emotional responses to their experience (e.g., anxiety, stress) as ours does, individuals can come to view a vast array of experiences as psychologically traumatizing and requiring psychological treatment. Some historians believe that over time a particularly Western, even American, emphasis on emotion as a mark of personal authenticity, combined with an erosion of belief in overarching systems of meaning such as religion and politics, have prepared the ground for our subjective sense of vulnerability and our current preoccupation with trauma.[19] Trauma stands for the psychological *effect* of the event on the person who experiences or witnesses it, as book titles like *Tools for Transforming Trauma* and *Assessing and Treating Trauma* show. But it's not the traumatic situation that's being transformed or assessed and treated; it's the person who has to be fixed. The reaction and the event itself end up being collapsed into each other. Suffering and trauma become one, just as "stress" and "stressor" are often fused, enabling trauma to take on protean forms.

As the idea of psychological trauma has been stretched to encompass so many phenomena, it has become less and less useful. How, for example, are we to interpret the following statement by Annette M. La Greca, Ph.D., chair of the American Psychological Association's (APA) Task Force on PTSD in Children: "As many as 50 percent of children experience trauma before their eighteenth birthdays"?[20] It is now assumed that certain events are traumatic for everyone, and evidence to the contrary isn't always well received. When Bruce Rind and his colleagues published a paper analyzing 59 studies of the long-term psychological effects of childhood sexual abuse (CSA) in a respected journal,[21] they could not have imagined the firestorm that would ensue: that their paper would be unanimously condemned by the Congress of the United States, attacked by mental health professionals, and savaged by radio talk celebrity "Dr. Laura." Why? Their analysis, demonstrating that college-age adults who had been sexually abused as children were doing almost as well from a psychological standpoint as their peers who had not been abused, ran strongly counter to the established view that because CSA is morally wrong it must necessarily be traumatically harmful to everyone exposed to it.[22]

Medicalization Revisited

Is suffering normal or not? Are people *expected* to cope in the face of difficulties and even horrors? Perhaps, as Boone and Richardson suggest, a person who suffers should not have to choose between being designated as "feisty survivor" or a "medicalized victim."[23] The questions that Summerfield poses—"what kind of adversity someone can face and still be 'normal'; what is reasonable risk; what is acceptable behavior at a time of crisis...and whether restitution is due"[24]—are questions each society answers in its own way. In the West, as more and more types of suffering have been labeled mental health disorders, the answers to these questions are usually provided by people in the "psy" professions. The degree of traumatization is for the experts to decide, and so is the assessment of whether treatment is necessary.

The pairing of stress and trauma in the 1980s had everything to do with the expansion both of the psychological professions and of a therapeutic culture that embraces an interventionist perspective. In Chapter 3, I discussed some of the ways we talk about the relationship between stress and *physical* disease, but medicalization has also forged a close association between stress and *mental disorders*. As we proceed to look at posttraumatic stress, it's helpful to keep in mind Kleinman's take on psychiatric diagnosis as only "an interpretation of an individual's experience."[25] Diagnosis is a way of seeing things and, sometimes, a way of getting others to see things in a certain way (this is true particularly when people seek compensation for injuries sustained). It doesn't explain anything about what is really wrong.[26]

Social change can lead societies to "uncover" new stresses and new forms of disorder.[27] There's a common idea that PTSD has always been with us, and some historians see evidence of PTSD in everything from the nightmares chronicled in Shakespeare's *Henry IV* to the description of the Great Fire of London described in Samuel Pepys' *Diary*, and more.[28] But posttraumatic stress as it is diagnosed today is hardly a timeless, universal condition.[29] Yes, it is true that medical men were talking about mental and physical reactions to horrifying events from the late nineteenth century onward. But the symptoms physicians described long ago are not the same as today's symptoms of PTSD.[30] Eric Caplan has shown how attempts to explain a condition called "railway spine" that uninjured passengers developed after being exposed to railroad accidents, symptoms of which included paralysis and headaches, set medical men on a journey that took them from the body to the brain, and, eventually, in Freud's time and beyond, to the mind.[31] During the Civil War, physicians described soldiers' symptoms of lethargy and isolation as evidence of "nostalgia" or homesickness. They talked mainly of physical symptoms such as "irritable heart." During World War I, British soldiers were commonly described as having symptoms such as tremors, seizures, spasms, blindness, and muteness that doctors said indicated problems in the nervous system. In the Second World War, too, most symptoms were viewed as somatic rather than psychological. Today, the emphasis is almost entirely on the *psychological* effects of adverse events. We call reactions to the atrocities of war *stress*, a condition that's everywhere and nowhere, as we have seen. But is *stress* really the term that best describes "the constant danger of dying, grief over the loss of friends, nightmarish situations of moral conflict, and a sense of powerlessness and helplessness that being at war creates for so many," described by Paula Caplan in her book *When Johnny and Jane Come Marching Home*?[32] Here's what Brigadier General Donald M. Campbell, Jr., spokesman for U.S. forces in Iraq, is reported to have said about what led to the killing by American troops of 24 unarmed Iraqi civilians in Haditha: "It's stress, fear, isolation, and in some cases, they're just upset."[33] Stress? Upset? That's how people talk about spilling coffee on their favorite t-shirt. But these are the euphemisms we depend on to describe reactions to killing and death.

The Vietnam era was not, by far, the first time that soldiers' reactions to the horrors of war were taken seriously. That thousands upon thousands of soldiers who were diagnosed with shell shock, neurasthenia, and "effort syndrome" were paid war pensions following World War I attests to the fact that it was no new thing for physicians to concern themselves with the effects of combat on soldiers.[34] But those effects were considered *abnormal* reactions. The establishment of PTSD as an official diagnosis changed the way we explained how war affects people.[35] The PTSD era ushered in the idea that, in Scott's words, "it is normal to be traumatized by the abnormal events typical of war."[36] In the past, as Summerfield has said, war was not conceived of as "a sort of public health emergency."[37] But when the World Health Organization refers to "psychological trauma" as "a major mental health problem,"[38] why should war be exempt?

The military often seems to want it both ways. On the one hand, soldiers are diagnosed and treated for PTSD, a mental illness. On the other hand, as Capt. Robert L. Koffman, navy psychiatrist, said in 2004, "We do not want to pathologize combat stress.... Individuals are not patients.... [Combat stress is] a relatively normal reaction by a normal person to an abnormal, horrific situation."[39] Capt. Koffman may not want to turn soldiers into patients, but the military *does* medicalize stress; at every turn, military personnel mention "stress injury" and "stress illness."[40] At the 23rd annual meeting of International Society for Traumatic Stress Studies there was even a workshop entitled "Preventing Psychological and Moral Injury in Military Service." It's certain that Mr. C. would have known one can't "prevent" morality from kicking in, and surely not by talking about moral qualms as "injuries."

Why all the talk of "normal" reactions to "abnormal" situations? We can't conceptualize PTSD as a "normal" response to trauma and a disorder at the same time. But this is just what some therapists have done in an attempt to normalize symptoms women may develop following rape or physical or sexual assault. PTSD is a preferred diagnosis among many feminist therapists (truth to tell, I, too, used to favor the diagnosis) because, by focusing on external events, it seems less blaming and stigmatizing than some other diagnoses. Here's a fairly typical statement by a therapist Jeanne Marecek interviewed for a study on "trauma talk."

> Almost all my clients have PTSD and I tell them what it means. I say, "This means you are having a normal reaction to trauma. You're not having a sick reaction to trauma. You're having a normal reaction to trauma." The reason I like PTSD as a diagnosis and I'm glad it's there is that it says

right in the definition that this is a normal response to trauma that most people would have.[41]

If PTSD were a "normal reaction to trauma," then it would stand to reason that most people who are exposed to traumatic events would develop it. But they don't, as we'll soon see. The effort to separate the "abnormal" act (e.g., rape) from the un-blameworthy person by calling her reaction to it "normal" is commendable, but there's only one problem: giving her a diagnosis that implies she is disordered can't possibly accomplish that aim.

THE BIRTH OF PTSD: A POLITICAL STORY

In the first *Diagnostic and Statistical Manual of Mental Disorders* (*DSM-I*) a slim volume published in 1952 and consulted by virtually no one, there was a category called "gross stress reaction," a temporary reaction in otherwise normal individuals caused by extreme stress in the environment. In the *DSM-II* of 1968 there was no reference to stress or traumatic stress at all; it was assumed that diagnoses already in use—depression, alcoholism, schizophrenia—would suffice for people who were responding symptomatically to highly stressful events. By 2000, the *DSM-IV-TR* (text revision) was consulted by every mental health professional in the United States (and many globally) and weighed in at a bloated 3.7 pounds and 943 pages. The PTSD diagnosis was not only established fact but was achieving a growth rate and influence that hasn't been matched yet in this century. The story of how that diagnosis was created started in 1969, when the United States had been involved in the Vietnam War for four years, and it isn't over yet.[42]

As historian Wilbur Scott tells it, soon after Sarah Haley, a newly minted social worker, arrived at the Boston Veterans Administration Hospital in 1969, she interviewed a veteran who was complaining of being extremely frightened and unable to sleep. The veteran told her that his friends were out to kill him and said that his company had killed a lot of women and children in a village called My Lai. He hadn't shot anyone (in fact, he hadn't fired his weapon at all), but following the shootings several men in his company said they would kill him if he ever told what they had done. Haley took the case to a staff meeting at which the man's diagnosis and treatment plan were to be formulated. The consensus? The veteran was delusional and psychotic: he had paranoid schizophrenia. As Haley tells the story:

> I argued that there were no other signs of this if one took his story seriously. I was laughed out of the room. I was told that it was my first day and just didn't understand how things worked.... I was aghast. These professionals denied the reality of combat.[43]

Haley's take on the combat experiences of the veterans with whom she worked attracted the interest of antiwar psychiatrists Robert Lifton and Chaim Shatan and a group of vets calling themselves Vietnam Veterans Against the War (VVAW). Shatan, tremendously moved by the highly publicized fate of Congressional Medal of Honor winner Dwight Johnson, who had been killed when he tried to rob a store at gunpoint, wrote about a "post-Vietnam syndrome" that he theorized was a delayed response to trauma, expressed through rage, guilt, psychological numbing, and other symptoms. Headlines like such as "Vietnam Veteran Releases Hostages and Gives Up in Ohio After 9 Hours" and movies like *Taxi Driver* and *Apocalypse Now* hammered out a media message about the meaningless of the Vietnam War and depicted the veteran as an angry psychotic. Veterans themselves often painted a picture of their suffering as qualitatively different from that of veterans in past wars.[44] Vets and their advocates were not the only proponents of a posttrauma diagnosis; the strengthening women's movement provided a great deal of muscle in the fight. In an unusual move, quite a few conservative politicians took up the movement's cause, advocating greater power for law enforcement against perpetrators in cases of rape and wife battering (law enforcement needed to be able to show that women had been damaged even when the victims had no outward scars to prove it).[45]

The ball that Lifton and Shatan started rolling eventually led them to the door of Robert Spitzer, chief editor of *DSM-III*, which was then in the works. It was an anxious time for American psychiatry. Research funding was drying up. Other professional groups—psychologists, social workers—were staking claims to psychiatry's turf. Many psychiatrists were anxious to detach themselves from their profession's long connection with psychoanalysis and to establish their discipline as purely scientific. They counted on a new diagnostic manual that they claimed would be based on empirical research and would owe allegiance to no particular set of theories to get them there. That manual was to be *DSM-III*.[46]

When Shatan and Lifton talked to Spitzer, they learned there were no plans to include a combat-related disorder diagnosis in the new manual. Spitzer said he was willing to be persuaded, but he needed evidence that PTSD was an essential diagnostic category. To that end, Lifton, Shatan, and others formed a working group to gather data in support of a "post-combat disorder" diagnosis. Eventually, Spitzer himself appointed a committee to take up the investigation and report back to the entire *DSM-III* task force. By 1978, the committee had recommended that a diagnosis of PTSD be included in the manual. When *DSM-III* came out in 1980, three forms of PTSD—acute, chronic, and delayed—were listed in the "Anxiety Disorders" section. The manual clearly stated that in order to be diagnosed with PTSD, a person had to have experienced "a psychologically traumatic event that is generally outside the range of such common experiences as simple bereavement, chronic illness, business losses, or marital conflict."[47] Of course, whether an event is inside or outside the range of usual human experience can't be determined in a vacuum. As Allan Young contends, there are many factors to consider—principally, what the event means in the context of the person's life, how often it occurs in the community in which the person lives, the moral values and standards for conduct in that community and whether the person accepts those values and standards, among other factors.[48]

PTSD was—and is still—one of a very few diagnoses in any version of the *DSM* that has a direct relationship to an event in the external environment. It is viewed as resulting from the psyche's inability to process an overwhelming event or events, since the traumatic nature of the event(s) provokes dissociation by interfering with normal awareness, cognition, and emotion. As a result, memories return in the present as if they *are* present, suspended in time. Dissociation can result in a person's reexperiencing the trauma via intruding memories, having recurrent dreams of the traumatic event, feeling numb (emotionally detached from and disinterested in things going on around her/him), avoiding whatever might bring up memories of the event(s), and possibly experiencing survivor guilt, sleep problems, and hyperalertness. The business of determining the accuracy of memories of a traumatic event years after the event has taken place isn't easy. Many of us remember the heated debates of the 1990s—the so-called "memory wars"—over repressed (some said false) memories of child sexual abuse, debates that haven't been settled yet.[49]

Trauma by Proxy?

The newly fashioned PTSD diagnosis said nothing about symptoms specific to the stress of combat, and there has never been a sub-classification of the disorder tied to war experiences. Responses to the trauma of war, rape trauma, civilian disasters, torture, and other events were lumped together into one disorder, ignoring the social, cultural, and environmental contexts in which they occurred and, as historian Ben Shephard points out, leaving intact the main emphasis on the "stressor" and the "stressed."[50]

In *DSM-III*, among the examples of traumatic stressors that might produce the disorder were rape, combat, torture, airplane crashes, and earthquakes. A revised version, *DSM-III-R*, published in 1987, stated definitively that the stressor must be "a psychologically distressing event...outside the range of usual human experience."[51] Every version of *DSM* has made changes to one or another facet of the PTSD diagnosis, but no change has been as radical as the one that occurred in 1994 with the publication of *DSM-IV*, when the traumatic stressor was completely redefined. *DSM-IV* states that in order to qualify for the diagnosis, the person must have "*experienced, witnessed, or* [*been*] *confronted with* an event or events that involved actual or threatened death or serious injury, or a threat to the physical integrity of self or others" [italics added]. Also, for the first time, significant distress and impairment in social role functioning was necessary for diagnosis: the person's response had to have involved "intense fear, helplessness, or horror."[52] According to this version of *DSM*, responding with horror on hearing that a friend has been in an accident is a potentially traumatic stressor.[53] Breslau and Kessler have argued that trauma takes a very different shape in this two-part definition, as the subjective reactions of the person have now come to overshadow the elements of the traumatic stressor.[54] Paradoxically, then, the more real estate the concept of psychological trauma consumes in the PTSD diagnosis, the less important it becomes to emphasize the stressful event itself.

Put in historical context, the viral spread of PTSD-related talk in the public arena may rival that of hysteria and neurasthenia in the late nineteenth century. And PTSD itself is often referred to as if it were a virus; as something one can "get;" something that "can be lethal."[55] Rates of PTSD diagnosis are rising along with the talk, with the latest national epidemiological survey estimating that the lifetime prevalence among all American adults is 6.8 percent,[56] as compared with roughly 1 percent in 1985.[57] As the list of potential stressors has lengthened, the number of people in the United States who consider that they have been exposed to at least one traumatic event has reached almost 90 percent, by some counts.[58] And the radical change in the definition of the traumatic event in 1994 has created a situation in which millions more people became eligible for a PTSD diagnosis.[59] For women, this has proven, at best, a mixed blessing. Feminists had argued that the *DSM-III* definition of the stressor for PTSD as outside the range of usual human experience excluded many women who had been sexually and physically abused from being diagnosed with PTSD, since these experiences are common in women's lives. A diagnosis that recognized the psychological effects of abuse seemed a refreshing change from the traditional view that the aftereffects of abuse were women's intrapsychic problems to solve. Over time, however, the consequences of opening up the PTSD diagnosis to millions of women who otherwise never would have received it are becoming more distressingly apparent.[60]

Now, granted, there are many people who don't qualify for a PTSD diagnosis. The person who receives the diagnosis must still have a minimum number of symptoms. But since there are 175 ways to combine criteria such that a PTSD diagnosis can be reached,[61] it may not be as difficult for a person to qualify for the diagnosis as it might seem. And, as I've pointed out elsewhere, now that the PTSD tent has been enlarged, many of the people who fit under it have virtually no symptoms in common with each other.[62] The larger *DSM-IV-TR* tent also holds more business for mental health professionals than *DSM-III's* smaller one, and the *DSM-5* version may prove to be the Superdome, if proposals for both broadening the criteria and creating a new preschool version of the diagnosis are accepted.[63] There has also been plenty of work for academic researchers, if this is judged by the steady, yearly rise in the number of academic publications devoted to trauma and PTSD since 1979.[64]

Ever since the criteria for PTSD were broadened, the question of whether PTSD is a valid diagnosis has kept reemerging. In 1995, the fact that a "pure" form of PTSD is quite rare suggested to Yehuda and McFarlane that extreme stress can provoke many different kinds of symptoms and syndromes, and that people who are predisposed to depression and anxiety may be the people most likely to develop the constellation of symptoms we now call PTSD.[65] Several recent studies seem to support this idea. In one, Alexander Bodkin and his colleagues compared two groups of patients, both suffering from major depression. Members of one group reported that they had experienced traumatic events; members of the other said they had not. When the two groups were assessed for symptoms of PTSD, the rate of PTSD was found to be identical for each group—78 percent.[66] What did Bodkin and colleagues have to say about such results? Pretty much what Yehuda and McFarlane had said over a decade earlier: "the symptom cluster currently attributed to PTSD may be a non-specific group of symptoms widely observed in patients with mood and anxiety disorders, regardless of trauma history."[67]

Most studies of PTSD rely on reports that research subjects make to interviewers about their past experiences, and the accuracy of memory retrieval depends on a variety of conditions, including the state a person is in at the time of the interview.[68] This is especially important in PTSD research because what we know about PTSD depends on the association between a person's memories of an event and the symptoms the person is reporting or exhibiting. Paul McHugh and Glenn Treisman describe how, when diagnosing PTSD, clinicians often take a "top down" approach, searching, in essence, for symptoms that match the criteria.[69] Sleep problems, for instance, may be symptoms of PTSD, but they are also symptoms of major depression and other disorders. Once a patient reports having been exposed to a traumatic event or events, symptoms that are not specific to PTSD are viewed as definitive signs: phobias become "avoidance behaviors": depressive ruminations become "reexperiences."[70] But just because a person may have these symptoms, it doesn't necessarily follow that they are caused by the traumatic event. As McHugh and Treisman suggest, symptoms can be caused by "the onset of a depressive illness, progress of an addiction, or even a search for the 'sick role' now promoted in the patient by the social rewards and suggestive attitudes of physicians and other mental health workers single-mindedly engrossed with PTSD."[71] It might come as a surprise to some, given all the media attention devoted to PTSD, that most people, even victims of violent assault, who have experienced what we now call traumatic events never develop PTSD.[72]

At the height of the Vietnam War, before many combat soldiers had come home for good, there was a certain amount of crowing over how few men were afflicted with psychiatric problems related to "combat stress." A *Time* magazine article from 1969 reported a rate of 1 in 100 psychiatric casualties, noting that "most of the victims rejoin their units within two days.... Combat psychiatrists see the battlefield not so much as a special environment but as a kind of telescoped, infinitely more stressful version of ordinary life."[73] This take on things would soon change, as more and more soldiers returned home and reports of lingering posttraumatic symptoms rose. And shortly after George W. Bush declared "mission accomplished" in Iraq, when it seemed there would be few actual American casualties, the media signaled that there would be large numbers of military returning home with PTSD.[74] By 2004, newspaper headlines like "A Deluge of Troubled Soldiers Is in the Offing, Experts Predict" and "1 in 6 Veterans Is Found to Have Stress-Related Disorder" were common.[75]

As Simon Wessely has remarked, Americans' shame over having made Vietnam veterans scapegoats for angry feelings about the war may have made us loathe to question anything those vets have said about their experience during and after the war.[76] This includes questioning the data on the number of Vietnam veterans who actually have PTSD. For decades, researchers and journalists have been reporting that over 30 percent of all Vietnam veterans eventually developed PTSD and that over 15 percent developed partial PTSD. These figures were taken from the 1988 National Vietnam Veterans Readjustment Study (NVVRS) mandated by Congress, the most important epidemiological survey of Vietnam veterans ever undertaken.[77] The figures indicate a phenomenally high rate of PTSD (all the more so when one considers that only 15 percent of vets with PTSD had combat roles during the war), and they remained undisputed for years.[78] But in 2006 Bruce Dohrenwend and his colleagues reviewed the original NVVRS data, checking it against the vets' military records and records of combat exposure.[79] Although there has been some research showing that a significant number of Vietnam veterans lied about having been in combat in order to receive compensation,[80] Dohrenwend did not find much evidence of this kind of falsification. What he *did* find was that some veterans whose exposure to traumatic events could not be documented and some who had suffered only slight impairments in functioning had been included in the 1988 study. Dohrenwend's conclusion was that 18.7 percent of the vets—not over 30 percent, as originally reported—had had PTSD and that 9.1 percent were suffering from PTSD more than 10 years after the war ended. This is no insignificant number, as the authors of the study pointed out.[81] But Dohrenwend's major argument was that the majority of the soldiers who had been exposed to severe stressors in the war zone didn't develop PTSD. For most who did, symptoms improved rapidly or disappeared altogether. Even the vets who still had problems weren't having severe problems when they were reinterviewed later. Because fewer than half the vets with PTSD had never had any treatment, psychiatric intervention could not explain what Dohrenwend and his colleagues referred to as the "trend toward recovery over time."

Even though Dohrenwend's data has been available since 2006 and has been reported in the press,[82] the 30 percent figure has never died. I found it, for example, in this 2010 discussion of the raging epidemic of PTSD among soldiers returning from Iraq and Afghanistan: "Studies estimate that nearly 30 percent of Vietnam veterans (some 830,000) have experienced some level of PTSD. Today, more than 150,000 veterans of the Iraq and Afghanistan wars have been officially diagnosed with PTSD. The number likely is higher...."[83]

Dialing for PTSD: The 9/11 Epidemic That Wasn't

On December 7, 1941, the day Pearl Harbor was bombed, there were almost no allusions to the possibility that the events of that day might affect Americans' mental health. In fact, as *Time* magazine reported on that day, "There were a few people, then a throng, looking intently...out to the Pacific where the enemy was. There was no visible excitement, no hysteria, and no release of words for the emotions behind the grim, determined faces."[84] Sixty years later, just days after the events of September 11, 2001, somewhere around 9,000 counselors descended on lower Manhattan,[85] and parents were warned that children watching television coverage of the attacks hundreds of miles away from the World Trade Center and the Pentagon might develop PTSD. In New York City, a Board of Education study found that "tens of thousands of children" were having anxiety, nightmares, and other fears, quickly labeled "mental health problems."[86] There were debates over whether all the children who went to school near the World Trade Center should be screened for mental health problems.[87] *U.S. News and World Report* warned of a "second wave" of problems—a "siege on body and mind," visited on hapless citizens less than a month after the terrorist attacks.[88] Long-term effects seemed certain. Spencer Eth, a longtime specialist on trauma in children, said "Those kids affected and untreated will go on to have potentially lifelong difficulties directly related to 9/11, in the form of educational handicaps, substance abuse, antisocial behavior."[89]

Within days after the events of 9/11, Mark Schuster and his colleagues were randomly phoning adults about their reactions to the attacks. Not surprisingly, many people reported symptoms of stress. This led the researchers to conclude that "the psychological effects of the recent terrorism are unlikely to disappear soon," and that "if there are further attacks, clinicians should anticipate that even people far from the attacks will have trauma-related symptoms of stress."[90] This didn't happen. Many found the research flawed: Schuster and others who were doing phone surveys were only, it seemed, assessing what they called "probable PTSD" because they couldn't perform complete assessments over the telephone. Tolin and Foa cautioned researchers that a person who is still having nightmares and unwanted memories of the event, when asked a question in an epidemiological survey such as "Have you ever experienced a terrorist attack?" might be more likely to answer "yes."[91] Even if one accepts that trolling for "probable PTSD" is a reasonable method for gathering data, the results of these phone surveys aren't impressive. One of the largest of the epidemiological studies showed that less than one percent of New York City residents met the criteria for PTSD six months after the terrorist attacks.[92] By the second month after the attacks, clinical symptoms in the U.S. population as a whole were judged to be within normal limits.[93]

By May 2003, Project Liberty, a huge federally funded program to provide crisis counseling following the September 11 attacks, still had about $90 million left unspent. Of the 2.5 million people expected to request short-term counseling, only 643,710 people had shown up.[94] Veterans, who, it was thought, would make heavy use of mental health services in New York and Washington following 9/11, didn't.[95] Yet another surprise was that, despite Big Pharma's heavy advertising after 9/11, there was no spike in the use of psychotropic medications following the terrorist attacks.[96] When interviewed, Robert Rosenheck, lead author of the study that had found no increase in the vets' use of services, said that this finding, among others, should cause researchers to rethink the methods they use to distinguish a stress disorder from normal emotional distress. He remarked, "It's ingrained in our culture to express the horror of something by saying it's so bad that it causes mental illness."[97]

In December 2010, Congress passed the James Zadroga 9/11 Health and Compensation Act, setting aside $4.3 billion for treatment of and compensation to people who had developed illnesses as a result of the terrorist attacks. The funds cover emergency responders and residents exposed to the dust cloud, many of whom have developed severe illnesses in the wake of the attacks. But the funds also cover people like Stanley Mieses, a 58-year-old freelance writer who lived in the shadow of the World Trade Center and was quickly evacuated from the area but continued to return to his dust-filled apartment regularly to feed his cats. In the period following 9/11, his mother died, his girlfriend left him, and, with less work coming in, he had to move for financial reasons. His doctor isn't sure whether Mr. Mieses's shortness of breath was caused by the dust or his 20 years of smoking, and it will probably never be clear whether his self-reported PTSD symptoms are a direct result of the events of September 11, 2001.[98]

Although their predictions of long-term mental health problems in the aftermath of 9/11 turned out to be misguided, it has taken a decade for psychologists to acknowledge this publicly. On the 10-year anniversary of 9/11, in September 2011, a special issue of the *American Psychologist* came out, reviewing a mountain of 9/11 psychological research. This review showed that, other than rescue and recovery workers and direct witnesses of the events near the site of the World Trade Center,[99] most people did not develop significant

PTSD symptoms following the terrorist attacks. For the majority of those who did, symptoms decreased over time. The authors of this review concluded, as have many others, that the reason people showed few if any effects after 9/11was because they were resilient, with "an impressive capacity to adapt to extremely adverse situations." But the review authors still described people who *did* develop symptoms (even though these symptoms decreased or vanished over time) as "traumatized individuals [who] do not continue to manifest long-term psychological difficulties."[100] Like many of their fellow researchers who failed to find an epidemic of traumatic psychopathology after 9/11, they never question the original ideas about trauma that led them astray in the first place. They are still viewing people as "traumatized individuals," resilient or not, symptoms or no symptoms, even though, as Breslau and McNally remark, every time resilience is brought into the picture, this assumes that a pathological response to extremely stressful events is actually the "normal" response.[101]

Psychotherapy and Big Pharma in the Big Muddy

There is almost no evidence to show that intervention in the month or so following a catastrophic event, beyond offering practical help and connecting people to resources, is helpful.[102] Whereas people's "processing" their experience by describing both the event and their emotional reactions to it in some detail right after a disaster used to be considered very important, this practice of *critical stress incident debriefing* is now considered counterproductive and has pretty much been discontinued.[103] As some studies on treatment outcomes for veterans with PTSD show, sometimes even a long-term focus on the emotional processing of past events isn't helpful, as it can distract from problems in the present that must be solved if the veteran is to manage in her or his daily life.[104]

By June 2008, according to Army estimates, there were some 20,000 troops in Iraq and Afghanistan taking antidepressants like Prozac and Zoloft and sleeping pills like Ambien. Whereas the military was referring to "temporary stress injuries" and longer-term "stress illnesses," a *Time* reporter pinpointed long and (often) multiple redeployments, as well as the Army's desperate need not to lose soldiers from the front lines, as the sources of the Army's need to medicate troops.[105] One army colonel told the reporter that "in the Persian Gulf War we didn't have these medications, so our basic philosophy was 'three hots and cot'.... If they didn't get better right away, they'd need to head to the rear and probably out of theater." But in 2006 the colonel had an epiphany when he met a soldier whose job it was to guard Iraqi detainees:

> He was distraught while he was having high-level interactions with detainees, having emotional confrontations with them—and carrying weapons. But he was part of a highly trained team, and we didn't want to lose him. So we put him on an SSRI [antidepressant], and within a week, *he was a new person*, and we got him back to full duty. (italics added)

The Iraq War Clinician Guide, put out by the Veterans Administration in 2004, refers to antidepressants as "first line medications" for PTSD and counsels military clinicians to "balance the mission requirements with the best interest of the patient." However, as Paula Caplan points out, the *Guide* never details how this should be done.[106]

The results of a 2008 report on PTSD treatment commissioned by the Veterans Administration itself were less than stunning. In that report, a review of research since 1980 on treatments for PTSD, the committee of the Institute of Medicine concluded that there were "significant gaps in the evidence that made it impossible to reach conclusions establishing the efficacy of most treatment modalities." They said that "this result was unexpected and may surprise VA and others interested in the disorder."[107] The report came out that October. Three months later, the American Psychological Association published a piece in the *Monitor on Psychology* entitled "PTSD Treatments Grow in Evidence, Effectiveness," marshaling "expert" opinion against the report's conclusions:

> "I think [the Institute of Medicine panel] raised the bar too high and they're not realistic about what PTSD is and how hard it is to study and keep people in treatment," says PTSD expert Barbara O. Rothbaum, PhD, director of the Trauma and Anxiety Recovery Program at Emory University. "High dropout is endemic in PTSD."... In addition, the panel's findings are at odds with many reviews already done in the field, Rothbaum says. As one example, the committee did not support

the evidence base on any drug at all, even though the Food and Drug Administration has approved … Paxil and … Zoloft to treat PTSD.[108]

What that piece in the *Monitor*, full of news about new drug treatments and the "virtual-reality simulations" that "beef up" the effectiveness of "proven treatments,"[109] omitted to say was that the Institute of Medicine committee had also reported that most of the PTSD drug studies had been funded by Big Pharma and that many of the studies of psychotherapy interventions for PTSD were conducted by the very researchers involved in working on the techniques under investigation.

In our therapeutic culture, the pairing of suffering and mental illness leads to the natural conclusion that professionals are the only people qualified to help people deal with their distress. Paula Caplan writes that the standard response from family and friends when vets talk about their problems is: "You need to see a psychiatrist, because I am not trained to deal with a mental illness."[110] This common view is a boon to professionals seeking to maintain their credibility as well as their incomes.

POSTTRAUMATIC INEQUALITY: PREDISPOSITION, RISK, AND PTSD

Ever since World War I, the question of what, if any, part individual predispositions and vulnerabilities play in the development of posttrauma problems has bedeviled psychiatry. But, for all their head-scratching, in the many years since that war, researchers have not managed to find a single stressful event in response to which most individuals develop PTSD,[111] and the debate over whether some people are simply more vulnerable than others to developing symptoms in the face of exposure to extreme events or conditions lingers on. In the 1980 version of PTSD, it was implied that conditions of war alone could be a sufficient cause of psychological breakdown. This diverged from earlier perspectives that took soldiers' personalities and backgrounds into account in theorizing the nature and development of combat-related symptoms.[112]

Shephard makes the point that it was the Vietnam War that divided the psychiatric community over the question of whether soldiers who developed severe problems were particularly vulnerable as a result of a history of previous trauma, depression, and/or low intelligence, and whether all soldiers should be screened prior to entering the service. It was decided not to screen soldiers going to Vietnam—and yet there *was* one default criterion that, to a large extent, did determine their selection, and that was social class. Many of the men who "volunteered" to fight in Vietnam went to war only because they were afraid they would be drafted. Three-quarters of the volunteers were poor or working class, whereas thousands of middle- and upper-class young men, including George W. Bush and Bill Clinton, played whatever cards and pulled whatever strings they needed in order to evade the draft.[113] At the time, literary critic Leslie Fiedler commented acerbically that Vietnam was "a war fought for us by our servants."[114] More recently, low troop levels in Iraq and Afghanistan meant that "an obscenely small portion of our population" carried the "terrible burden of these conflicts," as Bob Herbert has written in the *New York Times*.[115] These days, the press often refers to the Army as the "volunteer Army."[116] In Herbert's words, "the country soothes its conscience and tamps down its guilt with the cowardly invocation: "Oh, they're *volunteers*. They knew what they were getting into."[117] At the same time, the troops are repeatedly described as heroes. Perhaps this helps alleviate a sense of guilt on the part of those whose burden they carry; perhaps it helps avoid the collective projection of anger about the war onto our troops that occurred in the aftermath of the Vietnam debacle; perhaps it offers a glimpse of something unsoiled by the mess and uncertainty that characterizes modern warfare and political life.[118] The PTSD diagnosis fits better than "depression" with the idea of soldier as hero. It carries no taint of cowardice, weakness, or malingering; it's just a "disease," and the equal opportunity every soldier appears to have of "getting" it is consistent with our democratic ideals.

Posttraumatic Inequality

But is PTSD really democratic? Who *are* the people most likely to "get" it? Something interesting but not wholly unpredictable happened as researchers began pulling together data on the mental health impact of 9/11 that might help answer this question: it began to look as though risk for developing PTSD depended not just on degree of exposure to distressing events, but also on gender, ethnicity, race, and/ or socioeconomic status.[119] In one 9/11 study, women, Hispanics, and African Americans were found to be at greatest risk, and survivors of the terrorist attacks with incomes under $25,000 were eight times likelier to have PTSD than survivors earning over $100,000.[120] In that study, poverty was the most potent of all risk factors for mental health problems following the events of 9/11. But what did the researchers say about why this was so? "Potential explanations for this relation include findings that poor populations tend to avoid seeking or receiving treatment from mental health specialists, as well as broader sociologic [sic] theories on the effect of marginalization, lack of resources, and powerlessness on [sic] coping with negative life events."[121]

In the eyes of these researchers, there was an overall "coping" problem: poor people don't seek treatment, and their position in society makes them lousy at dealing with "negative life events." As I argued in Chapter 3, there are problems with this way of thinking about the relationship between stress and poverty, and even though we're now talking about *traumatic* stress and poverty, the problems remain the same. We need to look beyond coping, a cognitive and behavioral process, in order to focus on the very inequalities the researchers themselves named—marginalization, lack of resources, powerlessness—in order to understand what the effects of exposure to a "traumatic" event means to people.

There has been broad acceptance in the psychological community of Ronnie Janoff-Bulman's claim that traumatic events universally shatter our assumptions about ourselves and our world, causing us to feel a new sense of vulnerability.[122] This idea, of course, assumes that there is a level playing field such that everyone feels equally *invulnerable* when traumatic events occur. Recall from Chapter 2 how researchers found that what seems on the surface a relatively small loss—a washing machine breakdown, for example—could precipitate a full-blown crisis for women in poverty. This study was based on Stevan Hobfoll's Conservation of Resources (COR) theory, according to which people try very hard to build up what they value, and experience psychological stress when they lose or are threatened with loss of those resources, whether the resources are conditions of life (e.g., financial security), personal characteristics (e.g., optimism), material possessions, or energies (e.g., time, money, knowledge).[123] What Hobfoll and his colleagues found in their research on New York City residents' responses to 9/11 was that what had come before 9/11—previous exposure to other stressful events, a history of abuse, strong or weak social support—had little to do with the development of PTSD symptoms. These were "water under the bridge" compared to the loss of crucial resources that *followed* exposure to the events of 9/11.[124] This signals how problems in coping can result from a loss, rather than causing it.

Gender Differences and PTSD

In Chapter 2, I talked about nineteenth-century physicians' insistence on the differences between men's and women's nervous illnesses. Because hysteria wasn't considered manly, men's hysteria simply couldn't be diagnosed or talked about as much as women's.[125] George Beard even made a distinction between men's "cerebresthenia" and women's "myelasthenia," the former brought on by mental overload, the second by trauma.[126] Women were considered more susceptible to developing symptoms following catastrophic events because of their innate nervous weakness and the sensitivity of their reproductive systems.[127] Gender differences were also found in the causes of traumatization.[128] Early in his career as a psychoanalyst, Freud believed that hysterical symptoms in his (mostly women) patients were caused by repressed memories of early childhood seduction and rape by adults.[129] But later, he theorized (or recanted his "seduction theory" under pressure, depending on one's view)[130] that the "memories" were fantasies based on the women's unconscious desires.

As I discussed in Chapter 4, the seemingly insatiable need to find differences between men and women has not abated, and PTSD research is no exception. There are studies that stretch credulity in their efforts to explain the connection between gender and PTSD. Take this article in the *Archives of Women's Mental Health*, "Trauma and PTSD—An Overlooked Pathogenic Pathway for Premenstrual Dysphoric Disorder [PMDD]?"[131] PMDD, if you haven't already guessed, is what we used to call PMS before Big Pharma and *DSM* got hold of it. The combination of an incredibly low number of study participants (10) combined with a "subthreshold" version of the already suspect PMDD diagnosis (add trauma and stir) makes for the kind of gender difference research that causes even hardy academics to wince.[132] There are more such studies, but I won't go on.[133]

To date, substantive research studies on gender differences in PTSD agree on only a couple of points: that although men encounter and experience more traumatic events than women, women develop PTSD more often than men,[134] and that the type of event to which men and women are more often exposed differs (men more often suffer physical attacks, combat, and serious accidents; women, sexual abuse and rape). There are many theories about why women develop more symptoms even though they are exposed to fewer traumatic stressors: they find it easier to report symptoms; rape and sexual assault are more devastating because they are "man-made"; women's "emotion-focused" coping style leaves them at greater risk than men's "problem-focused" style; hormonal and other biological changes and differences might be at work, and so on.[135]

What Tolin and Foa found in their extensive review of studies on gender differences in trauma and PTSD, though, was that there were enormous differences in the studies' methods, and that the highest prevalence of PTSD in women was found in studies using the expanded 1994 *DSM* criteria, as one might have predicted. In Tolin and Foa's analysis, the hypothesis that women might have more PTSD symptoms because of the particular characteristics of sexual assault wasn't borne out. One explanation that Tolin and Foa put forward for the differences in prevalance of PTSD has to do with differences in the ways men and women express distress. For a long time now, we've known that because of the ways women and men "do" gender[136] in our society (see Chapter 4), women are more likely to have "internalizing" disorders such as depression and anxiety, whereas men are likely to "externalize" distress in the form of violence and excessive drug or alcohol use.[137] Beyond Tolin and Foa's explanation, Hobfoll's Conservation of Resources theory suggests another hypothesis: that because women throughout the world have fewer material resources than men, extremely stressful events may hit them particularly hard and pull them into a vortex of further losses.[138]

No exploration of gender differences would be complete without a discussion of biology, and women's hormonal differences in response to traumatic events have been associated with PTSD in some studies.[139] Of course, associations are not the same as causal connections, but there are other compelling reasons to be wary of jumping on the biological bandwagon when it comes to explanations for the higher rates of PTSD in women. It's not so much that biology is the villain of the piece; it's that we should be wary of allowing biological explanations of the effects of violence against women to preempt our understanding of this violence as rooted in mainstream American society. And the problem of male-to-female violence—violence that often leads to women's physical, psychological, and material suffering—is among the many problems the PTSD diagnosis has not solved. So rather than chasing chimerical gender differences in the rates and causes of PTSD, we'd be far better off working actively toward better enforcement of laws that offer women protection from men's violence and, in the long term, eradicating men's violence toward women altogether. This latter goal requires thinking about how the way masculinity, as practiced in the West, contributes to physical and sexual abuse and assault. Eileen Zurbriggen argues that our society's need to create successful soldiers demands that we socialize boys to become men who are aggressive, tough, powerful, in control, and emotionally constricted—the very same characteristics that can create the capacity for rape.[140]

ENTER—OR REENTER—BIOLOGY; EXIT SOCIAL CONTEXT

The biological bandwagon rolls along, making PTSD connections as it goes. According to Rachel Yehuda, a neuroscientist who has published widely on PTSD since the 1990s, stress responses can begin in the womb. Parents with low cortisol levels beget children with low cortisol levels.[141] Although Yehuda is careful to assert that there is only an *association* between the cortisol levels and PTSD, not everyone is so cautious when it comes to making claims about neurobiology. As one *Newsweek* reporter put it:

> Doctors now *know* that PTSD is the product of subtle biological changes that occur in the brain in response to extreme stress. Using sophisticated imaging techniques, researchers now believe that extreme stress alters the way memory is stored, … [burning] vivid memories that are capable of activating the amygdala, or fear center, in the brain. *People can*

get PTSD, doctors say, when that mechanism works too well. Instead of creating protective memories (ducking at the sound of gunfire), says Dr. Roger Pitman, a psychiatry professor at Harvard Medical School, "the rush of adrenaline creates memories that intrude on everyday life and without treatment, can actually hinder survival" (italics added).

Why some people get PTSD and others don't remains a mystery. Recent studies suggest that a predisposition to the disorder may be genetic and that previous traumatic experiences can make soldiers more vulnerable to it. Once a soldier has it, though, says Dr. Matthew Friedman, executive director of the Department of Veterans Affairs National Center for PTSD, the good news is that the medical community now knows that "PTSD is very real and very treatable."[142]

In the space of a couple of paragraphs, the reporter has signaled that PTSD is a physical disease (people can "get it" as they might catch a cold), that extreme stress alters the brain in specific ways that result in intrusive memories, and that PTSD "may be genetic." All of these factors imply that PTSD is "real" *because* it has been scientifically proven to be a disease, and that it is "treatable" *because* it is "real." The science behind PTSD, however, hasn't been able to spell out the exact relationship between trauma and the brain, regardless of the myriad studies that have attempted to do this.

The idea that PTSD comes about because horrifying events are "encoded into memory" differently from the usual way memories are retained is very widespread.[143] This idea has been put forward and elaborated over a period of many years by Bessel van der Kolk and his colleagues, who base much of their work on animal models. They assert that "imprints of traumatic experiences are initially dissociated, and retrieved as sensory fragments."[144] These "imprints" of "reality," as they call them, are divorced from the meaning the experiences have for the person, as well as the context of those experiences. Ruth Leys holds van der Kolk principally responsible for turning research attention from the mind to the body through his neurobiological explanations of traumatic memory. Although his ideas are often treated as fact, they have not been widely substantiated, and even van der Kolk himself is careful to couch his observations and conclusions in conditional terms.[145]

Van der Kolk has spent a lot of time examining flashbacks, or memories of a traumatic event that burst unbidden into consciousness, and he assumes that flashbacks are essential and timeless symptoms of PTSD. But according to Edgar Jones, flashbacks were rarely observed in the nineteenth century. Jones and his associates, poring over records of UK servicemen from 1854 onward, found almost no reports of flashbacks before World War I and only a handful of cases in World War II.[146] Their results support the contention that PTSD is only one in a long line of ideas about human responses to danger and horror.

Researchers like van der Kolk who study animals under conditions of inescapable stress or shock in their quest to understand the biology of trauma are restricted to studying the fear response, as other responses such as guilt and shame that can follow in the wake of combat or rape can't be measured in nonhumans.[147] Douglas Bremner, who has written extensively on PTSD, depends heavily on animal research to support his theorizing; in fact, his conclusion that high levels of cortisol released during stressful experiences can damage people's brains by producing atrophy in the hippocampus (a part of the brain that helps regulate short- and long-term memory) is based on the work of Robert Sapolsky and others who study primates' responses to stressful conditions.[148] There's more than one problem with Bremner's conclusion: for one thing, it simply doesn't jibe with recent studies showing that people with PTSD have normal or lower than normal cortisol levels.[149] For another, there's also evidence that cortisol is not a direct "marker" for PTSD, and that the hippocampi of people with and without PTSD are the same size.[150] In fact, Mark Gilbertson and his colleagues, studying pairs of twins, only one of whom had seen combat, found that the twins who were war veterans but hadn't developed PTSD had *larger* hippocampi than their brothers who hadn't been in combat.[151] It seems that humans' reactions to traumatic events are more complex than the *DSM* would have us believe.[152] As Nancy Andreason has remarked, in a world that places an inordinate value "on standardization and objectivity, subtlety and complexity are imperiled" at the cost of over-valuing the "biological markers" or "neurobiological substrates" that presumably validate psychiatric diagnoses.[153]

It is very difficult to map psychological states onto biological or neurobiological phenomena. Psychological processes and mental actions can only be inferred; they are not "out there" to be observed. A person moves and behaves in a certain way and shows certain emotions, and we make inferences on the basis of whatever signs and symptoms the person exhibits or reports. William Uttal has argued that after a century's worth of research, even though we know that there are *different* regions of the brain, we still can't reliably connect most higher order cognitive functions to *specific* regions.[154] What we infer may have less to do with brain processes and more to do with researchers' preferences and theories. Uttal believes that we should think hard about what the result would be if we *could* map every psychological process to a particular part of the brain; he doesn't think this would tell us much about how our minds actually work.[155]

Despite the indeterminacy of information on the biology of PTSD and the warnings about the limited applicability of that information, we still read headlines like this one—"Study Links Heart Health and Post-Traumatic Stress"—in the *New York Times*, even when the article that follows reports that "the exact mechanism through which post-traumatic stress might affect heart health is not known."[156] Judith Herman, a pioneer in researching the abuse of women and girls and bringing it to public awareness, issued the following warning about the increasing biologization of trauma and PTSD in an updated afterword to her classic book *Trauma and Recovery*:

> Legitimacy…can be a mixed blessing. The next generation of researchers may lack the passionate intellectual and social commitment that inspired many of the most creative earlier investigations. In this new, more conventional phase of scientific inquiry, there is some cause for concern that integrative concepts and contextual understanding of psychological trauma may be lost, even as more precise and specific knowledge is gained. The very strength of the recent biological findings in PTSD may foster a narrowed, predominantly biological focus of research.[157]

Bremner, who has set out a model of what he calls "trauma-spectrum-disorders" that may have a "common neurological deficit,"[158] has this to say about environmental influence on trauma-induced psychopathology: "Most likely, a *combination* of genetic and environmental, of nature and nurture, is involved in the development of psychopathology. In terms of possible environmental causes of psychopathology, stress is a good candidate."[159] Since stress is not itself part of the environment, it can hardly be considered the "environmental cause" of anything. We've seen how the stress concept has come to stand for psychological responses to events *in* the environment. But in Bremner's equation, where stress stands *for* the environment, psychology seems to beget psychology. The environment, as we've seen, is not just the way we perceive or feel about it. Current trauma theories, however, would have us view the social world as a set of "social factors" that can be measured individually, and would have us view "social support," as Patrick Bracken points out, as just one more set of factors that acts from the outside to protect people from the force of extremely stressful events. Because they rely on universal psychological laws to structure the way trauma can be studied, these theories have not made a place for the part that social or historical forces play in shaping people's responses to horrific events.[160]

WHAT'S NEXT? MORE TRAUMA DISORDERS?

In 2009, after years spent working on a task force to craft a new diagnosis called "Developmental Trauma Disorder" (DTD) that he believed would capture the problems of chronically abused children and adolescents better than the PTSD diagnosis has done, Bessel van der Kolk brought it to the *DSM-5* Trauma, PTSD, and Dissociative Disorders work group for consideration.[161] Van der Kolk branded the work group's rejection of the proposal[162] highly political, railing: "If you say that your disorder...includes elements from several other diagnoses, then you'd have to rearrange your lab, your concepts, your funding...and you also have to confront the fact that if children are terrified and abandoned by caregivers, this will affect their brains, minds and behavior."[163] Regardless of the work group's rejection of this particular proposal of van der Kolk's, it seems almost certain that, if the stirrings of the press and the blogosphere are on point, the soon-to-be-published *DSM-5* will be expanding the universe of human problems considered pathological, further cementing the cultural role of individual diagnosis in a social world.

The creation of trauma as a psychological problem has taken a familiar trajectory from public health risk to diagnosis to intervention.

As the PTSD diagnosis has broadened, so has the perception of which human experiences are traumatically stressful. New posttraumatic diagnoses are being created by fiat even as we speak. How about, for instance, Posttraumatic Embitterment Disorder,[164] a disorder described in publication materials as "characterized not by a particular type of stressful events [sic], but by...experiences of injustice and violation of basic beliefs and by a highly specific psychopathological profile?" According to the book's authors, "PTED is seen more frequently in times of societal changes [sic] which force people to cope with reorganizations [sic] of their lives and prospects." By this account, it won't be long before people hard hit by the recent economic downturn are diagnosed with PTED. Perhaps Congress can dispense medication for PTED, rather than considering ways to improve the economy.

Whereas it is true that some injustices are horrible and horrifying, not all injustice needs to be considered traumatic. Loss can be sad and may result in suffering, but loss is usually not traumatic. Change can bring despair, but it generally doesn't. We call people who don't adjust well to change "disordered," and those who do, "resilient." As the idea of trauma has taken root, we have begun to see potential damage to our health or mental health everywhere. In our therapeutic culture, this situation is unlikely to change any time soon. The grip of the "psy" establishment is firm, as is the grip of Big Pharma. And, as Audre Lorde has so succinctly put it, "the master's tools will never dismantle the master's house."[165]

One of the defining features of PTSD as it is now conceptualized is that symptoms must persist in order for the diagnosis to be made. At the same time, posttraumatic stress is believed to be pathological because symptoms do persist, leaving the impression that it isn't normal for individuals who have been traumatized to continue to suffer. Implicit in the PTSD diagnosis is the idea that we humans should not have to endure suffering; in fact, we need endure nothing; as Kleinman ironically suggests, we can even "work through" our memories.[166] New theories about "posttraumatic growth"[167] are seductive in that they focus on the meaning events have for people; yet the talk of "coping styles," rebuilding, and recovery is fixed in the medical/psychological lexicon. Some people who cope well in their daily lives still can say, as Mr. C. did, "There is no end to it, you know. No way to close it out." But living with existential doubt and a sense that there may be no "closure" seems positively un-American.

Perhaps people don't have to suffer; perhaps we can simply *train* them to be resilient. This is exactly what the U.S. Army proposed to do in 2008 when, in the face of high rates of depression, divorce, PTSD, and suicide in the military, Chief of Staff General George W. Casey, Jr., approached Martin Seligman, prominent research psychologist, past president of the American Psychological Association, and father of the positive psychology movement. In view of his sense that constant rotation between war zones and the home front had brought on "cumulative levels of stress impacting [soldiers'] performance, their readiness, and—in many cases—their personal relationships,"[168] Casey and his advisors at the Pentagon turned to Seligman for help, just as the Army had once turned to Hans Selye, father of the modern stress concept.[169] As Seligman tells it, the Army brass was particularly concerned about a study published in the *British Medical Journal* showing that the 15 percent of personnel who were the least mentally and physically fit made up 58 percent of all PTSD cases. Casey was looking to create "a resilient fighting force in our small, all-volunteer Army that would be capable of meeting the challenge of persistent warfare and repeated redeployments that loom in the Army's future."[170] Seligman took on the job of creating a program for "Comprehensive Soldier Fitness" that includes "resilience training" and positive psychology training[171] aimed at outfitting soldiers with "a well-oiled emotional resilience system in place from the start."[172] Perhaps we feel less guilty about sending soldiers into combat if we equip them with both hand grenades and emotional resilience.

If it seems to you that Seligman jumped into the breach only to help maintain the status quo, you're not alone. The results of the Army's $125 million investment may not be in yet, but criticisms of the "soldier fitness" programs are. Some say that psychology has clearly lost its moral compass.[173] As one psychologist has put it:

> Can we use resilience training and other forms of stress inoculation to immunize our soldiers against the stresses of war? Should we? . . . If we can train our soldiers to experience more death, destruction, and depredation with less distress, is that a positive outcome? The prospect of creating

a psychologically invulnerable soldier sounds...more reminiscent of...
A Clockwork Orange or... [*The*] *Manchurian Candidate*.[174]

We probably can't train people not to suffer and we certainly can't outlaw suffering. People who are diagnosed with PTSD certainly suffer, and professionals who treat them are well intentioned; I don't mean to imply otherwise. But what we need to consider is whether thinking about stress and trauma in the ways we have been doing—medicalizing the aftereffects of horrific experience as we call suffering pathological, and widening the range of the experiences that we consider traumatic—is helping us in the long run. There is no contradiction between the fact of PTSD as a "real" disorder and the fact of PTSD as a production of society. As Ian Hacking conceives it, PTSD is a disorder that is real as people experience it—and as they use it to receive insurance reimbursement for psychotherapy, or financial compensation for injury, a pension, or as part of a legal defense. And yet, at the same time, it is something "made up" at a specific time in history.[175] We have just seen how PTSD was created through a highly political process that could only have occurred in a certain time and place. That place is America, and that time is a period in our history when the uses of stress are everywhere.

CHAPTER 7
Afterword: Vulnerability Reexamined

Although, on the face of it, the building-a-better soldier approach to easing "combat stress" seems qualitatively different from the take-a-soothing-bath-and-relax protocol for reducing working mothers' "work-life conflict" or the therapy-and-medication intervention for lessening the miseries of poverty, this is not so. Each of these solutions is based on the proposition that problems created by social forces can and should be solved through the individual management of stress. The psychologists who are fitting out our troops for resilience in the face of the stresses of combat don't acknowledge the part that class and privilege play in soldiers' ability to *become* resilient. The "emotional fitness" approach papers over inequalities in wealth and opportunity that make our present "all volunteer army" hardly representative of the class-free society that Americans have always prided themselves on, just as psychologizing poverty obscures class inequalities, and the take-a-relaxing-bath approach to working motherhood conceals gender inequities in care work. Whether or not vulnerability to stress is defined as a mental "fitness" problem, or a tendency to become "frazzled," or a dearth of "cognitive-emotional resources," it remains a personal characteristic. But vulnerability is not tied merely to genes or personality or subjective experience; it is also an outgrowth of human ecology, from family, neighborhood, and community to societal institutions, policies, and dominant ideologies.

In the nineteenth century, neurasthenia gave Americans a way to talk about transformations in institutions and the relationships people had with them. It fit with the story of American individualism that is the cornerstone of the American dream of progress as a straight diagonal upward. Now stress gives us a way to talk about unsettling transformations in American life: growing income inequality, tectonic shifts in gender arrangements, war in the age of terrorism. We call the plunge into poverty during recession "financial stress"; we call the sometimes crushing responsibility for equal investment in work and family the stress of "work-family conflict"; we call suicidal reactions to the unnamable horrors of war "posttraumatic stress." George Beard and his fellow physicians prescribed medical treatments and lifestyle transformations for the symptoms of neurasthenia; "psy" professionals in the twenty-first century, with the addition of new medications and new psychological therapies, don't prescribe much differently. Both academic researchers and media commentators offer the consistent message that societal change can be countered through adjustment, both of psyche and lifestyle. "Balance," whether in immune system functioning or in the relationship between work and family, is what we are supposed to be seeking. What seems to be required is an internal gyroscope that will keep us functioning well no matter the tempests we face. Not to be able to adjust, not to be able to achieve balance, means we're not coping well. We may or may not receive a psychiatric diagnosis, but we'll definitely need help.

When the social world is just a set of social factors and the "environment" is just one of many influences, it is easy to marginalize the impact of these on all of us and train our scientific gaze on the changes in brain and behavior that accompany "stress." What is outside comes in, to be explained in terms of individual or group differences in evaluating and responding to the circumstances in which people find themselves. Stress gives us a way to talk with each other about our troubles at the same time as it keeps our travails uniquely our own. The working mother may feel "stressed," but she mustn't let any ball hit the ground when she's juggling, and she mustn't show the strain; the person who lives in poverty must cope with the appalling conditions of a "financially stressful" life out of view of the rest of us. Although we don't all experience the same kind or quality of stress, and we don't all have the same means to deal with it, we share the moral obligation to do so.

DREAM ON: STRESS AND THE AMERICAN DREAM

In the United States, we pride ourselves on our persistent attachment to the idea of equality. Indeed, the American Dream is built on this foundational idea. From a legal standpoint, equality is achieved through equal treatment, and equal treatment means the same treatment for all. But the idea of equality as identical treatment for everyone depends on a sameness of social condition and a sameness of opportunity that simply don't exist.[1] We can keep talking about who is more vulnerable to stress—men or women, resilient soldiers or less "mentally fit" soldiers, poor people with strong "social supports" or poor people with few "social resources." We can worry about our own exposure to risk, disaster, old age, and death. And to the extent that the stress concept supports a preoccupation with these questions and concerns, and as long as the middle class continues to be seduced into believing that we just need to pull ourselves and others up to the level of the least stressed or vulnerable among us through exhortation or public health campaigns or medication and psychotherapy, it is unlikely that we will take on the work of reducing inequalities in our society. Risk and the fear it engenders have played a large part in the middle-class embrace of the stress concept, and stressism[2] fosters the illusion that, in the push toward improved adjustment, human vulnerability must be battled one person at a time. But there's another way to think about vulnerability.

As legal scholar Martha Albertson Fineman suggests, the term *vulnerability*, stripped of its negative connotations, has the potential to describe "a universal, inevitable, enduring aspect of the human condition that must be at the heart of social and state responsibility."[3] This is not a vulnerability that implies weakness. The only thing it implies, as Harry Stack Sullivan[4] famously said, is that "we are all much more simply human than otherwise." But to accept this revised notion of universal vulnerability means, paradoxically, living with both less fear and more: less, in the sense that recognizing universal vulnerability can lead to creating greater safety for everyone in a society; and more, because embracing this way of thinking about vulnerability means accepting that there are risks, uncertainties, and dangers in life that can't be vanquished through reengineering ourselves, no matter how disciplined, persistent, or courageous we are.

Lately the media have carried prominent stories about the rising income gap between White households and Hispanic and black households.[5] The Occupy Wall Street Movement (a predominantly white movement so far) has attracted attention to the vast inequality in wealth between the 1 percent of the wealthiest Americans and the other "99 percent." There has been news about how, although the recession initially hit men harder than women, women are losing more jobs in the current recovery than men and are in increasing economic peril.[6] It seems that Americans are taking a harder look at social conditions in our country than we have in a long time. But it's too soon to know whether the era in which we are living, this latest incarnation of the most stressful times ever, will induce us as a society to take greater responsibility for dealing with the tensions of the twenty-first century, or whether it will yield yet more individual prescriptions for grappling with our all-American stress.

NOTES

CHAPTER 1

1. Publications include articles, books, book chapters, and essays. In 2010 alone there were 2,604. These figures resulted from a PsychInfo search of journal articles, book chapters, and dissertations in psychology and related disciplines (e.g., sociology, education, medicine, law, physiology, psychiatry, and anthropology).

2. Becky Barrow, "Stress 'Is Top Cause of Workplace Sickness' and Is So Widespread It's Dubbed the 'Black Death of the 21st Century,'" *MailOnline*, October 5, 2011. http://www.dailymail.co.uk/health/article-2045309/Str ess-Top-cause-workplace-sickness-dubbed-Black-Death-21st-century.html (accessed October 3, 2011).

3. Robert Kugelmann, *Stress: The Nature and History of Engineered Grief* (Westport, CT: Praeger, 1992), 15.

4. Ibid., 15–16.

5. In the seventeenth century, Robert Hook created the engineering concepts of "load," "stress" and "strain." See Richard S. Lazarus, "From Psychological Stress to the Emotions: A History of Changing Outlooks," *Annual Review of Psychology* 44 (1993): 1–21, esp. 2. See also Serge Doublet, *The Stress Myth* (Chesterfield, MO: Science & Humanities Press, 1999–2000).

6. http://oxforddictionaries.com/definition/stress.

7. Steven Lukes, *Individualism* (New York: Harper & Row, 1973), esp. 26.

8. Charles Taylor lays out in detail the progression of historical thought that has led to modern notions of the self. See Charles Taylor, *Sources of the Self: The Making of the Modern Identity* (Cambridge, MA: Harvard University Press, 1989).

9. Nikolas Rose, *Governing the Soul: The Shaping of the Private Self* (London: Routledge, 1990), 218.

10. Ibid., 228.

11. Ian Hacking, "Making Up People," in *Reconstructing Individualism: Autonomy, Individuality, and the Self in Western Thought*, eds. Thomas C. Heller, Morton Sosna, and David E. Wellbery (Stanford: Stanford University Press, 1986), 222–252.

12. These ideas are part of Hacking's historical ontology. See Ian Hacking, *Historical Ontology* (Cambridge, MA: Harvard University Press, 2002); see

also Jeff Sugarman, "Historical Ontology and Psychological Description," *Journal of Theoretical and Philosophical Psychology* 29, no. 1 (2009): 5–15.

13. Luther H. Martin, Huck Gutman, and Patrick H. Hutton, eds., *Technologies of the Self: A Seminar with Michel Foucault* (Amherst: University of Massachusetts Press, 1988).

14. Reid Kanaley, "Smartphone Apps Help Manage Your Stress," *The Philadelphia Inquirer*, October 20, 2011, A26–27 (Business).

15. This is how Nikolas Rose refers to psychiatry, psychology, social work, counseling, and other "psychological" professions.

16. Arthur Kleinman and Erin Fitz-Henry, "The Experiential Basis of Subjectivity: How Individuals Change in the Context of Societal Transformation," in *Subjectivity: Ethnographic Investigations*, eds. Joao Biehl, Byron Good, and Arthur Kleinman (Berkeley: University of California Press, 2007), 52–65.

17. See Charles Rosenberg, *No Other Gods: On Science and American Social Thought* (Baltimore: Johns Hopkins University Press, [1976]1997).

18. Nikolas Rose, *The Politics of Life Itself: Biomedicine, Power, and Subjectivity in the Twenty-First Century* (Princeton: Princeton University Press, 2007).

19. PBS National Geographic Special, *Stress: Portrait of a Killer*, September 23, 2008.

20. Susan Sontag, *Illness as Metaphor* (New York: Doubleday, 1977), esp. 72.

21. "How to Handle Stress: 'Learn to Enjoy It," Time, November 29, 1963. http://www.time.com/time/magazine/article/0,9171,875385,00.html. (accessed January 10, 2009).

22. Mary Carmichael, "Who Says Stress Is Bad For You?" *Newsweek*, February 23, 2009. http://www.thedailybeast.com/newsweek/2009/02/13/who-says-stress-is-bad-for-you.html (accessed May 18, 2010).

23. Jane Weaver, "Can Stress Actually Be Good For You?" MSNBC.com, December 20, 2006.http://www.msnbc.msn.com/id/15818153/ns/health-mental_health/t/can-stress-actually-be-good-you/#.TqGezHJrMTA (accessed May 31, 2008).

24. National Geographic Special, *Stress: Portrait of a Killer*.

25. Dr. Mehmet Oz, "Sex on the Brain," *AARP Magazine* (September/October, 2011): 28.

26. Steven D. Brown, "Stress as Regimen: Critical Readings of Self-Help Literature," in *Applied Discourse Analysis: Social and Psychological Interventions* (Philadelphia: Open University Press, 1999), ed. Carla Willig, 22–43, esp. 35.

27. Eliza McCarthy, "Kids and Stress," *Elle* (January 2005), 89.

28. Another example is the pairing, in bold font, of cancer and stress, along with the warning that "the evidence linking stress to cancer is limited." For this example, see Dr. Ranit Mishori, "Can Stress Make You Sick?" *Parade*, October 25, 2009, 20.

29. Elissa S. Epel et al., "Accelerated Telomere Shortening in Response to Life Stress," *Proceedings of the National Academy of Sciences* 101, no. 49 (2004): 17312–17315.

30. As it turns out, mothers of chronically ill children were compared with women who were mothers of healthy children.

31. Camille Sweeney, "When Stress Takes a Toll on the Teeth," *New York Times*, October 8, 2009, E1, E3 (Thursday Styles).

32. Benedict Carey, "Stress and Distress May Give Your Genes Gray Hair," *New York Times*, November 30, 2004, F5.

33. "Fountain of Youth? Try Washing Your Face," *New York Times*, December 27, 2007, G–3 (Styles).

34. Julie Wheldon, "Stress May Be Causing Infertility in Women," *Daily Mail*, June 21, 2006. http://www.dailymail.co.uk/health/article-391616/Stress-causing-infertility-women.html.This article describes Sarah Berga's research on fertility risks to women who have stressful jobs.

35. Laura Spinney, "Born Scared," *New Scientist*, November 27, 2010. http://www.lexisnexis.com/.

36. "I Am Just a Poor Boy Though My Story's Seldom Told," *The Economist*, April 2, 2009. http://www.economist.com/node/13403177. This is a report on Martha Farah's research on the effects of the stress of poverty on children's working memories. The subtitle of the article is "How poverty passes from generation to generation is now becoming clearer. The answer lies in the effect of stress on two particular parts of the brain."

37. Jodie Mailander Farrell, "Generation Stress: Blackberry-Toting Toddlers. Sleep-Deprived Teens. Are Our Overbooked Lives Killing Our Kids?" *Miami Herald*, October 15, 2006. http://www.lexisnexis.com/.

38. Sian Beilock, "Back to School: Dealing with Academic Stress," *Psychological Science Agenda*, September 2011. http://www.apa.org/science/about/psa/2011/09/academic-stress.aspx.

39. Pam Belluck, "With Mayhem at Home, They Call a Parent Coach," *New York Times*, March 13, 2005, A1, A33.

40. Sara Rimer, "Less Homework, More Yoga, From a Principal Who Hates Stress," *New York Times*, October 29, 2007, A1, A16.

41. This was the conclusion reached by the American College Health Association. See Mary Duenwald, "Students Find Another Staple of Campus Life: Stress," *New York Times*, September 17, 2002, F5 (Health & Fitness).

42. Joann Klimkiewicz, "The Angst of the 20s," *Philadelphia Inquirer*, July 24, 2001. http://articles.philly.com/2001–07–24/news/25315008_1_associate-degrees-abby-wilner-quarterlife-crisis. See also Rick Marin, "Is This the Face of a Midlife Crisis?" *New York Times*, June 24, 2001, 9–1, 9–2 (Sunday Styles).

43. See *Monitor on Psychology* 39, no. 2 (February, 2008): 9; Sadie F. Dingfelder, "An Uncertain Future for America's Work Force," *Monitor on Psychology* 42, no. 8 (September, 2011): 42–46.

44. Frank Furedi, *Therapy Culture: Cultivating Vulnerability in an Uncertain Age* (New York: Routledge, 2004) esp. 5. There were also massive increases in the use of the words *self-esteem, trauma, syndrome,* and *counseling.*

45. Gregg Easterbrook, "The Nation: Wages of Wealth; All This Progress Is Killing Us, Bite by Bite," *New York Times*, March 14, 2004. http://www.nytimes.com/2004/03/14/weekinreview/the-nation-wages-of-wealth-all-this-progress-is-killing-us-bite-by-bite.html?pagewanted=all&src=pm (accessed September 26, 2011); Tori DeAngelis, "America: A Toxic Lifestyle?" *Monitor on Psychology* 38, no. 4 (April, 2007): 50, 51.

46. Roger Walsh, "Lifestyle and Mental Health," *American Psychologist* 66, no. 7 (2011): 579–592.

47. "Calling Dr. Feel-Good: How to Keep Financial Stress from Harming Your Health," was the cover headline of the *AARP Magazine*, January/February 2009.

48. For more on "lifestyle" as a middle-class development, see Robert N. Bellah et al., *Habits of the Heart: Individualism and Commitment in American Life* (Berkeley: University of California Press, [1985]1996).

49. Brown, 24.

50. Betsey Stevenson and Justin Wolfers, "The Paradox of Declining Female Happiness," *American Economic Journal: Economic Policy* 1, no. 2 (2009): 190–225.

51. Ross Douthat, "Liberated and Unhappy," *New York Times*, May 25, 2009 (Op-Ed). http://www.nytimes.com/2009/05/26/opinion/26douthat.html.

52. Barbara Ehrenreich, "Are Women Getting Unhappier? Don't Make Me Laugh," *Los Angeles Times*, October 14, 2009. http://articles.latimes.com/2009/oct/14/opinion/oe-ehrenreich14.

53. Anna North, "'Declining Female Happiness' May Be Just Another Way to Sell Shit," October 14, 2009. http://jezebel.com/5381638/declining-female-happiness-may-be-just-another-way-to-sell-shit (accessed August 20, 2011).

54. Rachael Combe, "No Way Out?" *Elle* (December 2009), 296, 300.

55. "Fat & Stress," *Time*, January 28, 1957. http://www.time.com/time/magazine/article/0,9171,808997,00.html.

56. Zak Stambor, "Stressed Out Nation," *Monitor on Psychology* 37, no. 4 (April 2006): 28.

57. Sara Reistad-Long, "Diagnose and Manage Your Stress Type," AOL Living (Health). http://www.aolhealth.com/healthy-living/longevity/stress-type?feed=1 (accessed February 11, 2010). See also "Size Up Your Stress Style," *Self* (May 2010), 171.

58. Reistad-Long. In this piece, "fatigue, lack of energy, nervousness and sleeplessness" are attributed to "comfort" eating to reduce stress.

59. "10 Ways to Lost 5 Pounds," *InStyle Magazine* (September 2008), 325. See also "Eat-Right Flash," *Self* (September 2006), 144.

60. "Quick Stress Relievers," *Cooking Light* (November 2010), 80.

61. "The State of the American Woman," *Time*, October 14, 2009. http://www.time.com/time/specials/packages/article/0,28804,1930277_1930145_1930309,00/html.

62. See Rebecca M. Jordan-Young, *Brainstorm: The Flaws in the Science of Sex Differences* (Cambridge, MA: Harvard University Press, 2011).

63. Stacey Burling, "Seasonal Highs and Lows," *Philadelphia Inquirer*, December 13, 2004, C1, C5 (Health & Science).

64. Mary Poovey, *Uneven Developments: The Ideological Work of Gender in Mid-Victorian England* (Chicago: University of Chicago Press, 1988).

65. See Hacking, *Historical Ontology*.

66. See Caryl L. Cooper and Philip Dewe, *Stress: A Brief History* (Oxford: Blackwell, 2004); Fiona Jones and Jim Bright, *Stress: Myth, Theory, and*

Research (Harlow, UK: Pearson Education, 2001); see also Doublet, *The Stress Myth*.

67. Beyond histories, there are certainly books that illuminate various facets of the stress concept and the way we have come to think about and use it, among them Angela Patmore's *The Truth about Stress* (London: Atlantic Books, 2009), which focuses primarily on problems in social and therapeutic attempts to solve the stress "problem"; Allan Young's *Harmony of Illusions: Inventing Post-Traumatic Stress Disorder* (Ewing, NJ: Princeton University Press, 1995), focusing on PTSD; Robert Kugelmann's *Stress: The Nature and History of Engineered Grief;* a chapter in Andrew Abbott's *Chaos of Disciplines* (Chicago: University of Chicago Press, 2001); Steven D. Brown's article, "Stress as Regimen: Critical Readings of Self-Help Literature," in *Applied Discourse Analysis: Social and Psychological Interventions;* and a chapter in Robert A. Aronowitz's *Making Sense of Illness: Science, Society, and Disease* (Cambridge: Cambridge University Press, 1998). None of these, however, is a full-length work that solely focuses on the social uses of the stress concept in the United States.

CHAPTER 2

1. I am indebted to the work of Charles Rosenberg for this "progress-and-pathology" framework and the phrase itself. See Charles E. Rosenberg, *Our Present Complaint: American Medicine, Then and Now* (Baltimore, MD: Johns Hopkins University Press, 2007), 90–91. See also Chapter 5.

2. See Andrew Abbott, *Chaos of Disciplines* (Chicago: University of Chicago Press, 2001), 41–43, for cogent arguments about the duality of stress and the "damage" and "adjustment" themes.

3. Abbott views the concept of stress as representing a "syncresis" (from the Greek), combining what are normally opposites—in this case, damage and maladjustment.

4. Ibid.

5. Roy F. Baumeister, *Meanings of Life* (New York: Guilford, 1991), 78; Robert N. Bellah, Richard Madsen, William M. Sullivan, Ann Swidler, and Steven M. Tipton, *Habits of the Heart: Individualism and Commitment in American Life* (Berkeley: University of California Press, [1985]1996).

6. See discussion of Mary Poovey's concept of "ideological work" in Chapter 1. *Uneven Developments: The Ideological Work of Gender in Mid-Victorian England* (Chicago: University of Chicago Press, 1988).

7. Abbott, 52.

8. Daniel J. Boorstein, *The Lost World of Thomas Jefferson* (Chicago: University of Chicago Press, 1993).

9. Ibid., 181; George Rosen, "Benjamin Rush on Health and the American Revolution," *American Journal of Public Health* 66 (1976): 387–398.

10. *Traitement morale*, so-named by Philippe Pinel, the French physician sometimes called the father of psychiatry (1745–1846), was based on the idea that under the guidance of experts, the mentally ill could learn self-control without the use of force.

11. Gerald N. Grob, *Mental Institutions in America: Social Policy to 1875* (New York: Free Press, 1973), 156.

12. Silas Weir Mitchell, *Wear and Tear, or Hints for the Overworked* (Philadelphia: J. B. Lippincott & Sons, 1871), 6.

13. Charles E. Rosenberg, *No Other Gods: On Science and American Social Thought* (Baltimore, MD: Johns Hopkins University Press, 1976/1997).

14. For a detailed discussion of the rise of the experts, see Barbara Ehrenreich and Deirdre English, *For Her Own Good: Two Centuries of the Experts' Advice to Women* (New York: Anchor Books, 1978), Chapter 3: "The Ascent of the Experts."

15. Beard was not the first to discuss the condition or to use the term, but beginning in 1869 his elucidation of the "condition," which indeed was a vast constellation of symptoms, did a great deal to make neurasthenia a widely discussed and diagnosed illness. Not all physicians or intellectuals accepted neurasthenia as an actual disease, however, as Rosenberg (2007) has noted.

16. George M. Beard, *American Nervousness: Its Causes and Consequences: A Supplement to Nervous Exhaustion* (New York: Arno Press, [1881]1972), 7–8.

17. Cynthia E. Russett, *Sexual Science: The Victorian Construction of Womanhood* (Cambridge, MA: Harvard University Press, 1989), 113.

18. See Russett, 107–112, for discussion about how Hermann von Helmholtz's mechanistic principles of conservation were transmuted into mechanistic notions of the body's "nerve force."

19. Beard, *American Nervousness*, 99.

20. From Beard's *Sexual Neurasthenia* (1884), cited in Russett, 115–116.

21. For a thorough discussion of the British debate over and experience of neurasthenia, see Janet Oppenheim, *"Shattered Nerves": Doctors, Patients, and Depression in Victorian England* (New York: Oxford University Press, 1991).

22. Beard, *American Nervousness*, vi.

23. Charles E. Rosenberg, "The Place of George M. Beard in Nineteenth-Century Psychiatry," *Bulletin of the History of Medicine* 36 (1961): 245–259, 256.

24. Beard, *American Nervousness*, ix.

25. F. G. Gosling, *Before Freud: Neurasthenia and the American Medical Community, 1870–1910* (Urbana: University of Illinois Press, 1987), 15.

26. Beard, *American Nervousness* (1881), 122.

27. Rosenberg, 1961.

28. Tom Lutz, *American Nervousness, 1903: An Anecdotal History* (Ithaca, NY: Cornell University Press, 1991).

29. David G. Schuster, *Neurasthenic Nation: America's Search for Health, Happiness, and Comfort, 1869–1920* (New Brunswick, NJ: Rutgers University Press, 2011).

30. And so it remained until the turn of the century, when the diagnosis became so widespread that it was applied increasingly to the poor. See Gosling, 161.

31. Eric Caplan, *Mind Games: American Culture and the Birth of Psychotherapy* (Berkeley: University of California Press, 1998), 38–39; Ann Douglas Wood, "'The Fashionable Diseases': Women's Complaints and Their Treatment in

Nineteenth-Century America," *Journal of Interdisciplinary History* IV, no. 1 (1973): 25–52.

32. Russett, 116; Elaine Showalter, "Hysteria, Feminism, and Gender," in *Hysteria beyond Freud*, eds. Sander L. Gilman, Helen King, Roy Porter, G. S. Rousseau, and Elaine Showalter (Berkeley: University of California Press, 1993), 293. Janet Oppenheim has pointed out, however, that economic metaphors were not "perfectly tailored to a capitalist system.... In some respects...they harked back to an older notion of wealth...as an inherited resource to be guarded rather than risked." *Shattered Nerves*, 85–86.

33. Mitchell, *Wear and Tear*, 5, 7.

34. Gosling, 85.

35. By the mid-1840s about half of all factory workes were women; by 1910, one out of five workers in the nonagricultural labor force were women. See Alice Kessler-Harris, *Gendering Labor History* (Chicago: University of Illinois Press, 2007), 101, 107. See also Karen Manners Smith, "New Paths to Power," in *No Small Courage: A History of Women in the United States*, ed. Nancy F. Cott (New York: Oxford University Press, 2000), 353–412.

36. Russett, 118–119. Herbert Spencer, in his well-known evolutionary theory of mental development, argued that puberty in girls, coming earlier than that of boys, robbed them of the final steps in nervous system development.

37. Gosling, xi.

38. Christopher Lasch, *Haven in a Heartless World: The Family Besieged* (New York: Basic Books, 1977).

39. Oppenheim speculates that "when middle-class Victorians thought about woman in the abstract, they may have chosen to emphasize her delicacy and dependence, but when they thought about her actually married and raising a family, they stressed very different qualities." *Shattered Nerves*, 207.

40. Bourdieu calls this a "space of transformation." See Pierre Bourdieu, *Distinction: A Social Critique of the Judgement of Taste* (Cambridge, MA: Harvard University Press, 1984).

41. Christopher Lasch, *The Culture of Narcissism* (New York: Norton, 1979), 56.

42. Barbara Sicherman, "The Uses of a Diagnosis: Doctors, Patients, and Neurasthenia," *Journal of the History of Medicine* (1977): 33–54, 42.

43. George M. Beard, *Nervous Exhaustion (Neurasthenia): Its Symptoms, Nature, Sequences, Treatment* (New York: E. B. Treat, 1888), 163.

44. Oppenheim, 157.

45. Ibid., 141, 150–151.

46. Gosling, 59

47. Beard, *Nervous Exhaustion*, 137. Havelock Ellis, cited in Russett, 119, stated that there were 14 neurasthenic women for every neurasthenic man, a figure even *he* admitted might be an overestimate.

48. See Sicherman.

49. Beard, *Nervous Exhaustion*, 138. See also Carroll Smith-Rosenberg and Charles Rosenberg, "The Hysterical Woman: Sex Roles in Nineteenth Century America," *Social Research* 39 (1973): 652–678; Showalter, *The Female Malady* (New York: Pantheon, 1985), 133. Smith-Rosenberg and

Rosenberg have viewed hysteria as a social role option for some middle-class women crushed by the pressure to take on two conflicting roles, that of the delicate, emotional "True Woman" and that of the strong, competent "Ideal Mother." For some women, the sick role provided respite from the stress (e.g., the agonies of childbirth, the isolation of domestic life, and the care of household and children) for which their indulged girlhoods and languid courtships had ill-prepared them. Physicians noted that women who felt most overwhelmed were most prone to develop nervous illness.

50. Cited in Sicherman, 41, from Silas Weir Mitchell's (1875) *Rest in Nervous Disease: Its Use and Abuse.*

51. See Oppenheim, Chapter 6.

52. See Wood, 31; Showalter, 297–300.

53. Wood.

54. Gosling, 59.

55. Ibid., 55. A minority attributed women's "nerves" to the monotony of domestic work and believed that breaking free of the hearth was the cure. John K. Mitchell, author of *Self Help for Nervous Women* (1909), held this belief. New Thought writers Elizabeth Towne and Helen Wilmans admitted a strong dislike for housework. See Gail Parker, *Mind Cure in New England: From the Civil War to World War I* (Hanover, NH: University Press of New England, 1973), 83.

56. Cited in Gosling, 56–57. Margaret A. Cleaves, "Neurasthenia and Its Relation to Diseases of Women," *Transactions of the Iowa State Medical Association*, 7 (1886): 165–166.

57. Silas Weir Mitchell, *Fat and Blood: And How to Make Them* (Philadelphia: J. B. Lippincott, 1887), 1.

58. Wood, 36–37. Even so, a certain number remained permanent invalids, an outcome that would hardly have been tolerated in men. Alice James, sister of two illustrious brothers, William and Henry, has become a famous example of female invalidism. Many believe that if Alice, by all accounts a bright, charming woman, had had the educational advantages of her brothers and their freedom to move in the world, she would have remained on her feet. See Jean Strouse, *Alice James: A Biography* (New York: Bantam Books, 1980).

59. Ehrenreich and English, 154.

60. John C. Burnham, *Paths into American Culture: Psychology, Medicine, and Morals* (Philadelphia: Temple University Press, 1988), 203. In 1908, Clifford Beers, an upper-class former insane asylum inhabitant, brought influential forces together with the aim of reforming the treatment of the mentally ill, and his efforts spawned the Mental Hygiene Movement.

61. Barbara A. Dreyer, "Adolf Meyer and Mental Hygiene: An Ideal for Public Health," *American Journal of Public Health* 66, no. 10 (1976): 998–1003, esp. 1000. Adolf Meyer, who had originally suggested the mental hygiene approach to Beers, was very familiar with Jane Addams's work with the poor and rejected many of Freud's ideas in favor of the new "social conscience."

62. For this discussion of Meyers and a history of the Mental Hygiene Movement through the 1940s, see Hans Pols, "'Beyond the Clinical Frontiers': The American Mental Hygiene Movement, 1910–1945," in *International Relations in Psychiatry: Britain, Germany, and the United States to World War II*, eds. Volker Roelcke, Paul J. Weindling, and Louise Westwood (Rochester, NY: University of Rochester Press, 2010), 111–133.

63. Ibid., 115.

64. John H. Ehrenreich, *The Altruistic Imagination: A History of Social Work and Social Policy in the United States* (Ithaca, NY: Cornell University Press, 1985), 42.

65. Fred Matthews, "Defense of Common Sense: Mental Hygiene as Ideology and Mentality in Twentieth-Century America," *Prospects*, no. 4 (1979): 459–516, esp. 481.

66. Ibid., 476.

67. Burnham, 204.

68. See Dreyer; see also J. Ehrenreich, 42.

69. J. Ehrenreich, 34–35.

70. Matthews, 476.

71. J. Ehrenreich, 67.

72. Ibid., 68.

73. Charlotte Perkins Gilman, *The Home: Its Work and Influence* (New York: McClure, Phillips & Co., 1903), 37.

74. Nancy F. Cott, *The Grounding of Modern Feminism* (New Haven, CT: Yale University Press, 1987), esp. 167.

75. Ibid., 39–40.

76. Joel Kovel, "The American Mental Health Industry," in *Critical Psychiatry: The Politics of Mental Health*, ed. David Ingleby (New York: Pantheon, 1980), 72–101, esp. 80.

77. L. E. Hinkle, "Stress and Disease: The Concept After 50 Years," *Social Science and Medicine* 25 (1987): 561–566. Psychosomatic medicine, as a field, was spurred on by Adolf Meyer's 1920s work in psychobiology.

78. Bernard famously said, "La fixité du milieu intérieur est la condition d'une vie libre et indépendente" (the constancy of the internal environment is the condition of a free and independent life). In Claude Bernard, *Lectures on the Phenomena Common to Animals and Plants,* trans. H. E. Hoff, R. Guillemin, L. Guillemin (Springfield, IL: Charles C. Thomas, 1974).

79. Cannon called it "adrenin."

80. Walter Cannon, *The Wisdom of the Body* (New York: W. W. Norton & Co., 1932), esp. 227.

81. Ibid., 230.

82. Caryl L. Cooper and Philip Dewe, *Stress: A Brief History* (Oxford: Blackwell, 2004), esp. 17. Because he defined stress in physiological terms, questions have been raised as to whether Cannon can justifiably be called the "founding father" of stress.

83. Doublet has argued that without the idea of homeostasis there would be no stress concept at all. See 71.

84. This idea of "Stone Agers in the fast lane," as Rosenberg has called it, has limitations. As Tim Newton has asked: If our biology had evolved enough, would we have no problems dealing with life in our time? Perhaps there is something wrong with the assumption that stress lies in our primitive instincts rather than in the complications of modern existence. See Tim Newton, *"Managing" Stress: Emotion and Power at Work* (London: Sage, 1995), 22.

85. They responded with ulceration both of the intestines and the adrenal cortex and atrophy of the thymus gland.

86. Russell Viner, "Putting Stress in Life: Hans Selye and the Making of Stress Theory," *Social Studies of Science* 29, no. 3 (1999): 391–410, esp. 393.

87. John W. Mason, "A Historical View of the Stress Field" (Part I), *Journal of Human Stress* (March, 1975): 6–12, esp. 9.

88. Hans Selye, *The Stress of Life* (New York: McGraw-Hill, 1956). On p. 41 Selye also calls it "the state which manifests itself by the G.A.S."

89. Ibid., 41

90. See Serge Doublet, *The Stress Myth* (Chesterfield, MO: Science & Humanities Press, 1999–2000), 76.

91. Cited in Mason, 7.

92. Cited in Newton, 41.

93. See Harrington, 152–155, for a fuller discussion of military involvement; see also Viner, 399–400.

94. Selye cited in Viner, 399.

95. Harringon, 153.

96. Selye, *The Stress of Life*, 276.

97. "The secret of success is not to avoid stress and thereby endure an uneventful, boring life, for then our wealth would do us no good, but to learn to use our capital wisely, to get maximal satisfaction at the lowest price." Hans Selye, *Stress Without Distress* (Philadelphia: J. B. Lippincott, 1974), 129.

98. Ibid., 281.

99. Ibid., 299.

100. Ibid., 299–300.

101. Newton, 26–27.

102. Viner, 400–401.

103. Selye, *The Stress of Life*, 12.

104. Selye, *Stress Without Distress*, 89.

105. Selye, *The Stress of Life*, vii.

106. Selye, *Stress Without Distress*.

107. Hans Selye, "History of the Stress Concept," in *Handbook of Stress* (2nd ed.), eds. Leo Goldberger and Shlomo Breznitz (New York: Free Press, 1993), 7–17, esp. 17.

108. Cannon, *The Wisdom of the Body*, 319; 320–321.

109. Selye, *Stress Without Distress*, 129.

110. "Dr. Selye Has Remedy for Stressful Life," *Montreal Gazette*, October 13, 1977. http://news.google.com/newspapers?nid=1946&dat=19771013&i

d=XE8xAAAAIBAJ&sjid=1aEFAAAAIBAJ&pg=5973,3244772 (accessed September 25, 2011).

111. "Medicine: Life & Stress, *Time*, December 3, 1956, 50. http://www.time.com/time/magazine/article/0,9171,808661.html.

112. Thomas H. Holmes and Richard H. Rahe, "The Social Readjustment Rating Scale," *Journal of Psychosomatic Research* 11, no. 2 (1967): 213–218.

113. A score over 200 indicated a strong risk and a score over 300 indicated critical risk for specific diseases.

114. Viner, 396. See also Viner, 404, for a summary of what later critics had to say about Selye's work.

115. Ibid., 402.

116. Ibid., 404.

117. Selye, *Stress Without Distress*, 91.

118. Viner, 405–406.

119. Lasch, *The Culture of Narcissism*, 54–57, 63

120. Harrington, 159.

121. Ibid., 160.

122. Osler was, among English speakers, the best-known physician of his day.

123. Elianne Riska, "The Rise and Fall of Type A Man," *Social Science & Medicine* 51 (2000): 1665–1674, esp. 1666.

124. *Time*, January 24, 1944, p. 48. http://www.time.com/time/magazine/article/0,9171, 803087,00.html.

125. Riska, 1667.

126. Meyer Friedman and Ray H. Rosenman, *Type A Behavior and Your Heart* (New York: Knopf, 1974), 54–55.

127. As Riska points out (p. 1667), when a grant proposal to study this behavior pattern had been turned down twice by the National Institutes of Health (NIH), an NIH representative suggested that they call the pattern "Type A" in order to strip it of any connection with psychology or psychiatry.

128. Ibid., 1667. In M. Friedman and R. H. Rosenman, "Association of Specific Overt Behavior Pattern with Blood and Cardiovascular Findings," *Journal of the American Medical Association*, 169 (1959): 1286–1295, esp. 1286.

129. Cited in Riska. R. H. Rosenman and M. Friedman, "The Central Nervous System and Coronary Heart Disease, *Hospital Practice* (October, 1971): 87–97, esp. 90.

130. Cited in Riska. Ray H. Rosenman, "The Interview Method of Assessment of Coronary-Prone Behavior Pattern," in *Coronary-Prone Behavior*, eds. T. M. Dembroski, S. M. Weiss, J. L. Shields, S. G. Hayes, and M. Feinleib (New York: Springer, 1978), 55–69, esp. 62.

131. Friedman and Rosenman, *Type A Behavior and Your Heart*, 75, 78.

132. Silas Weir Mitchell, *Wear and Tear*, 6.

133. Riska, 1670. See also Barbara Ehrenreich, *The Hearts of Men: American Dreams and the Flight from Commitment* (Garden City, NY: Anchor/Doubleday, 1983).

134. "The Cost of Getting Ahead," *Time*, May 16, 1960. http://www.time.com/time/magazine/article/0,9171,836957.00.html.

135. Rosenman and Friedman, 1974, 164.

136. Ibid., 62.

137. *New York Times,* July 21, 1958.

138. Fred Kerner, *Stress and Your Heart* (New York: Hawthorn Books, 1961), 76–77.

139. B. Ehrenreich, *The Hearts of Men,* 69–70.

140. Ibid., 69.

141. Suzanne B. Haynes and Manning Feinleib, "Women, Work and Coronary Heart Disease: Prospective Findings from the Framingham Heart Study," *American Journal of Public Health* 70, no. 2 (1980): 133–141.

142. Ibid., 133. The psychosocial questionnaire devised by the researchers was administered to men as well as women. 580 men, 350 housewives, and 387 working women participated. All had been free of CHD when they entered the study 8–9 years earlier.

143. Ibid., 138. The researchers were not actually surprised by this outcome, as it jibed with the results of three other surveys that had been conducted between 1960 to 1978.

144. Ibid., 140. Among the most salient of those cited were economic pressures, self-selection of certain personalities for clerical work, and the specific work context itself.

145. Glorian Sorensen, David R. Jacobs Jr., Phyllis Pirie, Arron Folson, Russell Luepker, and Richard Gillum, "Relationships Among Type A Behavior, Employment Experiences, and Gender: The Minnesota Heart Survey," *Journal of Behavioral Medicine,* 10 (1987): 323–336, esp. 334.

146. Jane Brody, "Study Suggests Changing Behavior May Prevent Heart Attack," *New York Times,* September, 16, 1980, C–1.

147. Ibid.

148. Just as in Mitchell's day, the lower classes were presumed to have a reduced incidence of stress-related illness (in this case CHD), a conclusion based more on class biases and class differences in access to healthcare than on anything else. See Robert A. Aronowitz, *Making Sense of Illness: Science, Society, and Disease* (Cambridge: Cambridge University Press, 1998), 164.

149. Riska, 1670. During the 1950s and early 1960s, the psychologists had much more clout in the medical schools and with the physicians than did the sociologists.

150. B. Ehrenreich, *The Hearts of Men,* 74.

151. I am indebted to Riska's analysis for the discussion that follows about the influence of psychology at this critical juncture; see 1670–1671.

152. Aronowitz, 161.

153. Jane Brody, "Heart Attacks and Behavior: Early Signs Are Found," *New York Times,* February 14, 1984, C1. In this Valentine's Day piece, research is cited that shows that Type A children may elicit a kind of pushy parenting from mothers that could cause individuals to be vulnerable to coronary heart disease as adults.

154. Aronowitz, 150.

155. See Michael Specter, "'Type A' Men More Likely Than 'Type B' to Survive Heart Disease," Study Says," *Washington Post*, A13; Jane Brody, "'Type A' Men Fair Better in Heart Attack Study," *New York Times*, January 14, 1988, B7.

156. "10 Ways to Improve Your Memory," *InStyle*, November, 2008, 231.

157. Phillip J. Brantley, Karen B. Grothe, and Gareth R. Dutton, "Stress, Anger, and Hostility in Coronary Heart Disease," in *Formulation and Treatment in Clinical Health Psychology*, eds. Ana V. Nikcevic, Andrej R. Kuczmierczyk, and Michael Bruch (New York: Routledge, 2006), 104–122, esp.105.

158. John Cloud, "Depressed? Angry? Your Heart May Suffer as a Result," *Time*, March 14, 2009. http://www.time.com/time/magazine/article/0,8599,1885257.00.html.

159. Laura Blue, "A Link between Anxiety and Heart Attacks," *Time* (January 8, 2008) http://www.time.com/time/magazine/article/0,8599,1701335.00.html.

160. "How Stress Harms the Heart," *Time*, October 9, 2007. http://www.time.com/time/health/article/0,8599,1669766,00.html.

161. See Riska, 2000, 1667.

162. Ray H. Rosenman, "Relationships of the Type A Behavior Pattern with Coronary Heart Disease," in *Handbook of Stress* (2nd ed.), eds. Leo Goldberger and Shlomo Breznitz (New York: The Free Press, 1993), 449–476.

163. I will not attempt to detail the history of Lazarus's complete research trajectory here. For an excellent summary of Lazarus's work, its impact, and the debates that it has spawned, see Caryl L. Cooper and Philip Dewe. *Stress: A Brief History* (Oxford: Blackwell, 2004), 67–84.

164. Richard S. Lazarus and Susan Folkman, *Stress, Appraisal and Coping* (New York: Springer, 1984), 19.

165. Susan Gore and Mary Ellen Colten, "Gender, Stress, and Distress," in *The Social Context of Coping*, ed. John Eckenrode (New York: Plenum, 1991), 139–163, esp. 157.

166. Lazarus and Folkman, 236.

167. See Paul T. Costa, Jr., and Robert R. McRae, "Personality: Another 'Hidden Factor' in Stress Research," *Psychological Inquiry* 1, no. 1(1990): 22–24.

168. Rudolf H. Moos and Ralph W. Swindle, Jr., "Person-Environment Transactions and the Stressor-Appraisal-Coping Process," *Psychological Inquiry* 1, no. 1 (1990): 30–32.

169. Gore and Colten, 144.

170. Richard S. Lazarus, "Why We Should Think of Stress as a Subset of Emotion," in *Handbook of Stress* (2nd ed.), eds. Leo Goldberger and Shlomo Breznitz (New York: The Free Press, 1993), 21–39.

171. Ibid., 26.

172. Ibid., 23.

173. "Stand Up for Yourself at Work, Warns a Heart-Attack Study," *Philadelphia Inquirer*, November 30, 2009, D2.

174. I am indebted to Aronowitz's discussion for what follows.

175. As Aronowitz points out, "interactive factors such as social incongruity, environmental factors such as housing, or population variables such as social cohesiveness may bear only an indirect relationship to individual behavior and risk and therefore are not easily assimilated into mechanistic models of disease, however strong the association at the group or population level" (p. 163).

176. Ibid., 165.

CHAPTER 3

1. Edmund Husserl, *The Crisis of the European Sciences and Transcendental Phenomenology* (Evanston, IL: Northwestern University Press, 1970), 6.

2. Emily Martin, *Flexible Bodies: The Role of Immunity in American Culture from the Days of Polio to the Age of AIDS* (Boston: Beacon Press, 1994), 240.

3. Susan Oyama, *Evolution's Eye: A Systems View of the Biology-Culture Divide* (Durham, NC: Duke University Press, 2000), 68.

4. Robert A. Aronowitz, *Making Sense of Illness: Science, Society, and Disease* (Cambridge: Cambridge University Press, 1998).

5. Ludwik Fleck, *Genesis and Development of a Scientific Fact* (Chicago: University of Chicago Press, 1979), 27–28, 37.

6. Neil Schneiderman, Gail Ironson, and Scott D. Siegel, "Stress and Health: Psychological, Behavioral, and Biological Determinants," in *Annual Review of Clinical Psychology*, 1 (2005): 607–628, esp. 621.

7. Stanley Aronowitz, *Science as Power: Discourse and Ideology in Modern Society* (Minneapolis: University of Minnesota Press, 1988), 335.

8. See Peter Conrad and Joseph W. Schneider, *Deviance and Medicalization: From Badness to Sickness* (Philadelphia: Temple University Press, 1992); Peter Conrad, *The Medicalization of Society: On the Transformation of Human Conditions into Treatable Disorders* (Baltimore, MD: Johns Hopkins University Press, 2007).

9. Claudine Herzlich and Janine Pierret, *Illness and Self in Society*, trans. Elborg Forster (Baltimore, MD: Johns Hopkins University Press, 1987).

10. Robert Crawford, "Healthism and the Medicalization of Everyday Life," *International Journal of Health Services* 10, no. 3 (1980): 365–388, esp. 368.

11. Alan Radley and Michael Billig, "Accounts of Health and Illness: Dilemmas and Representations," *Sociology of Health & Illness* 18, no. 2 (1996): 220–240.

12. Deborah Lupton, *The Imperative of Health: Public Health and the Regulated Body* (London: Sage, 1995).

13. For the following discussion, I rely on Crawford (1980); Lupton (1995); Marc Chrysanthou, "Transparency and Selfhood: Utopia and the Informed Body," *Social Science & Medicine* 54, no. 3 (2002): 469–479; Adele E. Clarke, Laura Mamo, Jennifer R. Fishman, Janet K. Shim, and Jennifer R. Fosket, "Biomedicalization: Technoscientific Transformations of Health, Illness, and U.S. Biomedicine," *Sociological Review* 68, no. 2 (2003): 161–194; Charles E. Rosenberg, *Our Present Complaint: American Medicine, Then and Now* (Baltimore, MD: Johns Hopkins University Press, 2007); Mike Bury and

Mike Wadsworth, "'The 'Biological Clock'? Ageing, Health and the Body across the Lifecourse," in *Debating Biology: Sociological Reflections on Health, Medicine and Society* (London: Routledge, 2003), eds. Simon J. Williams, Lynda Birke, and Gillian A. Bendelow, 109–119; Nikolas Rose and Carlos Novas, "Biological Citizenship," in *Global Assemblages: Technology, Politics, and Ethics as Anthropological Problems*, eds. Aihwa Ong and Stephen J. Collier (Oxford: Blackwell, 2005), 439–463; Ian Hacking, "Making Up People," in *Reconstructing Individualism: Autonomy, Individuality, and the Self in Western Thought*, eds. Thomas C. Heller, Morton Sosna, and David E. Wellbery (Stanford: Stanford University Press, 1986), 222–252.

14. Crawford, 380.
15. Rose and Novas, 445.
16. Lewis Thomas, "The Health Care System," *New England Journal of Medicine* 293 (1975): 1245–1246.
17. Robert Crawford, "The Ritual of Health Promotion," in *Health, Medicine, & Society: Key Theories, Future Agendas*, eds. Simon J. Williams, Jonathan Gabe, and Michael Calnan (London: Routledge, 2000), 219–235.
18. Charlie Davison, George Davey Smith, and Stephen Frankel, "Lay Epidemiology and the Prevention Paradox: The Implications of Coronary Candidacy for Health Education," *Sociology of Health & Illness* 13, no. 1 (1991): 1–19.
19. Harvey M. Sapolsky, "The Politics of Risk," *Daedalus* 119, no. 4 (1990): 83–96.
20. Mary Douglas, "Risk as a Forensic Resource," *Daedalus* 119, no. 4 (1990): 1–16, esp. 5.
21. David Armstrong, "The Rise of Surveillance Medicine," *Sociology of Health & Illness* 17 (1995): 393–404, esp. 400–401.
22. Ibid., 401.
23. Adele E. Clarke, Laura Mamo, Jennifer R. Fishman, Janet K. Shim, and Jennifer R. Fosket, "Biomedicalization: Technoscientific Transformations of Health, Illness, and U.S. Biomedicine," *Sociological Review* 68, no. 2 (2003): 161–194.
24. John-Arne Skolbekken, "The Risk Epidemic in Medical Journals," *Social Science and Medicine* 40, no. 3 (1995): 291–305.
25. Lupton, 79.
26. Mary Douglas claims that these differences of opinion are often treated as if power had nothing to do with them when, in fact, the "education" is often class-based.
27. Cited in Rosenberg, *Our Present Complaint*, 69.
28. Marshall H. Becker, "A Medical Sociologist Looks at Health Promotion," *Journal of Health and Social Behavior* 34 (1993): 1–6.
29. M. H. Becker, 4.
30. The cuts were recommended even though there was solid evidence from the U.S. Department of Agriculture and the Office of Management and Budget that the WIC program actually helps reduce healthcare costs.
31. Ibid., 4.

32. Lupton, 79–80.
33. Skolbekken, 301, 302.
34. Steve Sternberg, "9 Factors That Affect Your Heart's Health; [*sic*] Lifestyle, Not Heredity, Is the Biggest Culprit," *USA Today*, January, 9, 2006, 7D (Life section). http://www.lexisnexis.com/ (accessed February 2, 2009).
35. George M. Beard, *American Nervousness: Its Causes and Consequences: A Supplement to Nervous Exhaustion* (New York: Arno Press, [1881]1972).
36. Steve Sternberg, 7-D.
37. Charlie Davison, George Davey Smith, and Stephen Frankel, "Lay Epidemiology and the Prevention Paradox: The Implications of Coronary Candidacy for Health Education," *Sociology of Health & Illness* 13, no. 1 (1991): 1–19.
38. M. H. Becker, 3.
39. When Deena Weisberg and her colleagues performed a series of studies aimed at discovering the impact of irrelevant neuroscience information on explanations of psychological phenomena, they discovered that adding bogus neuroscientific information to the mix influenced people who weren't experts in the field to accept the psychological explanations. See Deena Skolnick Weisberg, Fank C. Keil, Joshua Goodstein, Elizabeth Rawson, and Jeremy R. Gray, "The Seductive Allure of Neuroscience Explanations, *Journal of Cognitive Neuroscience* 20, no. 3 (2008): 470–477.
40. Emily Martin, "Talking Back to Neuro-reductionism," in *Cultural Bodies: Ethnography and Theory*, eds. Helen Thomas and Jamilah Ahmed (Oxford: Blackwell, 2004), 190–211.
41. Martin, *Flexible Bodies*, 204.
42. Stanley Aronowitz.
43. Oyama, 156.
44. Rosenberg.
45. Martin, *Flexible Bodies*.
46. Ibid.; see also Anne Harrington, *The Cure Within: A History of Mind-Body Medicine* (New York: Norton, 2008).
47. Martin, 1994.
48. Ibid., 184–185.
49. Ibid., 38.
50. Cited in Martin, 186.
51. Richard S. Lazarus and Susan Folkman, *Stress, Appraisal and Coping* (New York: Springer, 1984).
52. A Lexis-Nexis search of major U.S. and world publications uncovered only 42 citations that included both the terms *stress* and *immune system,* as compared with 866 over the following 20 years.
53. See Esther M. Sternberg, *The Balance Within: The Science Connecting Health and Emotions* (New York: W. H. Freeman, 2001), esp. 131, 59; Schneiderman et al., 613, for these and other examples.
54. Donna J. Haraway, *Simians, Cyborgs, and Women* (New York: Routledge, 1991), 212.
55. Rosenberg, 86.
56. Hans Selye, *The Stress of Life* (New York: McGraw-Hill, 1956), vii–viii.

57. Schneiderman et al., 21.
58. Madonna G. Constantine and Derald Wing Sue, "Factors Contributing to Optimal Human Functioning in People of Color in the United States," *The Counseling Psychologist* 34 (2006): 228–244.
59. Amartya Sen, "The Possibility of Social Choice," *American Economic Review* 89, no. 3 (1999): 349–378, esp. 358.
60. Martin, 1994.
61. See Suzanne C. Segerstrom, and Gregory E. Miller, "Psychological Stress and the Human Immune System: A Meta-Analytic Study of 30 Years of Inquiry," *Psychological Bulletin* 130, no. 4 (2004): 601–630, especially 604. Segerstrom and Miller's article provides a very thorough explanation of how the immune system is thought to work.
62. Schneiderman et al., 612.
63. Ibid., 612–613.
64. For a more complete history and description, see Serge Doublet, *The Stress Myth* (Chesterfield, MO: Science & Humanities Press, 1999–2000), especially 203–229; see also Fiona Jones and Jim Bright, *Stress: Myth, Theory, and Research* (Harlow, UK: Pearson Education, 2001), esp. Chapter 4.
65. Segerstrom and Miller (604–605) say that "to resolve this paradox, some researchers have chosen to focus on how chronic stress might shift the balance of the immune response. The most well-known of these models hypothesizes that chronic stress elicits simultaneous enhancement and suppression of the immune response by altering patterns of cytokine secretion" (604–605). One class of cytokines (Th 1) that acts against many varieties of infection is suppressed, and this increases production of another class of cytokines (Th 2) that may exacerbate allergic and autoimmune reactions. Cortisol is thought to be the hormone that facilitates the transformation just described. But the researchers conclude that, in actuality, neither model has been able adequately to explain the connection between chronic stress and insufficient immunity that can lead to infectious disease or between chronic stress and the extreme activity of the immune system that can lead to autoimmune diseases.
66. Segerstrom and her colleague initially undertook the meta-analysis because they believed that studies in the domain of psychoneuroimmunology were vulnerable both to false positive (Type I) and false negative (Type II) errors as a result of the small sample sizes in many of the studies.
67. See Tomothy J. Loving, Kathi L. Hefner, Janice K. Kiecolt-Glaser, Ronald Glaser, and William B. Malarky, "Stress Hormone Changes and Marital Conflict: Spouses' Relative Power Makes a Difference," *Journal of Marriage and Family* 66 (2004): 595–612.
68. See Suzanne C. Segerstrom, "Social Networks and Immunosuppression During Stress: Relationship Conflict or Energy Conservation?" *Brain, Behavior, and Immunity* 22 (2008): 279–284.
69. Anne Scott, "A Metaphysics for Alternative Medicine: 'Translating' the Social and Biological Worlds," in *Debating Biology: Sociological Reflections on Health, Medicine and Society*, eds. Simon J. Williams, Lynda Birke, and Gillian A. Bendelow (London: Routledge, 2003), 298–310.

70. Sadie F. Dingfelder, "An Insidious Enemy," *Monitor on Psychology* 39, no. 9 (October 2008): 20–23, esp. 23.

71. Stress, whether physical or psychological, is said to activate the HPA axis and increase the secretion of cortisol.

72. Some longitudinal designs that use multiple assessments have been considered promising even by those who have been critical of other methods of studying stress. See Peggy A. Thoits, "Stress, Coping, and Social Support Processes: Where Are We? What Next?" *Journal of Health and Social Behavior* (extra issue, 1995): 3–79. See, for example David Almeida's method of combining daily telephone diary self-reports with twice-daily measurements of salivary cortisol. David Almeida, Katherine McGonagle, and Heather King, "Assessing Daily Stress Processes in Social Surveys by Combining Stressor Exposure and Salivary Cortisol," *Biodemography and Social Biology* 55, no.2 (2009): 219–237.

73. Hellhammer and his colleagues have cautioned researchers using salivary cortisol in stress research to be "aware of possible sources of variance, which may affect this measure." See Dirk H. Hellhammer, Sefan Wust, and Brigette M. Kudielka, "Salivary Cortisol as a Biomarker in Stress Research," *Psychoneuroendocrinology* 34 (2009); 163–171, esp. 168.

74. Segerstrom and Miller, 605.

75. Ibid., 616.

76. Howard S. Friedman, "The Multiple Linkages of Personality and Disease," *Brain, Behavior, and Immunity* 27 (2008): 668–675, esp. 668.

77. http://www.apa.org/releases/stress_immune.html.

78. Margaret E. Kemeny, "Psychobiological Responses to Social Threat: Evolution of a Psychological Model in Psychoneuroimmunology," *Brain, Behavior, and Immunity* 23 (2009): 1–9, esp. 2.

79. Ibid., 2.

80. Ibid., 3.

81. Fleck, 37.

82. Segerstrom and Miller, too, consider it a significant omission that the studies they analyzed did not measure individuals' subjective experience in order to explore the relationship between that experience and the immune response. Moreover, they maintain that research on stress, immunity, and disease needs to overcome the methodological limitations that have made relationships among these impossible to decipher.

83. Friedman, 669.

84. This is what Friedman suggests we should do, 670.

85. Oyama, 175.

86. Rebecca A. Clay, "One Heart—Many Threats," *Monitor on Psychology* 38, no. 1 (January 2007): 46–48, esp. 46.

87. Ibid., 47.

88. *Context-stripping* is a term coined by Eliot Mishler. See Eliot G. Mishler, "Meaning in Context: Is There Any Other Kind?" *Harvard Educational Review* 49 (1979): 1–19.

89. Linda Gallo and Karen A. Matthews, "Understanding the Association Between Socioeconomic Status and Physical Health: Do Negative Emotions Play a Role?" *Psychological* Bulletin 129, no. 1 (2003): 10–51, esp. 10.

90. Ibid., 33.
91. As Shinn and Toohey suggest, researchers, quite problematically, often aggregate individual reports on their attitudes or values and use these to characterize the community itself. See Marybeth Shinn and Siobhan M. Toohey, "Community Contexts of Human Welfare," *Annual Review of Psychology* 54 (2003): 427–459, esp. 450.
92. Angus Forbes and Steven P. Wainwright, "On the Methodological, Theoretical and Philosophical Context of Health Inequalities Research: A Critique," *Social Science & Medicine* 53 (2001): 801–816, esp. 807.
93. Gallo and Matthews, 35.
94. Linda C. Gallo, "Do Psychosocial Factors Contribute to Socioeconomic Health Disparities? Applications of the Reserve Capacity Model," *Psychological Science Agenda* 22, no. 8 (September 2008)www.apa.org/science/about/psa/2008/09/gallo.aspx (accessed September 29, 2008).
95. Francis Fukuyama, "Social Capital and Civil Society" (paper presented at The Institute of Public Policy, George Mason University, October 1, 1999). http://www.imf.org/external/pubs/ft/seminar/1999/reforms/fukuyama.htm; Robert Putnam, *Bowling Alone: The Collapse and Revival of American Community* (New York: Simon and Schuster, 2000).
96. Carl Muntaner and John Lynch, "Income Inequality, Social Cohesion, and Class Relations: A Critique of Wilkinson's Neo-Durkheimian Research Program," *International Journal of Health Services* 29, no. 1 (1999): 59–81.
97. Mildred Blaxter, *Health* (Cambridge, UK: Polity Press, 2004), 119–120.
98. John Lynch, "Income Inequality and Health: Expanding the Debate," *Social Science & Medicine* 51 (2000): 1001–1005, esp. 1004.
99. They define social stress as a combination of lifetime traumatic experiences, discrimination, and recent stressful events. See R. Jay Turner and William R. Avison, "Status Variations in Stress Exposure: Implications for the Interpretation of Research on Race, Socioeconomic Status, and Gender," *Journal of Health and Social Behavior* 44 (2003): 488–505, esp. 500. Psychologizing poverty is an example of what Shinn and Toohey have called a *context minimization error*.
100. Nicole E. Ennis, Stevan E. Hobfoll, and Kerstin E. E. Schroder, "Money Doesn't Talk, It Swears: How Economic Stress and Resistance Resources Impact Inner-City Women's Depressive Mood," *American Journal of Community Psychology* 28, no. 2 (2000): 149–173, esp. 150.
101. Stevan E. Hobfoll, "Conservation of Resources: A New Attempt at Conceptualizing Stress," *American Psychologist* 44, no. 3 (1989): 513–524.
102. Ennis et al., 169.
103. Peggy A. Thoits, "Conceptual, Methodological, and Theoretical Problems in Studying Social Support as a Buffer Against Life Stress," *Journal of Health and Social Behavior* 23 (1982): 145–159.
104. Deborah Belle, "Social Ties and Social Support" in *Lives in Stress: Women and Depression,* ed. Deborah Belle (Beverly Hills, CA: Sage, 1982), 133–144.
105. Thoits, "Stress, Coping," 67.

106. Andrew Solomon "A Cure for Poverty: What If You Could Help End People's Economic Problems by Treating Their Depression?" *New York Times Magazine*, May 6, 2001, 112–117.

107. Ibid., 114.

108. Sendhil Mullainathan and Eldar Shafir, "Savings Policy and Decision-Making in Low-Income Households," in *Insufficient Funds: Savings, Assets, Credit and Banking among Low-Income Households*, eds. Michael Barr and Rebecca Blank (New York: Russell Sage Foundation Press, 2009), 121–145, esp. 122.

109. Sandro Galea et al., "Estimated Deaths Attributable to Social Factors in the United States," http://ajph.aphapublications.org/cgi/content/abstract/AJPH.2010.300086v1 (accessed July 8, 2011).

110. Muntaner and Lynch.

111. Forbes and Wainwright; A. Schulz et al., "Social Stressors and Self Reported Health Status among African American and White Women in the Detroit Metropolitan Area," *Social Science & Medicine* 51 (2000): 1639–1653.

112. Shinn and Toohey, esp. 442.

113. Richard Wilkinson, "The Challenge of Prevention: A Response to Starfield's 'Commentary: Pathways of Influence on Equity in Health,'" *Social Science & Medicine* 64 (2007): 1367–1370, esp. 1368.

114. Sen, 358, 362–363.

115. Blaxter, 15.

CHAPTER 4

1. Charlotte Perkins Gilman, *The Home: Its Work and Influence* (New York: McClure, Phillips & Co., 1903), 152.

2. See Ann Douglas's trenchant account of how women's oppression was used to shore up the cultural values of a nation in *The Feminization of American Culture* (New York: Noonday Press, [1977]1998).

3. Michael Kimmel, *Manhood in America: A Cultural History* (2nd ed.) (New York: Oxford University Press, 2004).

4. Answers to that question further constrained women's opportunities for women's more extensive participation in public life. See Carroll Smith-Rosenberg, "The Cross and the Pedestal: Women, Anti-Ritualism, and the Emergence of the American Bourgeoisie," in *Disorderly Conduct: Visions of Gender in Victorian America* (New York: Alfred A. Knopf, 1985), 129–163.

5. Kimmel, 81, 216, 221.

6. John Gray, *Why Mars and Venus Collide: Improving Relationships by Understanding How Men and Women Cope Differently with Stress* (New York: HarperCollins, 2008), 13.

7. Deborah Cameron, *The Myth of Mars and Venus* (New York: Oxford, 2007), 177.

8. See Derek Thompson, "It's Not Just a Recession. It's a Mancession!" *The Atlantic*, July 9, 2009. http://www.theatlantic.com/business/archive/2009/07/its-not-just-a-recession-its-a-mancession/20991 (accessed September 19, 2010).

9. Nancy Gibbs, "What Women Want Now," *Time*, Oct. 14, 2009. http://www.time.com/time/specials/packages/article/0,28804,1930277_1930145_19 30309,00.html (accessed February 1, 2010).

10. Kimmel, 241.

11. Ibid.

12. Caryl Rivers, *Selling Anxiety: How the News Media Scare Women* (Hanover, NH: University Press of New England, 2007), 12, 13.

13. Michel Foucault, *Discipline and Punish: The Birth of the Prison* (New York: Vintage, 1977).

14. In Candace West and Don H. Zimmerman, "Doing Gender," *Gender and Society* 1, no. 2 (1987): 125–151.

15. Barbara J. Risman, *Gender Vertigo: American Families in Transition* (New Haven, CT: Yale University Press, 1998), 32. See also Sandra Bartky, "Foucault, Femininity, and the Modernization of Patriarchal Power," in *Reflections on Resistance: Feminism and Foucault*, eds. Irene Diamond and Lee Quinby (Boston: Northeastern University Press, 1988), 61–86; Biddy Martin, "Feminism, Criticism, and Foucault," in *Reflections on Resistance: Feminism and Foucault*, eds. Irene Diamond and Lee Quinby (Boston: Northeastern University Press, 1988), 3–19.

16. Silas Weir Mitchell, *Wear and Tear, or Hints for the Overworked* (Philadelphia: J. B. Lippincott & Sons, 1871), 18.

17. Deborah Belle and Joanne Doucet, "Poverty, Inequality, and Discrimination as Sources of Depression among U.S. Women," *Psychology of Women Quarterly*, 27 (2003): 101–113.

18. Regina Markell Morantz, "Making Women Modern: Middle Class Women and Health Reform in 19th Century America," *Journal of Social History* 10 (1977): 490–507 (both quotations are on p. 495).

19. Communication from Mrs. R. B. Gleason to Catherine Beecher, printed in Beecher's *Letters to People on Health and Happiness* (New York: Harper & Bros., 1855). Reprinted in Nancy F. Cott et al., *Root of Bitterness: Documents of the Social History of American Women* (2nd ed.) (Boston: Northeastern University Press, 1996), 295.

20. Rodrique Ngowi, "Nearly Half of Women in U.S. Admit to Indulging in Favorite Foods as Stress Piles On, Study Says," *MercuryNews.com*, December, 18, 2006. http://www.mercurynews.com/cI_4860968.

21. Catherine Lutz, "Cultural Politics by Other Means: Gender and Politics in Some American Psychologies of Emotions," in *Historical Dimensions of Psychological Discourse*, eds. Carl F. Graumann and Kenneth J. Gergen (Cambridge: Cambridge University Press, 1996), 125–144, esp. 139. Peter Freund makes the case that the kind of emotional control that will be brought to bear depends on a person's place in the social hierarchy. Women, of course, have not been at the apex of that hierarchy. See Peter E. S. Freund, "The Expressive Body: A Common Ground for the Sociology of Emotions and Health and Illness," *Sociology of Health & Illness* 12, no. 4 (1990): 452–477, esp. 470.

22. Stephanie A. Shields, *Speaking from the Heart: Gender and the Social Meaning of Emotion* (Cambridge: Cambridge University Press, 2002), 46–47.

23. Ibid., 106. See also Stephanie A. Shields, "Passionate Men, Emotional Women: Psychology Constructs Gender Difference in the Late 19th Century," *History of Psychology* 10, no. 2 (2007): 92–110, esp. 98–99.

24. Of course, these ideas applied only to white middle- and upper-class men and women.

25. Shields, "Passionate Men."

26. Stephanie A. Shields, "The Politics of Emotion in Everyday Life: 'Appropriate' Emotion and Claims on Identity," *Review of General Psychology* 9, no. 1 (2005): 3–15.

27. See n. 34.

28. Arlie R. Hochschild, *The Managed Heart: The Commercialization of Human Feeling* (Berkeley: University of California Press, 1983), 165. See also Hochschild's "Emotion Work, Feeling Rules, and Social Structure," *American Journal of Sociology* 85, no. 3 (1979): 551–575.

29. As Hochschild reminds us, service jobs traditionally occupied by women (teacher, social worker, receptionist, salesperson) require considerable emotion work, particularly with respect to the suppression of feelings (e.g., "always greet the customer with a smile").

30. See Joan C. Tronto, "Women and Caring: What Can Feminists Learn About Morality from Caring?" in *Gender/Body/Knowledge: Feminist Reconstructions of Being and Knowing,* eds. Alison M. Jaggar and Susan R. Bordo (New Brunswick, NJ: Rutgers University Press, 1989), 172–187, esp. 184.

31. See Dana Becker, "Women's Work.".

32. "Stress Hurts! A Wake-up Call for Women with Dr. Nancy Snyderman," ABC video, March 10, 2001.

33. See Dana Becker, *The Myth of Empowerment: Women and the Therapeutic Culture in America* (New York: New York University Press, 2005).

34. This seems to be the rate in developed countries, where the ratio of depressed women to depressed men rises to anywhere from 3:1 to 4:1. See Frances M. Culbertson, "Depression and Gender: An International Review," *American Psychologist* 52 (1997): 25–31.

35. Susan Nolen-Hoeksema, "Gender Differences in Depression," in *Handbook of Depression,* eds. Ian H. Gotlib and Constance L. Hammen (New York: Guilford, 2002), 492–509; Kristine Siefert, Phillip Bowman, Colleen M. Heflin, Sheldon Danziger, and David R. Williams, "Social and Environmental Predictors of Maternal Depression in Current and Recent Welfare Recipients," *American Journal of Orthopsychiatry* 70, no. 4 (2000): 510–522.

36. http://messageboards.ivillage.com/n/mb/message.asp?webtag=ivbhstress &msg=3841.1&ctx=128.

37. Some researchers, of course, have looked at the long-term effects of early stressful experiences on later depression. They have found that well over a third of women who suffer from depression have been physically and/ or sexually abused in childhood, and that abuse increases their reactivity to stress in adulthood. See Nolen-Hoeksema, "Gender Differences in Depression."

38. See Constance Hammen, "Stress and Depression," *Annual Review of Clinical Psychology*, 1 (2005): 293–319, esp. 297. What is considered "chronic," however, varies from study to study.

39. Susan Nolen-Hoeksema, Judith Larson, and Carla Grayson, "Explaining the Gender Difference in Depressive Symptoms," *Journal of Personality and Social Psychology* 77, no. 5 (1999): 1061–1072.

40. Bridget Murray Law, "Probing the Depression-Rumination Cycle," *Monitor on Psychology*, 36, no. 10 (2005): 38.

41. "Women's Blues," *Working Mother*, December 2000, 42.

42. See Susan Nolen-Hoeksema, *Women Who Think Too Much: How to Break Free of Overthinking and Reclaim Your Life* (New York: Henry Holt, 2003), viii, 4. As early as 2000, Nolen-Hoeksema's research was being tailored to that market, and she was helping the process along. See "Women's Blues," *Working Mother* (December 2000), 42, in which Nolen-Hoeksema's "tips to help stop a brewing depression before it stops" include going for a walk or signing up for adult classes at a community college.

43. See Siefert et al., p. 511.

44. Nicole E. Ennis, Stevan E. Hobfoll, and Kerstin E. E. Schroder, "Money Doesn't Talk, It Swears: How Economic Stress and Resistance Resources Impact Inner-City Women's Depressive Mood," *American Journal of Community Psychology* 28, no. 2 (2000): 149–173, esp. 151.

45. Many of the problems with the research on stress and depression are problems that have plagued stress research in general. What is stressful can be confounded with what is depressing, such that in some studies that attempt to examine how or to what extent stressful events influence the development of depression, stress and depression come to stand for the same thing. For a more detailed discussion of methodological problems in the measurement of stress, see Constance Hammen, "Stress and Depression."

46. See A. Bifulco, O. Bernazzani, P. M. Moran, and C. Ball, "Lifetime Stressors and Recurrent Depression: Preliminary Findings of the Adult Life Phase Interview (ALPHI)," *Social Psychiatry and Psychiatric Epidemiology* 35, no. 6 (2000): 264–275.

47. R. Jay Turner and William R. Avison, "Status Variations in Stress Exposure: Implications for the Interpretation of Research on Race, Socioeconomic Status, and Gender," *Journal of Health and Social Behavior* 44 (2003): 488–505. Turner and Avison found that although women had greater exposure to recent stressful life *events*, men had greater exposure to stress generally. They have concluded that using checklists listing only recent events "significantly overestimates total stress exposure among women relative to men" (p. 496). This underestimate also holds true for African Americans when compared to non-Hispanic whites, and for poor people when compared to those who are better off. In Turner's and Avison's study, most—over 80 percent—of the increase in depression among African Americans was tied to greater exposure to what the researchers call *social stress*—a combination of recent life events, traumatic events, chronic stress, and the stress of discrimination.

48. Siefert et al., 518.
49. Ibid., 516. Siefert et al. found that women with three or more risk factors constituted over a quarter of this very large sample of women. Beyond this, women with three or more risk factors accounted for almost half the women who were depressed, showing the cumulative effect of such risk factors. Carolyn Cutrona and her colleagues have also shown how disadvantage and crime at the neighborhood level contribute to depression in African American women. See Carolyn E. Cutrona, Daniel W. Russell, P. Adama Brown, Lee Anna Clark, Robert M. Hessling, and Kelli A. Gardner, "Neighborhood Context, Personality, and Stressful Life Events as Predictors of Depression among African American Women," *Journal of Abnormal Psychology*, 114, no. 1 (2005): 3–15.
50. Schulz and her colleagues found that the depression experienced by African American women living in extremely impoverished areas of Detroit was only partially tied to low income levels. Disorder in the neighborhood, as well as discrimination, influenced depression, apart from the women's low-income status. See Amy J. Schulz et al., " Psychosocial Stress and Social Support as Mediators of Relationships between Income, Length of Residence and Depressive Symptoms among African American Women on Detroit's Eastside," *Social Science & Medicine* 62, no. 2 (2006): 510–522.
51. For a discussion of the contemporary medicalization of welfare, see Sanford S. Schram, *After Welfare, The Culture of Postindustrial Social Policy* (New York: New York University Press, 2000), Chapter 3, "In the Clinic: The Medicalization of Welfare," 59–88.
52. See Andrew Solomon, "A Cure for Poverty: What If You Could Help End People's Economic Problems by Treating Their Depression?" *New York Times Magazine,* May 6, 2001, 112–117, esp. 114.
53. Ibid., p. 116.
54. The article, written by Helen Epstein, was entitled, "Enough to Make You Sick?" *New York Times Magazine,* October 12, 2003, 75–81, 98, 102–107. Also see a discussion of the medicalization of poverty in Dana Becker, *The Myth of Empowerment.*
55. Ibid., 81.
56. Ibid., 79.
57. Ibid., 81.
58. Ibid., 98.
59. Nikolas Rose, *Governing the Soul: The Shaping of the Private Self* (London: Routledge, 1990), 228.
60. Mark R. Somerfield and Robert R. McRae, "Stress and Coping Research: Methodological Challenges, Theoretical Advances, and Clinical Applications," *American Psychologist* 55, no. 6 (2000): 620–625.
61. Cited in Victoria L. Banyard and Sandra A, Graham-Bermann, "Can Women Cope? A Gender Analysis of Theories of Coping with Stress, *Psychology of Women Quarterly* 17 (1993): 303–318, esp. 305. In her 1991 study, Peggy Thoits found pretty weak support for stereotyped styles of coping. See Peggy A. Thoits, "Gender Differences in Coping with Emotional Distress," in *The Social Context of Coping,* ed. John Eckenrode (New York: Plenum, 1991), 107–138.

62. Banyard and Graham-Bermann.

63. Ennis et al., 165.

64. See a fairly typical example in Elaine Walker, Zainab Sabuwalla, Annie M. Bollini, and Deborah J. Walder, "Women and Stress," in *Women's Mental Health*, eds. Sarah E. Romans and Mary V. Seeman (New York: Lippincott, Williams and Wilkins, 2005), 35–47. Dedovic et al., in their review, have found virtually no studies focused on the influence of gender socialization on men's and women's responses to stress. See Katarina Dedovic, Mehereen Wadiwalla, Veronika Engert, and Jens C. Pruessner, "The Role of Sex and Gender Socialization in Stress Reactivity," *Developmental Psychology* 45, no. 1 (2009): 45–55.

65. "Diagnose and Manage Your Stress Type." http://www.aol.health.com/healthy-living/longevity/stress-type (accessed July 12, 2010).

66. *Self*, January 2008, 119, 102.

67. Rebecca Lee, *The SuperStress Solution* (New York: Random House, 2010), xiii.

68. For this "detox" talk, see Lee, *The SuperStress Solution*; see also Stephanie McClellan and Beth Hamilton, *So Stressed: The Ultimate Stress-Relief Plan for Women* (New York: Free Press, 2010).

69. Deborah Hutton, "How to Reduce Your Stress," *Harper's Bazaar*, September 2003, 274–278, esp. 274.

70. McClellan and Hamilton, *So Stressed*, 63.

71. http://messageboards.ivillage.com/n/mb/message.asp?webtag=iv-bhstress &msg=3841.1&ctx=128.

72. See also, on AOL's health website, "Your Stress Personality," with a picture gallery of angry, anxious, or overwhelmed women exemplifying different "personalities." http://www.aolhealth.com/2010/26/stress-type (accessed June 20, 2010).

73. Lisa Held, "Psychoanalysis Shapes Consumer Culture," *Monitor on Psychology* 40, no. 11 (December 2009): 32. http://www.apa.org/monitor/2009/12/consumer.aspx (accessed May 24, 2010).

74. In the 1990s the tobacco company used the slogans "It's a woman thing" and "Find your voice" to sell the brand.

75. Ann Douglas, 64.

76. See Claire Cain Miller, "Woman to Woman, Online," *New York Times*, August 14, 2008, C1; C9.

77. http://messageboards.ivillage.com/iv-bhstress?ice=ivl,searchmb. A sampling of its content predictably reflects the current media emphasis on the relationship between stress and disease.

78. Ellen Annandale, "Gender and Health Status: Does Biology Matter?" in *Debating Biology: Sociological Reflections on Health, Medicine and Society*, eds. Simon J. Williams, Lynda Birke, and Gillian A. Bendelow (London: Routledge, 2003), 84–95, esp. 91.

79. E. Lamont, "A Beautiful Mind," *Elle*, May 2005, 169.

80. http://www/time.com/time/specials/2007/article/0,28804,1638826 (accessed June 23, 2009).

81. This rationale is suggested in Mary C. Davis, Karen A. Matthews, and Elizabeth W. Twamley, "Is Life More Difficult on Mars or Venus? A

Meta-analytic Review of Sex Differences in Major and Minor Life Events," *Annals of Behavioral Medicine* 21, no. 1 (1999): 83–97.

82. Judith Lorber, *The Paradoxes of Gender* (New Haven, CT: Yale University Press, 1994).

83. Davis et al., 92.

84. A number of these are enumerated in R. Jay Turner and William R. Avison, "Status Variations in Stress Exposure: Implications for the Interpretation of Research on Race, Socioeconomic Status, and Gender," *Journal of Health and Social Behavior,* 44, no. 4 (2003): 488–505.

85. Leonard I. Pearlin, "The Sociological Study of Stress," *Journal of Health and Social Behavior* 30, no. 3 (1989): 241–256.

86. Davis et al., 83.

87. In terms of their responses to stress, men still seem to have more pronounced cardiovascular responses to stress and women to more depressive responses. See Walker et al., 35–47.

88. Ronald Kotulak, *Chicago Tribune* (Science), April 30, 2006. http://www.lex-isnexis.com/.

89. Lesley Rogers, *Sexing the Brain* (New York: Columbia University Press, 2001). See especially pp. 2–37.

90. Ibid., 20.

91. Ibid., 34–35.

92. Although Rogers talks about "sex" differences, the old distinction between "sex" as purely biological difference and "gender" as socially constructed difference is a distinction that becomes more and more difficult to make.

93. Ibid., 3.

94. See Rogers, 13; see also Stanley Aronowitz, *Science as Power: Discourse and Ideology in Modern Society* (Minneapolis: University of Minnesota Press, 1988). In Chapter 12, Aronowitz discusses the increasingly political nature of research priorities in the social sciences.

95. Simon Baron-Cohen, *Essential Differences: The Truth about the Male and Female Brain* (New York: Basic Books, 2003). See also Simon Baron-Cohen, "They Just Can't Help It," *The Guardian*, April 17, 2003. http://www.guard-ian.co.uk/education/2003/apr/17/research.higher education

96. Louann Brizendine, *The Female Brain* (New York: Morgan Road Books, 2006); *The Male Brain* (New York: Broadway Books, 2010).

97. He says that "others may worry that a theory like this stereotypes the sexes. But we need to distinguish stereotyping from the study of sex differences. The study simply looks at males and females as two groups, and asks why on average, differences are seen. There is no harm in that, and even some important scientific advances can come out of it.... The E-S theory does not stereotype. Rather it seeks to explain why individuals are typical or atypical for their sex." See Baron-Cohen, "They Just Can't Help It."

98. A critique of the science can be found in Deborah Cameron's *The Myth of Mars and Venus*, 2–9.

99. Brizendine has been criticized for exaggerating small sex differences for which there is no actual evidence. See Nicole M. Else-Quest, "Biological Determinism and the Never-ending Quest for Gender Differences," *Psychology of Women Quarterly* 31 (2007): 322–323.

100. Diane F. Halpern, *Sex Differences in Cognitive Abilities* (3rd ed.) (Mahway, NJ: Lawrence Erlbaum Associates, 2000), 17.

101. Janet Shibley Hyde, "The Gender Similarities Hypothesis," *American Psychologist* 60, no. 6 (2005): 581–592.

102. Rosalind Barnett and Caryl Rivers also argue that Baron-Cohen trivializes women's activities, for example, by calling gossip one of women's talents. See *Same Difference: How Gender Myths Are Hurting Our Relationships, Our Children, and Our Jobs* (New York: Basic Books, 2004), 185–186.

103. Gray, *Why Mars and Venus Collide*, 37.

104. Ibid., viii, 3–4; 6;italics added.

105. Ibid., 39.

106. Ibid., 40–41. Gray's scanty references on brain differences include a neuroscientific article published on the Internet in which the author himself states that the "discovery" that the corpus callosum is larger in women than in men, an oft-repeated assertion of Gray's, "has been challenged recently." See Renato M. E. Sabbatini, "Are There Differences between the Brains of Males and Females?" http://www.cerebromente.org.br/n11/mente/eisntein/cerebro-homens.html (accessed June 23, 2010).

107. Ibid., 81, 78.

108. Cameron, 12.

109. Ibid., 58.

110. Ibid., 63.

111. Ibid., 65.

112. Ibid., 73.

113. Ibid., 95–96.

114. Ibid., 71.

115. Gray may be referring to Taylor's discussion of Repetti's work in Shelley E. Taylor, *The Tending Instinct: How Nurturing Is Essential for Who We Are and How We Live* (New York: Henry Holt, 2002), 22–23. See also Rena L. Repetti, "Effects of Daily Workload on Subsequent Behavior During Marital Interaction: The Roles of Social Withdrawal and Spouse Support," *Journal of Personality and Social Psychology* 57 (1989): 651–659.

116. Naill Bolger, Anita DeLongis, Ronald C. Kessler, and Elaine Wethington, "The Contagion of Stress Across Multiple Roles," *Journal of Marriage and the Family* 51 (1989): 175–183.

117. Although both males and females of a variety of species secrete oxytocin, it is believed that in females estrogen amplifies oxytocin's effects.

118. Shelley E. Taylor, Laura Cousino Klein, Brian P. Lewis, Tara L. Gruenwald, Regan A. R. Gurung, and J. A. Updegraff, "Biobehavioral Responses to Stress in Females: Tend-and-Befriend, Not Fight or Flight," *Psychological Review* 109 (2000): 411–429.

119. Shelley E. Taylor, *The Tending Instinct: How Nurturing Is Essential for Who We Are and How We Live* (New York: Henry Holt, 2002). Although in her preface (pp. 3–4), Taylor claims she has used the term *instinct* with "cautious deliberation," knowing that "tending is not invariant or inevitable" in ways that would justify its being called an instinct, she still asserts that "it is insistent in ways that justify the term instinct." Taylor points out that women do more "tending" than men, although she is quick to say that "both genders have the capacity for tending." She states that she is well aware that "instinct is a loaded word" and that the combination of instinct and tending lead us to the "slippery slope to mothering instinct, women's destiny, and other terms . . . used to box women into roles they may not choose to play."

120. Taylor et al., "Biobehavioral Responses," 422.

121. Taylor, *The Tending Instinct*, 25.

122. Ibid., footnote 7, 203.

123. Ibid., 24.

124. Ibid., 24.

125. Ibid., 3.

126. Barnett and Rivers have made this argument with reference to Taylor's research in *Same Difference*, 139.

127. Ibid., footnote 33. Barnett and Rivers interviewed Sarah Knox; see 181 ff.

128. See Taylor, *The Tending Instinct*, 110.

129. Cordelia Fine, "Will Working Mothers' Brains Explode? The Popular New Genre of Neurosexism," *Neuroethics* 1 (2008): 69–72. See also Fine's *Delusions of Gender* (New York: W. W. Norton, 2010).

130. Shelley E. Taylor, "Tend and Befriend: Biobehavioral Bases of Affiliation under Stress," *Current Directions in Psychological Science* 15 (2006): 273–277, esp. 275, 276.

131. Tori DeAngelis, "The Two Faces of Oxytocin," *Monitor on Psychology* 39, no. 2 (2008): 30–32.

132. Marilia Duffles and Jeffrey Lord, "Why Hillary Talks Like Bill," *The American Spectator*, May 7, 2007. http://spectator.org/archives/2007/05/07/why-hillary-talks-like-bill/. See Liberman's language blog http://itre.cis.upenn.edu/~myl/languagelog/archives/004506.html, in which he says, "It would be easy to sneer at the *American Spectator*, . . . but the fact is, the rest of the media, from *The New York Times* to ABC's 20/20 to the BBC, has not been any better in covering the neuroscience of sex differences in general, and sex differences in communication in particular. . . . There are several effects that combine here to create a perfect storm of misinformation. One is the modern tendency to treat science as a source of morally instructive tales, not to be taken literally. Another is the generally abysmal level of scientific understanding among journalists and editors." http://itre.cis.upenn.edu/~myl/languagelog/archives/004506.html.

133. "Tend and Befriend Instead of Fight or Flight: A Woman's Response to Stress." www.the-heart-of-motherhood.com/tendandbefriend.html (accessed June 28, 2010). See the popular medical website *WebMD* for a

piece, "Why Men and Women Handle Stress Differently," that almost exclusively relies on hormonal and evolutionary arguments and prominently discusses Taylor's "tend-and-befriend" theory. http://women.webmd.com/features/stress-women-men-cope.

CHAPTER 5

1. Anna Richardson Steese, "The Lure of the Double Salary," *Woman's Home Companion*, May 1920. Cited in Grace L. Coyle, *Jobs and Marriage? Outlines for the Discussion of the Married Woman in Business* (New York: The Woman's Press, 1928), 32–33.

2. According to the U. S. Bureau of Labor Statistics, only about 17 percent of those in the workforce were married mothers. In 1985, 61 percent of married mothers were either working or seeking employment. By 1995, the rate of participation was 70 percent. See Sharon R. Cohany and Emy Sok, "Trends in Labor Forced Participation of Married Mothers of Infants," *Monthly Labor Review* (February 2007): 9. http: www.bls.gov/opuls/mlr/2007/02/art2full (accessed July 22, 2010).

3. Anita Shreve, "Careers and the Lure of Motherhood," *New York Times*, November 21, 1982, 38.

4. "We Did It! The Rich World's Quiet Revolution: Women Are Gradually Taking Over the Workplace," *The Economist*, December 30, 2009. http://www.economist.com/node/15174489 (accessed December 29, 2010).

5. "Female Power," *The Economist*, December 30, 2009, http://www.economist.com/node/15174418 (accessed December 29, 2010).

6. "Professor Marianne Bertrand Says Motherhood Explains Gender Pay Gap," *Booth School of Business News*. http://www.chicagobooth.edu/news/2009–03–05_bertrand-gls.aspx (accessed December 29, 2010).

7. Anita Ilta Garey, *Weaving Work and Motherhood* (Philadelphia: Temple University Press, 1999), 11.

8. Virginia E. Schein, *Working from the Margins: Voices of Mothers in Poverty* (Ithaca, NY: ILR Press, 1995), esp. 42.

9. Garey, 11.

10. Scott Coltrane, "Fatherhood, Gender, and Work-Family Policies," in *Gender Equality: Transforming Family Divisions of Labor*, eds. Janet C. Gornick and Marcia K. Meyers (London: Verso, 2009), 385–409, esp. 398.

11. For this discussion of the historical legacy of household labor, see Ann Crittenden, *The Price of Motherhood* (New York: Henry Holt, 2001), esp. 47–77; Myra Marx Ferree, "Beyond Separate Spheres: Feminism and Family Research," *Journal of Marriage and the Family*, 52 (1990): 866–884; and Nancy Folbre, "The Unproductive Housewife: Her Evolution in Nineteenth-Century Economic Thought," *Signs*, 16, no. 31 (1991): 463–484.

12. Cited in Folbre, p. 477, from *The Revolution*, eds. Susan B. Anthony and Elizabeth Cady Stanton (December 24, 1868), 393.

13. Ibid., 481. Of course, none of these explanations took account of unmarried women who had no men to count on for economic support.

14. Ferree, 873.

15. Folbre, 483.

16. Ferree, 871.

17. Joan Williams, *Unbending Gender: Why Family and Work Conflict and What to Do About It* (New York: Oxford University Press, 2000).

18. Arlie R. Hochschild, *The Second Shift: Working Parents and the Revolution at Home* (New York: Viking, 1989).

19. Ann Crittenden, *The Price of Motherhood* (New York: Henry Holt, 2001), 8.

20. Crittenden makes the point that not only have feminists overlooked inequalities in mothers' work, but women's organizations have abandoned mothers as well. See pp. 253–254.

21. Crittenden, 12, 23–24.

22. Ferree, 872.

23. Joan C. Williams, Jessica Manvell, and Stephanie Bornstein, *Report: "Opt Out" or Pushed Out?: How the Press Covers Work/Family Conflict* (San Francisco: University of California Hastings College of Law, Center for WorkLife Law, 2006), esp. 25.

24. Evidence is often marshaled to show that Americans are not working longer, but this is misleading, because women, who entered the workforce in large numbers during this period, are more likely than men to work part-time, thus reducing the average of hours per week worked. See Jared Bernstein and Karen Kornbluh, New America Foundation Research Paper, *Running Faster to Stay in Place: The Growth of Family Work Hours and Incomes* (Washington, DC: 2005), 1–10. http://newamerica.net/publications/policy/running_faster_to_stay_in_place (accessed May 21, 2009). Also, it appears that when households are studied rather than individuals, longer workweeks are concentrated among two-earner and single-parent families. See Kathleen Gerson and Jerry A. Jacobs, "Changing the Structure and Culture of Work: Work and Family Conflict, Work Flexibility, and Gender Equity in the Modern Workplace," in *Working Families: The Transformation of the American Home*, eds. Rosanna Hertz and Nancy L. Marshall (Berkeley: University of California Press, 2001), 207–226, esp. 208.

25. 57 percent and 54 percent, respectively. Ibid., 8–9.

26. Marybeth J. Mattingly and Liana C. Sayer, "Under Pressure: Gender Differences in the Relationship between Free Time and Feeling Rushed," *Journal of Marriage and Family*, 68 (2006): 205–221, esp. 208.

27. Ibid., 209.

28. Bernstein and Kornbluh, 9–10.

29. Ibid., 209.

30. Suzanne M. Bianchi, Melissa A. Milkie, Liana C. Sayer, and John P. Robinson, "Is Anyone Doing the Housework? Trends in the Gender Division of Household Labor," *Social Forces* 79, no. 1 (2000): 191–228. Nancy Folbre and colleagues clocked the average amount of parental time (both active and passive) devoted to children from birth to age eleven at 41.3 hours a week. See Nancy Folbre, *Valuing Children: Rethinking the Economics of the Family* (Cambridge, MA: Harvard University Press, 2008), 114.

31. Liana C. Sayer, "Gender, Time and Inequality: Trends in Women's and Men's Paid Work, Unpaid Work and Free Time," *Social Forces* 84, no. 1 (2005):

285–303. According to the U.S. Department of Labor's Bureau of Labor Statistics report, *American Time Use Survey*, 2009, on an average day, 20 percent of men did housework as compared with 51 percent of women, and on days when they did household labor, women spent 2.6 hours on it compared with men's 2.0 hours. Men were more likely to engage in sports, exercise, or recreation on a given day than were women, and they spent more time engaged in these activities when they did participate. http://www.bls.gov/news.release/atus.nr0.htm (accessed January 13, 2011).

32. Suzanne M. Bianchi and Sara B. Raley, "Time Allocation in Families," in *Work, Family, Health, and Well-Being*, eds. Suzanne M. Bianchi, Lynne M. Casper, and Rosalind Berkowitz King (Mahwah, NJ: Lawrence Erlbaum, 2005), 21–42, esp. 31. Also see Scott Coltrane, "Fatherhood, Gender, and Work-Family Policies," in *Gender Equality: Transforming Family Divisions of Labor*, eds. Janet C. Gornick and Marcia K. Meyers (London: Verso, 2009), 385–409, esp. 387.

33. Sayer, 287.

34. Rosalind C. Barnett and Yu-Chu Shen, "Gender, High- and Low-Schedule-Control Housework Tasks, and Psychological Distress: A Study of Dual-Earner Couples," *Journal of Family Issues* 18 (1997): 403–428.

35. Cynthia Fuchs Epstein, "Border Crossings: The Constraints of Time Norms in Transgressions of Gender and Professional Roles," in *Fighting for Time: Shifting Boundaries of Work and Social Life*, eds. Cynthia Fuchs Epstein and Arne L. Kalleberg, (New York: Russell Sage Foundation, 2004), 317–340, esp. 332–333.

36. Jerry A. Jacobs and Kathleen Gerson, "Understanding Changes in American Working Time: A Synthesis," in *Fighting for Time: Shifting Boundaries of Work and Social Life*, eds. Cynthia Fuchs Epstein and Arne L. Kalleberg (New York: Russell Sage Foundation, 2004), 25–45, esp. 26.

37. Ibid., 217, 34.

38. Schein, 83.

39. Garey, 95.

40. Julia R. Henly, H. Luke Shaefer, and Elaine Waxman, "Nonstandard Work Schedules: Employer- and Employee-Driven Flexibility in Retail Jobs," *Social Service Review* 80, no. 4 (2006): 609–634.

41. David M. Almeida and Daniel A. McDonald, "The National Story: How Americans Spend Their Time on Work, Family, and Community," in *Unfinished Work: Building Equality and Democracy in an Era of Working Families*, eds. Jody Heymann and Christopher Beem (New York: The New Press, 2005), 180–203. Also see Harriet B. Presser, "Employment in a 24/7 Economy: Challenges for the Family," in *Fighting for Time: Shifting Boundaries of Work and Social Life*, eds. Cynthia Fuchs Epstein and Arne L. Kalleberg (New York: Russell Sage Foundation, 2004), 46–76. Maureen Perry-Jenkins and her colleagues found that working nonstandard shifts resulted in depression and conflict for many new parents. See Maureen Perry-Jenkins, Abbie E. Goldberg, Courtney P. Pierce, and Aline G. Sayer, "Shift Work, Role Overload, and the Transition to Parenthood," *Journal of Marriage and the Family* 69, no. 1 (2007): 123–138.

42. Susan J. Douglas and Meredith W. Michaels, *The Mommy Myth: The Idealization of Motherhood and How It Has Undermined Women* (New York: Free Press, 2004).

43. Sharon Hays, *The Cultural Contradictions of Motherhood* (New Haven, CT: Yale University Press, 1996).

44. See Judith Warner, *Perfect Madness: Motherhood in the Age of Anxiety* (New York: Riverhead, 2005). Also see Joan Williams, *Unbending Gender*.

45. See Hays; Warner. See also Annette Lareau, *Unequal Childhoods: Class, Race, and Family Life* (Berkeley: University of California Press, 2003).

46. Williams, Manvell, and Bornstein, 23.

47. Warner, 132.

48. Molly McElroy, "Less Depression for Working Moms Who Expect That They Can't 'Do It All,'" *UW Today*, August 22, 2011. http://www.washington.edu/news/articles/less-depression-for-working-moms-who-expect-that-they-2018can2019t-do-it-all2019 (accessed August 29, 2011).

49. Ibid., 124.

50. In their study, "Relative Fairness and the Division of Housework: The Importance of Options," AJS, 100 (1994): 506–531, Mary Clare Lennon and Sarah Rosenfeld found that the perception of unfairness depended on whether or not women believed they had options (e.g., that could support themselves if not married). The women who viewed the inequality in the division of housework as fair were not worried that they would descend into poverty if they were divorced, whereas their counterparts who saw few, if any, options, viewed the inequality as unfair and were likely to be depressed.

51. Sabrina F. Askari, Mirian Liss, Mindy J. Erchull, Samantha E. Staebell, and Sarah J. Axelson, "Men Want Equality, but Women Don't Expect it: Young Adults' Expectations for Participation in Household and Child Care Chores," *Psychology of Women Quarterly* 34 (2010): 243–252.

52. Lara Descartes and Conrad P. Kottak, *Media and Middle-Class Moms* (New York: Routledge, 2009), 94.

53. Elizabeth Miklya Legerski and Marie Cornwall, "Working-Class Job Loss, Gender, and the Negotiation of Household Labor," *Gender & Society* 24 (2010): 447–474, esp. 457–458.

54. Sayer, 287.

55. Ferree, 876.

56. Francine M. Deutsch, *Halving It All: How Equally Shared Parenting Works* (Cambridge, MA: Harvard University Press, 1999).

57. Carmen Knudson-Martin and Anne Rankin Mahoney, "Language and Processes in the Construction of Equality in New Marriages," *Family Relations* 47, no. 1 (1998): 81–91.

58. Deutsch, quoted by Lisa Belkin, in "When Mom and Dad Share It All," *New York Times Magazine*, June 15, 2008, 44–51, 74, 78, esp. 47–48.

59. Ferree, 876, 877.

60. S. Colón and S. Nayyar, "25 Stories of Stellar Moms," *Working Mother*, November 2004, 44–56, esp. 54.

61. Denise Di Fulco, "How She Does It," *Working Mother*, November 2004, 15–16, esp. 16.

62. Colón and Nayyar, 47.
63. Joyce K. Fletcher, "Gender Perspectives on Work and Personal Life Research," in *Work, Family, Health, and Well-Being*, eds. Suzanne M. Bianchi, Lynne M. Casper, and Rosalind Berkowitz King (Mahwah, NJ: Lawrence Erlbaum, 2005), 329–341, esp. 331.
64. Colón and Nayyar, 52.
65. Joseph G. Gryzywacz, Adam B. Butler, and David M. Almeida, "Work, Family, and Health: Work-Family Balance as a Protective Factor Against Stresses of Daily Life," in *The Changing Realities of Work and Family: A Multidisciplinary Approach*, eds. Amy Marcus-Newhall, Diane F. Halpern, and Sherylle J. Tan, (Chichester, UK: Blackwell, 2008), 194–215, esp. 194–195.
66. John MacInness, "Work-Life Balance: Three Terms in Search of a Definition," in *Work Less, Live More? Critical Analysis of the Work-Life Boundary*, eds. Chris Warhurst, Doris Ruth Eikhof and Axel Haunschild (Basingstoke, UK: Palgrave Macmillan, 2008), 44–61, esp. 45; Christopher Lasch, *Haven in a Heartless world: The Family Besieged* (New York: Basic Books, 1977).
67. Decartes and Kottak, 47.
68. R. W. Connell, "A Really Good Husband: Work/Life Balance, Gender Equity and Social Change," *Australian Journal of Social Issues* 40, no. 3(2005): 369–383, esp. 375.
69. Cynthia Fuchs Epstein, "Border Crossings: The Constraints of Time Norms in Transgressions of Gender and Professional Roles," in *Fighting for Time: Shifting Boundaries of Work and Social Life*, eds. Cynthia Fuchs Epstein and Arne L. Kalleberg, (New York: Russell Sage Foundation, 2004), 317–340, esp. 326, 331.
70. Ibid., 160–162, for a discussion of research on positive aspects of multiple role occupancy. See also Rena Repetti, "A Psychological Perspective on the Health and Well-Being Consequences of Parental Employment," in *Work, Family, Health, and Well-Being*, eds. Suzanne M. Bianchi, Lynne M. Casper, and Rosalind Berkowitz King (Mahwah, NJ: Lawrence Erlbaum, 2005), 245–258.
71. Maureen Perry-Jenkins, Rena L. Repetti, and Ann C. Crouter, "Work and Family in the 1990s." *Journal of Marriage and the Family* 62, no. 4 (2000): 981–998, esp. 987–988.
72. Peggy McDonough, Vivienne Walters, and Lisa Strohschein, "Chronic Stress and the Patterning of Women's Health in Canada," *Social Science & Medicine* 54 (2002): 767–782, esp. 769.
73. See Sylvia Ann Hewlett, *Off-Ramps and On-Ramps* (Boston: Harvard Business School Press, 2007), 36. African American women spend, on average, 12.4 hours more on such care than White women, and many African American professional women are caring for their own families, extended families, and members of the community who are in need.
74. Tarani Chandola, Hannah Kuper, Archana Singh-Manoux, Mel Bartley, and Michael Marmot, "The Effect of Control at Home on CHD Events in the Whitehall II Study: Gender Differences in Psychosocial Domestic Pathways to Social Inequalities in CHD," *Social Science & Medicine* 58 (2004): 1501–1509.

75. Sarah P. Wamala, Murray A. Mittleman, Myrian Horstein, Karin Schenck-Gustafson, and Kristina Orth-Gomer, "Job Stress and the Occupational Gradient in Coronary Heart Disease Risk in Women," *Social Science & Medicine* 51 (2000): 481–489.

76. Nancy E. Moss, "Gender Equity and Socioeconomic Inequality: A Framework for the Patterning of Women's Health," *Social Science & Medicine* 54 (2002): 649–661, esp. 656. Gender inequalities are among the factors that adversely affect women's health; see Donna M. Strobino, Holly Grason, and Cynthia Minkovitz, "Charting a Course for the Future of Women's Health in the United States: Concepts, Findings and Recommendations," *Social Science & Medicine* 54 (2002): 839–848.

77. Lois Bryson, Penny Warner-Smith, Peter Brown, and Leanne Fray, "Managing the Work-Life Roller-Coaster: Private Stress or Public Health Issue?" *Social Science & Medicine* 65 (2007): 1142–1153, esp. 1151.

78. Faye J. Crosby and Karen L. Jaskar, "Women and Men at Home and at Work: Realities and Illusions," in *Gender Issues in Contemporary Society*, eds. Stuart Oskamp and Mark Costanzo (Newbury Park, CA: Sage, 1993), 143–171.

79. Faye J. Crosby, *Juggling: The Unexpected Advantages of Balancing Career and Home for Women and Their Families* (New York: Free Press, 1991), esp. 17.

80. Ibid., 11.

81. Kim Parker, "The Harried Life of the Working Mother," PewResearchCenter Social & Demographic Trends (Washington, DC: 2009). http://pewsocial-trends.org/2009/10/01/the-harried-life-of-the-working-mother/#prc-jump (accessed May 11, 2011).

82. Crosby, 195.

83. MacInness, 46.

84. For an extensive discussion and critique of stress management techniques, see Angela Patmore's *The Truth About Stress* (London: Atlantic Books, 2009).

85. Jeffrey H. Greenhaus and Saroj Parasuraman, "The Allocation of Time to Work and Family Roles," in *Gender, Work Stress, and Health*, eds. Debra L. Nelson and Ronald J. Burke (Washington, DC: American Psychological Association, 2002), 115–128, esp. 123.

86. Work-family conflict has been associated with depression, alcoholism, hypertension, and other health problems. But, as Gryzywacz et al. point out (pp. 197–198), "it is becoming increasingly clear that stressors can act on health in complex and multifaceted ways, suggesting that a simple 'direct effects' model may not adequately capture the health effects of work-family balance."

87. Ibid., 205. Something they *did* find, however, was that work-family *imbalance* did not make women more vulnerable to illness, whereas when work and family were not well balanced *men's* exposure to stress had a significant impact on their distress.

88. Melissa A. Milkie and Pia Peltola, "Playing All the Roles: Gender and the Work-Family Balancing Act," *Journal of Marriage and the Family* 61, no. 2 (1999): 476–490.

89. Pew Research Center Social & Demographic Trends Report, *From 1997 to 2007: Fewer Mothers Prefer Full-time Work* (Washington, DC: 2007), http://pewresearch.org/assets/social/pdf/WomenWorking.pdf (accessed May 11, 2011). In 1997, 32 percent of working mothers said that part-time work would be "ideal" for them, as compared with 60 percent in 2007.

90. Hewlett, 30.

91. Pew Research Center, 4.

92. Garey, 107.

93. The Urban Institute, Economic Policy Institute Brief #155, Jeffrey Wenger, *The Continuing Problems [sic] with Part-Time Jobs* (Washington, DC: 2001). http://www.epi.org/publications/entry/issuebriefs_ib155 (accessed September 14, 2010).

94. See Joan C. Williams, "What Psychologists Need to Know about Family Responsibilities Discrimination," in *The Changing Realities of Work and Family: A Multidisciplinary Approach*, eds. Amy Marcus-Newhall, Diane F. Halpern, and Sherylle J. Tan (Chichester, UK: John Wiley & Sons, 2008), 255–276, especially 255–256. Williams points out that "while the wage gap between men and women has been narrowing, the gap between working women without children and working women with children has actually increased.... It is greatest for single mothers."

95. Strong evidence exists that there is widespread employer discrimination against mothers. See Shelley J. Correll, Stephen Benard, and In Paik, "Getting a Job: Is There a Motherhood Penalty?" *American Journal of Sociology* 112, no. 5 (2007): 1297–1338, esp. 1332.

96. Jane Waldfogel, "The Effect of Children on Women's Wages," *American Sociological Review* 62 (1997): 209–217.

97. Gerson and Jacobs, "Changing the Structure," 213–214.

98. Meryl Gordon, "Sarah Jessica Parker Gets Real," *Parade*, August 21, 2011, 6–8, 11–13.

99. Karen Crouse, "A Simpler Time," *New York Times*, August 1, 2010, Sports Sunday, 1, 8.

100. See Douglas and Michaels.

101. See Diana Tietjens Meyers, *Gender in the Mirror: Cultural Imagery and Women's Agency* (New York: Oxford University Press, 2002), esp. Chapter 2, for an acute analysis of why the decision to become a mother is so culturally freighted.

102. Sanford F. Schram, *After Welfare: The Culture of Postindustrial Social Policy* (New York: New York University Press, 2000), 39–40.

103. Epstein, 333.

104. Hewlett, esp.7–9.

105. Sara Eckel, "Time-out for the Type A," *Philadelphia Inquirer*, January 4, 2005, D-1, D-8.

106. Stewart D. Friedman and Jeffrey Greenhaus, *Work and Family—Allies or Enemies? What Happens When Business Professionals Confront Life Choices* (New York: Oxford University Press, 2000), esp. 124, 126.

107. Ibid., 31–32. To be scrupulously fair, Friedman and Greenhaus do acknowledge that there are some constraints on women's choices as well as inequities in childcare and domestic labor.
108. Ibid., 32.
109. Linda R. Hirshman, *Get to Work: A Manifesto for Women of the World* (New York: Viking, 2006), esp. 17.
110. Nikolas Rose, *Inventing Ourselves: Psychology, Power, and Personhood* (Cambridge: Cambridge University Press, 1998), esp. 227.
111. Barbara J. Risman, *Gender Vertigo: American Families in Transition* (New Haven, CT: Yale University Press, 1998), especially 32, 34–35.
112. Martha Albertson Fineman, *The Autonomy Myth: A Theory of Dependency* (New York: The New Press, 2004), 41.
113. Diane Kobrynowicz and Monica Biernat, "Decoding Subjective Evaluations: How Stereotypes Provide Shifting Standards," *Journal of Experimental Social Psychology* 33 (1997): 579–601, esp. 592–593.
114. Cited in Williams, Manvell, and Bornstein.
115. Hewlett, esp. 7–9.
116. Arielle Kuperberg and Pamela Stone, "The Media Depiction of Women Who Opt Out," *Gender & Society* 22, no. 4 (2008): 497–517, esp. 502.
117. Hewlett, 36–37.
118. Pamela Stone, *Opting Out? Why Women Really Quit Careers and Head Home* (Berkeley: University of California Press, 2007), 68.
119. Ibid., 77–78.
120. John Dixon and Margaret Wetherell, "On Discourse and Dirty Nappies: Gender, the Division of Household Labour and the Social Psychology of Distributive Justice," *Theory & Psychology* 14, no. 2 (2004): 167–189, esp. 179.
121. See Joan C. Williams, *Reshaping the Work-Family Debate: Why Men and Class Matter* (Cambridge, MA: Harvard University Press, 2010), esp. 81.
122. Ibid., G1-2.
123. Sue Falter Mennino and April Brayfield, "Job-family Trade-Offs: The Multidimensional Effects of Gender," *Work and Occupations* 29 (2002): 226–256. See also Gerson and Jacobs, "Changing the Structure," 210.
124. Williams, *Reshaping*, 81.
125. Ibid., 83.
126. Ibid., 83.
127. See U.S. Bureau of Labor Statistics for July 2011. http://www.bls.gov/news.release/empsit.t02.htm (accessed August 10, 2011).
128. Lynette Clemetson, "Work vs. Family, Complicated by Race," *New York Times*, February 9, 2006, G1-2.
129. Ibid., G1-2.
130. Joy Bennett Kinnon, "A Divided Duty," *Ebony*, July 2003, 30.
131. Clemetson, G2.
132. See typical examples of such advice in the special section "Take a Breath and… Calm Down, Chill Out," in *O, The Oprah Magazine*, October 2002, 240–259.

133. "Make Time for Yourself to Relieve Stress, Fatigue," *Indianapolis Recorder*, April 13, 2001, D-10. See also Karen De Witt, "Turn Chaos into Calm," *Essence*, January 2003, 99–102.

134. "Modern Mothers," *Ebony* (special issue, "The New Frontier"), August 1993, 60.

135. "Guarding gainst the Stress of Success," *Black Enterprise* (February 2003). www.blackenterprise.com/February-2003 (accessed July 6, 2010).

136. Connell, 378.

137. See John MacInness, 58.

138. Coverage was extended in 1997 to include participation in children's educational activities and taking elderly relatives to appointments.

139. Catherine Albiston, "Anti-Essentialism and the Work/Family Dilemma," *Berkeley Journal of Gender, Law, & Social Justice* 20 (2005): 30–50.

140. Cited in Erin Gielow, "Equality in the Workplace: Why Family Leave Does Not Work," *Southern California Law Review* 75 (2002): 1529–1551, esp. 1543.

141. Ibid.

142. Malin, cited in Gielow, 1545.

143. For a lengthy exposition of the subject of de-gendering care, see Judith Lorber, *Breaking the Bowls: Degendering and Feminist Change* (New York: Norton, 2005), esp. Chapter 2.

144. Kate Zernicke, "Gains, and Drawbacks, for Female Professors" (National, *New York Times*, March 21, 2011), A15.

145. Anita Shreve, "Careers and the Lure of Motherhood," *New York Times*, November 21, 1982, 38.

146. Fineman, 10.

147. Deanna Chityat, Psychology International UN Report, *Gender Equity in Caregiving: The United Nations Response*. http://apa.org/international/pi/2009/07/un-gender.aspx (accessed July 31, 2009).

148. Ibid., 239.

149. MacInness, 58.

150. Huffington Post Blog; "Sleep Challenge 2010: Women, It's Time to Sleep Our Way to the Top. Literally," blog entry by Arianna Huffington and Cindi Leive, January 4, 2010, http://www.huffingtonpost.com/arianna-huffington/sleep-challenge-2010-wome_b_409973.html (accessed August 3, 2011).

151. Erin L. Kelly, Samantha K. Ammons, Kelly Chermack, and Phyllis Moen, "Gendered Challenge, Gendered Response: Confronting the Ideal Worker Norm in a White-Collar Organization," *Gender & Society* 24, no. 3 (2010): 281–303.

152. Ibid., 290–291.

153. Ibid., 289; also 294.

154. Ibid., 298.

155. Gerson and Jacobs, "Changing the Structure," 221.

156. Ibid., 221.

CHAPTER 6

1. From *On the Genealogy of Morals*, cited in Ian Hacking, *Rewriting the Soul: Multiple Personality and the Sciences of Memory* (Princeton, NJ: Princeton University Press, 1998).
2. Statement made at the Battle of Fredericksburg, December 13, 1862.
3. http://www.cnn.com/2007/SHOWBIZ/TV/06/27/king.hilton.transcript/index.html (accessed September 22, 2011).
4. In Arthur Kleinman, *What Really Matters: Living a Moral Life Amidst Uncertainty and Danger* (Oxford: Oxford University Press, 2006), 32.
5. Ibid., 33.
6. Ibid., 35.
7. Ibid., 36.
8. Ibid., 42.
9. Hacking, *Rewriting the Soul*; see also Jeff Sugarman, "Historical Ontology and Psychological Description," *Journal of Theoretical and Philosophical Psychology* 29, no. 1 (2009): 5–15.
10. See Scott Shane, "A Deluge of Troubled Soldiers Is in the Offing, Experts Predict," *New York Times*, December 16, 2004, A1. http://www.lexisnexis.com/; Lizette Alvarez and Erik Eckholm, "Purple Heart Is Ruled Out for Traumatic Stress," *New York Times* January 8, 2009. http://www.lexisnexis.com/ (accessed July 23, 2011).
11. Katherine N. Boone and Frank C. Richardson, "War Neurosis: A Cultural Historical and Theoretical Inquiry," *Journal of Theoretical and Philosophical Psychology* 30, no. 2 (2010): 109–121.
12. Derek Summerfield, "Cross-Cultural Perspectives on the Medicalization of Human Suffering," in *Posttraumatic Stress Disorder: Issues and Controversies*, ed. Gerald Rosen (Hoboken, NJ: Wiley, 2004), 233–245, esp. 241.
13. Cited in Patrick J. Bracken, *Trauma: Culture, Meaning and Philosophy* (London: Whurr Publishers, 2002), 73.
14. Amy Novotny, "Calming the Tremors: Psychologists Provide Expertise in the Aftermath of the Earthquakes in Haiti and Chile," *Monitor on Psychology* 41, no. 4 (2010): 20–22.
15. See Ethan Watters, *Crazy Like Us: The Globalisation of the American Psyche* (Carlton North, Victoria, Australia: Scribe Publications, 2010).
16. Hanna Kienzler, "Debating War-Trauma and Post-Traumatic Stress Disorder (PTSD) in an Interdisciplinary Arena," *Social Science and Medicine* 67 (2008): 218–277, esp. 225. Medical anthropologist Arthur Kleinman has called this process "social suffering." See Arthur Kleinman, *Writing at the Margin: Discourse between Anthropology and Medicine* (Berkeley: University of California Press, 1995).
17. Derek Summerfield, "The Invention of Post-Traumatic Stress Disorder and the Social Usefulness of a Psychiatric Category," *British Medical Journal* 322 (2001): 95–98.
18. Summerfield, "Cross-Cultural Perspectives."
19. Ibid., 234–235. Also see Frank Furedi, *Therapy Culture: Cultivating Vulnerability in an Uncertain Age* (New York: Routledge, 2004), esp. 129.

20. Sadie F. Dingfelder, "The Smallest Survivors," *Monitor on Psychology* 39, no. 9 (2008): 34–35, esp. 34.

21. Bruce Rind, Philip Tromovitch, and Robert Bauserman, "A Meta-Analytic Examination of Assumed Properties of Child Sexual Abuse Using College Samples," *Psychological Bulletin* 124 (1998): 22–53.

22. See Richard J. McNally, "Progress and Controversy in the Study of Posttraumatic Stress Disorder," *Annual Review of Psychology* 54 (2003): 229–252, esp. 245–246, for a complete account of the episode and its sequelae.

23. Boone and Richardson, 119.

24. Derek Summerfield, "Cross-Cultural Perspectives," 234.

25. Arthur Kleinman, *Rethinking Psychiatry: From Cultural Category to Personal Experience* (New York: Free Press, 1988), esp. 7.

26. Summerfield, "Cross-Cultural Perspectives," 237.

27. For an uncannily prescient analysis of the relationship between stress and disorder, see Richard A. Cloward and Frances Fox Piven, "Hidden Protest: The Channeling of Female Innovation and Protest," *Signs* 4, no. 4 (1979): 651–669.

28. Michael R. Trimble is in this camp. See his chapter "Post-traumatic Stress Disorder: History of a Concept," in *Trauma and Its Wake: The Study and Treatment of Post-Traumatic Stress Disorder*, ed. Charles R. Figley (New York: Brunner/Mazel, 1995), 5–14.

29. For a discussion of the debates, see Ruth Leys, *Trauma: A Genealogy* (Chicago: University of Chicago Press, 2000); see also Mark S. Micale and Paul Lerner, "Trauma, Psychiatry, and History," in *Traumatic Pasts: History, Psychiatry, and Trauma in the Modern Age, 1870–1930*, eds. Mark S. Micale and Paul Lerner (Cambridge: Cambridge University Press, 2001), 1–27.

30. Bracken, 65–67.

31. Railroad accidents were quite frequent during the several decades after the expansion of the railway system. For a full examination of "railway spine," see Eric Caplan, *Mind Games: American Culture and the Birth of Psychotherapy* (Berkeley: University of California Press, 1998), esp. Chapter 2. See also F. G. Gosling, *Before Freud: Neurasthenia and the American Medical Community, 1870–1910* (Urbana: University of Illinois Press, 1987), ff. 91, for a discussion of traumatic neurasthenia.

32. Paula J. Caplan, *When Johnny and Jane Come Marching Home* (Cambridge, MA: MIT Press, 2011), esp. 117.

33. Jonathan Finer, "Frontline Care for 'At Risk' Soldiers; Army Effort Treats Psychological Trauma at Source," *Washington Post*, June 8, 2006, A1. http://www.lexisnexis.com/ (accessed July 23, 2011).

34. Simon Wessely, "War Stories: Invited Commentary on 'Documented Combat Exposure of US Veterans Seeking Treatment for Combat-Related Post-Traumatic Stress Disorder,'" *British Journal of Psychiatry* 186 (2005): 473–475.

35. Ibid., 475.

36. Wilbur J. Scott, "PTSD in DSM-III: A Case in the Politics of Diagnosis and Disease," *Social Problems* 37, no. 3 (1990): 294–310, esp. 308.

37. Summerfield, "Cross-Cultural Perspectives," 239.
38. Dan J. Stein, Wai Tat Chiu, Irving Hwang, et al. "Cross-National Analysis of the Associations between Traumatic Events and Suicidal Behavior: Findings from the WHO World Mental Health Surveys," 2010. PLoS ONE 5(5): e10574. doi:10.1371/journal.pone.0010574 (accessed September 12, 2011).
39. Patrick Peterson, "United States Tries New Combat-Stress Treatment," *Philadelphia Inquirer*, April 27, 2004, A12. http://www.lexisnexis.com/ (accessed July 23, 2011).
40. Gregg Zoroya, "Order Would Require Troubled Marines To Be Checked for Stress," *USA Today*, October 2, 2007, 10A. http://www.lexisnexis.com/ (accessed July 23, 2011); Mark Thompson, "America's Medicated Army," *Time*, June 5, 2008. http://www.time.com/time/magazine/article/0,9171,1812055,00.html (accessed June 23, 2009).
41. Jeanne Marecek, "Trauma Talk in Feminist Clinical Practice," in *New Versions of Victims: Feminists Struggle with the Concept*, ed. Sharon Lamb (New York: New York University Press, 1999), 158–182, esp. 163.
42. For the history of the development PTSD diagnosis, I rely on the following accounts: Wilbur J. Scott, "PTSD in DSM-III"; Edgar Jones and Simon Wessely, "A Paradigm Shift in the Conceptualization of Psychological Trauma in the 20th Century," *Journal of Anxiety Disorders* 21 (2007): 164–175; Allan Young, *The Harmony of Illusions: Inventing Post-Traumatic Stress Disorder* (Ewing, NJ: Princeton University Press, 1995).
43. Scott, 298.
44. Eric T. Dean, Jr., *Shook over Hell: Post-Traumatic Stress, Vietnam, and the Civil War* (Cambridge, MA: Harvard University Press, 1997), 14.
45. Herb Kutchins and Stuart A. Kirk, *Making Us Crazy: DSM: The Psychiatric Bible and the Creation of Mental Disorders* (New York: Free Press, 1997), 116.
46. For a more comprehensive discussion of the *DSM*, see Dana Becker, *Through the Looking Glass: Women and Borderline Personality Disorder* (Boulder, CO: Westview, 1997), 34–36.
47. American Psychiatric Association, *Diagnostic and Statistical Manual of Mental Disorders*, 3rd ed. (Washington, DC: Author, 1980), 236.
48. Young, 129.
49. On one side of the debate, see Elizabeth F. Loftus, *The Myth of Repressed Memory* (New York: St. Martin's Press, 1994); on the other, see Jennifer Freyd, *Betrayal Trauma* (Cambridge, MA: Harvard University Press, 1996). For a more recent consideration of the debates, see Robert F. Belli, ed., *True and False Recovered Memories: Toward a Reconciliation of the Debate* (New York: Springer, 2012).
50. See Ben Shephard, "Risk Factors and PTSD: A Historian's Perspective," in *Posttraumatic Stress Disorder: Issues and Controversies*, ed. Gerald Rosen (Hoboken, NJ: Wiley, 2004), 39–61.
51. American Psychiatric Association, *Diagnostic and Statistical Manual of Mental Disorders*, 3rd ed., revised (Washington, DC: Author, 1987), 247.

52. American Psychiatric Association, *Diagnostic and Statistical Manual of Mental Disorders*, 4th ed. (Washington, DC: Author, 1994), 427–428.

53. Ibid., 424, for examples of traumatic events.

54. Naomi Breslau and Ronald C. Kessler, "The Stressor Criterion in DSM-IV Posttraumatic Stress Disorder: An Empirical Investigation," *Biological Psychiatry* 50 (2001): 699–704.

55. Peg Tyre, "Battling the Effects of War," *Newsweek*, December 6, 2004, 68 (cover story).

56. This figure comes from *The National Comorbidity Survey Replication (NCS-R)*. http://www.ptsd.va.gov/professional/pages/epidemiological-facts-ptsd.asp (accessed October 3, 2011).

57. John E. Helzer, Lee N. Robins, and Lawrence T. McEvoy, "Post-Traumatic Stress Disorder in the General Population: Findings of the Epidemiological Catchment Area Survey," *New England Journal of Medicine* 317, no. 26 (1987): 1630–1634.

58. Breslau and Kessler, 699.

59. Richard McNally calls the expansion of diagnostic criteria "conceptual bracket creep." See Richard J. McNally, "Progress and Controversy," 231.

60. Herb Kutchins and Stuart A. Kirk, Making us Crazy: DSM: The Psychiatric Bible and the Creation of Mental Disorders (New York: Free Press, 1997).

61. Kutchins and Kirk, 124.

62. Dana Becker, "When She Was Bad: Borderline Personality Disorder in a Posttraumatic Age," *American Journal of Orthopsychiatry* 70, no. 4 (2000): 422–432.

63. See the proposed changes on the American Psychiatric Association's *DSM-5* Development website, http://www.dsm5.org/ProposedRevisions/Pages/proposedrevision.aspx?rid=165 (accessed September 20, 2011).

64. See Paul R. McHugh and Glenn Treisman, "PTSD: A Problematic Diagnostic Category," *Journal of Anxiety Disorders* 21 (2007): 211–222, esp. 217, for a graph showing PTSD publications from 1979 to 2005. The *Journal of Traumatic Stress* was first published in 1988.

65. Rachel Yehuda and Alexander C. McFarlane, "Conflict between Current Knowledge about Posttraumatic Stress Disorder and Its Original Conceptual Basis," *American Journal of Psychiatry* 152 (1995): 1705–1713.

66. J. Alexander Bodkin, Harrison G. Pope, Michael J. Detke, and James I. Hudson, "Is PTSD Caused by Traumatic Stress?" *Journal of Anxiety Disorders* 21 (2007): 176–182. See also Sari D. Gold, Brian P. Marx, Jose M. Soler-Baillo, and Denise M. Sloan, "Is Life Stress More Traumatic Than Traumatic Stress?" *Anxiety Disorders* 19 (2005): 687–698. In Gold et al.'s study in which one group of students reported a history of one or more traumatic events and a second group reported experiencing an event that would not be considered traumatic under the current PTSD diagnosis, the second group reported more PTSD symptoms than the first. Yet another study of 1,498 adults showed similar results: people who reported that their "worst" event was a life event such as a marital problem, unemployment, or chronic illness had more PTSD symptoms than people who reported an event defined as traumatic in the terms of the *DSM*. For this study,

see Saskia S. L. Mol, Arnoud Arntz, Job F. M. Metsemakers, et al., "Symptoms of Post-Traumatic Stress Disorder After Non-Traumatic Events: Evidence from an Open Population Study," *British Journal of Psychiatry* 186 (2005): 494–499.

67. Bodkin et al., 182.

68. McNally, "Progress and Controversy," 234.

69. McHugh and Treisman, 217.

70. Young, 120.

71. McHugh and Treisman, 220.

72. Naomi Breslau, Holly C. Wilcox, Carla L. Storr et al., "Trauma Exposure and Posttraumatic Stress Disorder: A Study of Youths in Urban America," *Journal of Urban Health: Bulletin of the New York Academy of Medicine* 81, no. 4 (2004): 530–544.

73. "Psychiatry: Dividend from Viet Nam," *Time*, October 10, 1969. http://www.time.com/time/magazine/article/0,9171,839053,00.html (accessed June 23, 2009).

74. See for example, a piece on MSNBC's health website (June 23, 2004) in which Dr. Matthew J. Friedman, executive director of the Department of Veterans Affairs' National Center for Post-Traumatic Stress Disorder, was quoted as saying that an estimate of 1 in 8 military personnel with mental health problems was probably too low. http://www.msnbc.msn.com/id/5334479/ns/health-mental_health/t/returning-soldiers-suffers-ptsd/#.ToN2POw0G (accessed September 28, 2011).

75. Scott Shane, "A Deluge of Troubled Soldiers Is in the Offing, Experts Predict," *New York Times*, December 16, 2004, A1. http://www.lexisnexis.com/ (accessed July 23, 2011); Anahad O'Connor, "1 in 6 Veterans Is Found to Have Stress-Related Disorder," *New York Times*, July 1, 2004, A12. http://www.lexisnexis.com/ (accessed August 18, 2011).

76. Wessely, "War Stories," 474.

77. See Richard J. McNally, "Can We Solve the Mysteries of the National Vietnam Veterans Readjustment Study?" *Journal of Anxiety Disorders* 21 (2007): 192–200; see also Bruce P. Dohrenwend, J. Blake Turner, Nicholas A. Turse, et al., "The Psychological Risks of Vietnam for U.S. Vets: A Revisit with New Data and Methods," *Science* 18 (August 2006): 979–982.

78. Young (p. 111) points out that most of the research on PTSD has been based on Vietnam veterans. These figures, then, had a particularly large impact.

79. Dohrenwend et al.

80. B. Christopher Frueh, Jon D. Elhai, Anouk L. Grubaugh et al., "Documented Combat Exposure of U.S. Veterans Seeking Treatment for Combat-Related Post-Traumatic Stress Disorder," *The British Journal of Psychiatry* 186 (2005): 467–472.

81. One must, of course, put the figures in context. When McNally compares them with estimates of psychiatric casualties in World War II (from 28 to 101 per 1,000 soldiers) and the Korean war (37 per 1,000), the Vietnam figure does not look so huge. See McNally, "Progress and Controversy," 230.

82. Benedict Carey, "Review of Landmark Study Finds Fewer Vietnam Veterans with Post-Traumatic Stress," *New York* Times, August 18, 2006.http://www.

nytimes.com/2006/08/18/health/policy/18psych.html (accessed March 19, 2009).

83. Brad Knickerbocker, "PTSD: New Regs [sic] Will Make It Easier for War Veterans to Get Help," *Christian Science Monitor*, July 10, 2010. http://www. lexisnexis.com/ (accessed July 23, 2011).

84. Quotation in Scott A. Baldwin, Daniel C. Williams, and Arthur C. Houts, "The Creation, Expansion, and Embodiment of Posttraumatic Stress Disorder: A Case Study in Historical Critical Psychopathology," *The Scientific Review of Mental Health Practice* 3, no. 1 (2004), 33–57, esp. 46.

85. Christina Hoff Sommers and Sally Satel, *One Nation Under Therapy* (New York: St. Martin's Press, 2005).

86. Abby Goodnough, "Post-9/11 Pain Found to Linger in Young Minds," *New York Times*, May 2, 2002. http://www.nytimes.com/2002/05/02/nyregion/ post-9-11-pain-found-to-linger-in-young-minds.html (accessed September 13, 2011).

87. David J. Hoff, "A Year Later, Impact of 9/11 Lingers," *Education Week*, September 11, 2002.

88. Amanda Spake and Marianne Szegedy-Maszak, "The Second Wave," *U.S. News and World Report*, October 8, 2001, 50. http://www.lexisnexis.com/ (accessed January 28, 2009).

89. See Joyce Purnick, "In Schools, A Hidden Toll of Sept. 11," *New York Times*, May 13, 2002, B1 (Metropolitan Desk).

90. Mark A. Schuster et al., "A National Survey of Stress Reactions After the September 11, 2001, Terrorist Attacks," *New England Journal of Medicine* 345, no. 20 (2001): 1507–1212, esp. 1511.

91. David F. Tolin and Edna B. Foa, "Sex Differences in Trauma and Posttraumatic Stress Disorder: A Quantitative Review of 25 Years of Research," *Psychological Bulletin* 132, no. 6 (2006): 959–992, esp. 979.

92. Even in the face of this low prevalence rate, however, the authors of the study were quick to assert that "in the general population of the NYC metropolitan area this is equivalent to approximately 142,000 persons…a substantial proportion of whom may be expected to have long-term symptoms." See Sandro Galea et al., "Post-Traumatic Stress Symptoms in the General Population after a Disaster: Implications for Public Health," in *9/11: Mental Health in the Wake of Terrorist Attacks*, eds. Yuval Neria, Raz Gross, and Randall D. Marshall (Cambridge: Cambridge University Press, 2006), 19–44, esp. 29, 39.

93. William E. Schlenger et al., "Psychological Reactions to Terrorist Attacks: Findings from the National Study of Americans' Reactions to September 11," *Journal of the American Medical Association* 288, no. 5 (2002): 581–588.

94. Greg Gittrich, "9-11 Trauma Aid in Limbo," *New York Daily News*, May 27, 2003. http://www.nydailynews.com/archives/news/2003/05/27/2003-05-27_9-11_trauma_aid_in_limbo__mi.html (accessed September 12, 2011).

95. Robert Rosenheck and Alan Fontana, "Use of Mental Health Services by Veterans with PTSD After the Terrorist Attacks of September 11," *American Journal of Psychiatry* 160 (2003): 1684–1690.

96. See advertising supplement, *New York Times Sunday Magazine*, October 28, 2001; see also Benjamin C. Druss and Steven C. Marcus, "Use of Psychotropic Medications Before and After Sept. 11, 2001," *American Journal of Psychiatry* 161 (2004): 1377–1383.

97. Erica Goode, "Calculating the Toll of Trauma," *New York Times*, September 9, 2003 (Health and Fitness). http://www.nytimes.com/2003/09/09/health/calculating-the-toll-of-trauma.html (accessed June 16, 2010).

98. This story is recounted in Anemona Hartocollis, "10 Years and a Diagnosis Later, 9/11 Demons Haunt Thousands," *New York Times*, August 9, 2011, A1.

99. Yuval Neria, Laura DiGrande, and Ben G. Adams, "Posttraumatic Stress Disorder Following the September 11, 2001, Terrorist Attacks," *American Psychologist* 66, no. 6 (2011): 429–446.

100. Ibid., 442.

101. Naomi Breslau and Richard J. McNally, "The Epidemiology of 9/11: Technological Advances and Conceptual Conundrums," in *9/11: Mental Health in the Wake of Terrorist Attacks*, eds. Yuval Neria, Raz Gross, and Randall D. Marshall (Cambridge: Cambridge University Press, 2006), 521–528, esp. 525–526.

102. Patricia J. Watson, Melissa J. Brymer, and George A. Bonanno, "Postdisaster Psychological Intervention Since 9/11," *American Psychologist* 66, no. 6 (2011): 482–494, esp. 485–486.

103. Among other studies on the subject, see Arnold A. P. van Emmerik et al., "Single Session Debriefing after Psychological Trauma: A Meta-analysis," *Lancet* 360 (2002): 766–771.

104. McHugh and Treisman (p. 219) list some of these studies, one of which was conducted by the National Center for PTSD.

105. Mark Thompson, "America's Medicated Army," *Time*, June 5, 2008. http://www.time.com/time/magazine/article/0,9171,1812055,00.html(accessed June 23, 2009).

106. Quotes are from *The Iraq War Clinician Guide*, cited in P. Caplan, 116–117. For more on the military's response to mental health problems, see Chapter 4 of Caplan's book.

107. Of all the treatments studied, exposure therapies seemed to have the most solid evidentiary basis; however, definitive evidence was lacking for all treatments. Board on Population Health and Public Health Practice, *Treatment of Posttraumatic Stress Disorder* (Washington, DC: Institute of Medicine, 2008), esp. ix.

108. Tori DeAngelis, "PTSD Treatments Grow in Evidence, Effectiveness," *Monitor on Psychology* 39, no. 1 (2008): 40–43, esp. 42.

109. Ibid., 41.

110. P. Caplan, 73.

111. Ronald C. Kessler et al., "Posttraumatic Stress Disorder in the National Comorbidity Survey," *Archives of General Psychiatry* 52, no. 12 (1995): 1048–1060.

112. See more on the subject of predisposition in Edgar Jones and Simon Wessely, "A Paradigm Shift."

113. See Shephard's discussion of the historical question of predisposition.
114. Cited in Shephard, 50. Shephard refers to a program instituted during the Vietnam War to help disadvantaged young men enter the military, in which 350,000 were recruited. About 40 percent of them were trained for combat, many with IQs well below average.
115. Bob Herbert, "War's Psychic Toll," *New York Times*, May 19, 2009, A23 (Op-Ed).
116. Gretel C. Kovach, "Combat's Inner Cost," *Newsweek*, November 5, 2007. http://www.lexisnexis.com/ (accessed July, 23, 2011).
117. Herbert, "War's Psychic Toll."
118. For an astringent discussion of the current fixation on troops as heroes, see William Deresiewicz, "An Empty Regard," *New York Times*, August 21, 2011, SR-1 (Sunday Review).
119. Laura DiGrande, Yuval Neria, Robert M. Brackbill, Paul Pulliam, and Sandro Galea, "Long-term Posttraumatic Stress Symptoms Among 3,271 Civilian Survivors of the September 11, 2001, Terrorist Attacks on the World Trade Center," *American Journal of Epidemiology* 173, no. 3 (2010): 271–281; Sandro Galea et al., "Hispanic Ethnicity and Post-traumatic Stress Disorder after a Disaster: Evidence from a General Population Survey after September 11, 2001," *Annals of Epidemiology* 14 (2004): 520–531.
120. DiGrande et al.
121. Ibid., 278.
122. Ronnie Janoff-Bulman, *Shattered Assumptions: Towards a New Psychology of Trauma* (New York: Free Press, 1992).
123. Stevan E. Hobfoll, "Conservation of Resources: A New Attempt at Conceptualizing Stress," *American Psychologist* 44, no. 3 (1989): 513–524.
124. Stevan E. Hobfoll, Melissa Tracy, and Sandro Galea, "The Impact of Resource Loss and Traumatic Growth on Probable PTSD and Depression Following Terrorist Attacks," *Journal of Traumatic Stress* 19, no. 6 (2006): 867–878.
125. Mark S. Micale, *Hysterical Men: The Hidden History of Male Nervous Illness* (Cambridge, MA: Harvard University Press, 2008).
126. Gosling, 97.
127. Ibid., 57–58.
128. From 1860 to 1890 there were more cases of "railway spine" found among men and more cases of hysteria brought on by the "pathological effects of their passions" in women. See Micale and Lerner, 22.
129. Freud's original paper, "The Aetiology of Hysteria," was read before the Society for Psychiatry and Neurology in Vienna on April 21, 1896.
130. See Jeffrey Moussaieff Masson, *The Assault on the Truth: Freud's Suppression of the Seduction Theory* (New York: Harper Collins, [1984]1992).
131. H.-U. Wittchen, A. Perkonigg, and H. Pfister, "Trauma and PTSD—An Overlooked Pathogenic Pathway for Premenstrual Dysphoric Disorder?" *Archives of Women's Mental Health* 6 (2003): 293–297.
132. In this study, the researchers read the charts on (but did not interview) 10 women who were diagnosed both with PTSD and "subthreshold PMDD"

(a few PMS symptoms) and who had been exposed to a traumatic experience or event in line with the current diagnostic criteria for PTSD. The findings? That "women with traumatic events [sic] and PTSD have an increased risk for secondary PMDD."

133. See, if you must, Judith A. Richman et al., "Effects on Alcohol Use and Anxiety of the September 11, 2001 Attacks and Chronic Work Stressors: A Longitudinal Study," *American Journal of Public Health* 94, no. 11 (2004): 2010–2015.

134. Maria Gavranidou and Rita Rosner, "The Weaker Sex? Gender and Post-Traumatic Stress Disorder," *Depression and Anxiety* 17 (2003): 130–139; Tolin and Foa; Ronald C. Kessler et al., "Posttraumatic Stress Disorder in the National Comorbidity Survey," *Archives of General Psychiatry* 52 (1995): 1048–1060; see also Breslau et al., "Trauma Exposure and Posttraumatic Stress Disorder." Only in the case of rape and sexual abuse do women and men appear to have the same probability of developing PTSD.

135. See Gavranidou and Rosner for an extended discussion of all these theories.

136. See Chapter 4 of this book for an explanation of "doing gender."

137. See Ronald C. Kessler, Wai Tat Chiu, Olga Demler, and Ellen E. Walters, "Prevalence, Severity, and Comorbidity of 12-Month DSM-IV Disorders in the National Comorbidity Survey Replication," *Archives of General Psychiatry* 62 (2005): 617–627. Although many accounts of PTSD in the military tie drug and alcohol abuse and violent behavior to PTSD, these are not listed in the *DSM* as criteria for the diagnosis.

138. In a study Hobfoll and his colleagues made of inner-city women with PTSD, they found that the most critical intervention to help reduce the women's PTSD symptoms was help in stopping the cycles of resource loss represented by the depletion of energy and money and the deterioration of family relationships. The authors made a point of remarking that the kind of help needed can be given by people who are not mental health professionals. See Kristen H. Walter and Stevan E. Hobfoll, "Resource Loss and Naturalistic Reduction of PTSD Among Inner-City Women," *Journal of Interpersonal Violence* 24, no. 3 (2009): 482–498.

139. Gavranidou and Rosner, 137; Ann M. Rasmusson and Matthew J. Friedman, "Gender Issues in the Neurobiology of PTSD," in *Gender and PTSD*, eds. Rachel Kimerling, Paige Ouimette, and Jessica Wolfe (New York: Guilford, 2002), 43–75; Meredith Melnick, "Why Are Women More Vulnerable to PTSD than Men?" *Time Healthland*, February 25, 2011. http://healthland. time.com/2011/02/25/are-women-more-vulnerable-to-ptsd-than-men (accessed September 21, 2011). Most studies of the biology of PTSD have been performed on male veterans, and gender effects are not usually what is being investigated.

140. Eileen L. Zurbriggen, "Rape, War, and the Socialization of Masculinity: Why Our Refusal to Give Up War Ensures That Rape Cannot Be Eradicated," *Psychology of Women Quarterly* 34 (2010): 538–549.

141. Laura Spinney, "Born Scared," *New Scientist*, November 27, 2010. http:// www.lexisnexis.com/hottopics/lnacademic (accessed August 15, 2011).

Yehuda studied a group of pregnant women who had been at or in the area of the World Trade Center on September 11, 2001 attacks. Of the 38 women she studied, the half of the group who had developed PTSD symptoms had lower cortisol levels than the other women, and at nine months old, so did their babies.

142. Peg Tyre, "Battling the Effects of War," Newsweek, December 6, 2004, 68 (cover story).

143. See DiGrande et al., "Long-term Posttraumatic Stress Symptoms," p. 278, for the following: "One potential explanation as to why those who witness horror are more susceptible to PTSD might lie in the biologic [sic] understanding of PTSD etiology, as images of grotesque and unimaginable scenes are encoded into memory and may be relived upon stimuli [sic]."

144. Bessel van der Kolk, Onno van der Hart, and Charles R. Marmar, "Dissociation and Information Processing in Posttraumatic Stress Disorder," in Traumatic Stress: The Effects of Overwhelming Experience on Mind, Body, and Society, eds. Bessel A. van der Kolk, Alexander C. McFarlane, and Lars Weisaeth (New York: Guilford, 1996), 303–327, esp. 313.

145. Leys, 6. For a thorough discussion and critique of van der Kolk's work, see Chapter 7, "The Science of the Literal: The Neurobiology of Trauma." Leys draws attention (p. 259) to van der Kolk's own statement that "the question of whether the brain is able to 'take pictures,' and whether some smells, images, sounds, or physical sensations may be etched onto the mind and remain unaltered by subsequent experience and by the passage of time, still remains to be answered." Leys responds: "His entire approach to traumatic memory rests on the assumption that the question can be answered in the affirmative." See also Young's detailed analysis and criticism of neurobiological research on PTSD in Harmony of Illusions, Chapter 8, esp. 276–285.

146. Edgar Jones et al., "Flashbacks and Post-Traumatic Stress Disorder: The Genesis of a 20th-Century Diagnosis," The British Journal of Psychiatry 182 (2003): 158–163.

147. McNally, "Progress and Controversy," 237.

148. J. Douglas Bremner, Does Stress Damage the Brain? (New York: W.W. Norton, 2002).

149. Rachel Yehuda et al., "Low Urinary Cortisol Excretion in Holocaust Survivors with Posttraumatic Stress Disorder," The American Journal of Psychiatry 152, no. 7 (1995): 982–986; John W. Mason et al., "Psychogenic Lowering of Urinary Cortisol Levels Linked to Increased Emotional Numbing and a Shame-Depressive Syndrome in Combat-Related Posttraumatic Stress Disorder," Psychosomatic Medicine 63 (2001): 387–401.

150. Mason et al., 399; Omer Bonne et al., "Longitudinal MRI Study of Hippocampal Volume in Trauma Survivors with PTSD," American Journal of Psychiatry 158, no. 8 (2001): 1248–1251.

151. Mark W. Gilbertson et al., "Smaller Hippocampal Volume Predicts Pathologic Vulnerability to Psychological Trauma," Nature Neuroscience 5, no. 11 (2002): 1242–1247.

152. Bracken, 80.
153. Nancy C. Andreason, "Posttraumatic Stress Disorder: Psychology, Biology, and the Manichean Warfare between False Dichotomies," *American Journal of Psychiatry* 152 (1995): 963–965.
154. William R. Uttal, *The New Phrenology: The Limits of Localizing Cognitive Processes in the Brain* (Cambridge, MA: MIT Press, 2001), esp. 25–26. See also Bracken's take on what he calls "cognitivism" and PTSD in Bracken, 55–60, particularly his discussion of Mardi Horowitz's information-processing approach.
155. Ibid., 26.
156. Nicholas Bakalar, "Study Links Heart Health and Post-Traumatic Stress," *New York Times*, January 2, 2007, F7.
157. Judith L. Herman, *Trauma and Recovery* (New York: Basic Books, 1992/1997), 240.
158. Bremner, 37.
159. Ibid., 32.
160. Bracken, 60, 61.
161. Mary Sykes Wylie, "The Long Shadow of Trauma," *Psychotherapy Networker* (March/April 2010): 20–27, 50–51, 54.
162. The group had rejected the proposed diagnosis principally on the grounds that the range of symptoms abused children and adolescents display is incredibly broad.
163. Ibid., 50.
164. Michael Linden et al., *Posttraumatic Embitterment Disorder* (Ashland, OH: Hogrefe & Huber, 2007).
165. Audre Lorde, *Sister Outsider: Essays and Speeches* (Berkeley, CA: Crossing Press, 1984).
166. Kleinman, *Writing at the Margin*.
167. Ronnie Janoff-Bulman, "Posttraumatic Growth: Three Explanatory Models," *Psychological Inquiry* 15, no. 1 (2004): 30–34.
168. George W. Casey Jr., "Comprehensive Soldier Fitness: A Vision for Psychological Resilience in the U.S. Army," *American Psychologist* 66, no. 1 (2011): 1–3.
169. On positive psychology's official website (University of Pennsylvania), positive psychology is defined as "the scientific study of the strengths and virtues that enable individuals and communities to thrive." www.ppc.sas.upenn.edu (accessed September 12, 2011). The positive psychology movement has been hotly debated among psychologists. For one critique of the movement, see Dana Becker and Jeanne Marecek, "Positive Psychology: History in the Remaking?" *Theory & Psychology* 18, no. 5 (2008): 591–604.
170. Martin E. P. Seligman and Raymond D. Fowler, "Comprehensive Soldier Fitness and the Future of Psychology," *American Psychologist* 66, no. 1 (2011): 82–86, esp. 84.
171. Ibid., 84.
172. See Sara B. Algoe and Barbara Fredrickson, "Emotional Fitness and the Movement of Affective Science from Lab to Field," *American Psychologist* 66, no. 1 (2011): 35–42, esp. 35.

173. Sean Phipps, "Comment. Positive Psychology and War: An Oxymoron," *American Psychologist* 66, no. 7 (2011): 641–642; also see the entire "Comment" section of this issue of *American Psychologist*, 641–647, for other critiques and for Seligman's response to those critiques.

174. Phipps, "Positive Psychology and War," 641.

175. Ian Hacking, *Rewriting the Soul: Multiple Personality and the Sciences of Memory* (Princeton, NJ: Princeton University Press, 1998), esp. 12; see also Ian Hacking, "Making Up People," in *Reconstructing Individualism: Autonomy, Individuality, and the Self in Western Thought*, eds. Thomas C. Heller, Morton Sosna, and David E. Wellbery (Stanford: Stanford University Press, 1986), 222–252.

CHAPTER 7

1. Martha Albertson Fineman, "The Vulnerable Subject and the Responsive State," Emory University School of Law, *Public Law & Legal Research Paper Series* no. 10–130, posted October 21, 2010. http://ssrn.com/abstract=1694740 (accessed August 19, 2011).

2. In Chapter 1, I defined stressism as a "belief that the tensions of contemporary life are primarily individual lifestyle problems to be solved through managing stress, as opposed to the belief that these tensions are linked to social forces and need to be resolved through social and political means."

3. Martha Albertson Fineman, "The Vulnerable Subject: Anchoring Equality in the Human Condition," *Yale Journal of Law and Feminism* 1 (2008): 1–21. http://web.gs.emory.edu/vulnerability/zpdfs/20_Yale_J.L.___Feminism_1__PDF (accessed March 12, 2009).

4. Sullivan (1892–1945) was a psychiatrist; the quotation can be found in his *Conceptions of Modern Psychiatry*, Psychiatric Foundation, 7.

5. D'Vera Cohn, "Adding Context to the Census Bureau's Income and Poverty Report," *Report of the Pew Research Center*, September 12, 2011. http://www.pewsocialtrends.org/2011/09/12/adding-context-to-the-census-bureaus-income-and-poverty-report/ (accessed September 23, 2011).

6. For an example of an early report, see Catherine Rampell, "As Layoffs Surge, Women May Pass Men in Job Force," *New York Times*, February 5, 2009. http://www.nytimes.com/2009/02/06/business/06women.html?pagewanted=all (accessed August 18, 2011). For a more recent account, see Rakesh Kochhar, "In Two Years of Economic Recovery, Women Lost Jobs, Men Found Them," Pew Research Center Publications, July 6, 2011.

INDEX

Soldiers. *See also* Posttraumatic Stress
    Disorder; War
  mental health problems of, 228 n.74
  valorization of, 231 n.118
Solomon, Andrew, 73, 91, 92, 93
Sontag, Susan, 8
Spencer, Herbert, 193 n.36
Spitzer, Robert, 158–159
Stanton, Elizabeth Cady, 118
Stay-at-home mothers. *See* Mothers
Stevenson, Betsey, 14
Stone, Pamela, 139, 140
Stress
  and adaptation, 51
  and adjustment theme, 20, 115, 131, 184
  and the American Dream, 184
  as beneficial, 8
  and biomedicine, 75
  and cancer, 7
  and caregiving, 130
  chameleon-like nature of, 2, 3, 17
  chronic, 87, 89, 203 n.65
  and combat, 155, 160. *See also*
    Posttraumatic Stress Disorder
  commodification of, 15, 99–101
  and coping, 10, 46, 94–95
  and coronary heart disease, 37, 43, 45,
    129–130. *See also* Coronary heart
    disease; Type A
  and damage theme, 20
  definitions of, 3–4
  and depression, 85–94
  and disease, 3, 10, 20, 36, 67–69
  embrace of concept, 35
  and emotion, 17, 47–48, 73
  and family work, 121
  fear of, 8–10, 81
  financial, 13–14
  and gender, 14–16, 80, 102–113, 209
    n.48, 212 n.88
  and health, 34, 50
  histories of, 17
  and hormones, 10, 64–65, 66, 103–106
  as ideological work, 17
  and the immune system, 10, 202 n.52, 203
    nn.61–62, 65, 67
  and the individual, 3, 7, 72–73, 89, 183
  and juggling, 129–131
  and lifestyle, 13–14
  management strategies, 6, 9–10

measurement of, 36, 47, 66, 89–90
media on, 81, 96–98
men's response to, 15, 212 n.88
and mental disorders, 154
as metaphor, 3, 8
methods of studying, 204 n. 72
as middle-class phenomenon, 13–14
and mind-body connection, 59
and moral domain, 7
and mothers, 16
neurobiology of, 103–106
popularity of concept, 37
and poverty, 14
and PTSD. *See* Posttraumatic Stress
    Disorder
psychological effects of, 132
as a psychological factor, 11
and the psychological professions,
    12–13
and psychopathology, 225 n.27
publications on, 2
research studies of, 11, 65, 209 n.46
primate, 10, 68
as risk factor, 58
and science, 6, 64–69
in seventeenth century, 187 n.5
social, 205 n.99, 209 n.48
and social change, 154
social functions of, 17, 75
and subjective experience, 204 n.82
and trauma, 154
as term, 33
and terrorism. *See* Terrorist attacks of 9/11
types, 65
and uncertainty, 3
and vulnerability, 72
and women, 15–16, 78–82
Stressism, 16–18, 184, 235 n.2
Stress management. *See* Advice
Stressor
  poverty as, 7, 92–93
  traumatic, 160
Subjectivity, 6
Success, American emphasis on, 20
Suffering
  and PTSD, 181
  social meaning of, 152
Sullivan, Harry Stack, 184, 235 n.4
Summerfield, Derek, 152, 154, 156
"Superwoman," 122